The Inventor Toolmaker

Extending Open Inventor™, Release 2

Josie Wernecke
Open Inventor Architecture Group

Addison-Wesley Publishing Company
Reading, Massachusetts   Menlo Park, California
New York   Don Mills, Ontario   Wokingham, England
Amsterdam   Bonn   Sydney   Singapore   Tokyo   Madrid
San Juan   Paris   Seoul   Milan   Mexico City   Taipei

Library of Congress Cataloging-in-Publication Data

Wernecke, Josie.
    The Inventor toolmaker : extending Open Inventor, release 2 /
Josie Wernecke.
        p.   cm.
    Includes index.
    ISBN 0-201-62493-1
        1. Object-oriented programming (Computer science)   2. Open
Inventor.   I. Title.
QA76.64.W49   1994
005.13'3--dc20   94-8378
                                                                                                        CIP

Author: Josie Wernecke
Sponsoring Editor: Keith Wollman
Project Manager: Joanne Clapp Fullagar
Cover Image: Rikk Carey
Cover Design: Jean Seal
Text Design: Electric Ink, Ltd., and Kay Maitz

Set in 10-point Stone Serif

Addison-Wesley books are available for bulk purchases by corporations, institutions, and other organizations. For more information, please contact the Corporate, Government and Special Sales Department at (800) 238-9682.

2 3 4 5 6 7-CRS-97969594
Second printing, August 1994

To Ruthie

Contents

Part II: Extending Interaction Classes

Examples

Figures

Tables

About This Book

The Inventor Toolmaker describes how to create new classes and how to customize existing classes in the Open Inventor Toolkit, an object-oriented toolkit used for interactive 3D graphics. This book is a companion to *The Inventor Mentor*, which describes how to write applications using the Open Inventor Toolkit.

There are several ways to extend the Inventor toolkit. The quickest way, and the only way available without using C++, is to use callback functions. Various classes, such as the **SoCallback** and **SoEventCallback** nodes and the **SoCallbackAction**, support callbacks to add user-defined behavior. To truly extend the system, however, requires C++ subclassing, which is the subject of this book.

Many Inventor classes and member functions are labeled as **SoEXTENDER**, which means they are available to programmers who wish to extend the toolkit. Note that these classes and functions are not documented in the *Open Inventor C++ Reference Manual*. Refer to header files and this book for information on them.

Other classes and methods are labeled as **SoINTERNAL**. These are used solely within the Open Inventor library and should not be used in applications. The labels **SoEXTENDER** and **SoINTERNAL** are for documentation purposes only and are not checked by the compiler.

What This Book Contains

This book is for the advanced programmer and describes how to create new Inventor classes and how to customize existing classes in the Open Inventor Toolkit.

The Inventor Toolmaker contains the following parts and chapters:

Part I, "**Extending Database Classes**," has seven chapters:

- Chapter 1, "**Key Concepts**," describes important background information on the Open Inventor Toolkit that was not needed in *The Inventor Mentor*. It introduces concepts such as the method list, state and elements, the stack index, caching, runtime typing, and using extender macros. If you are creating any database class (described in Chapters 2 through 6), it is required reading.

- Chapter 2, "**Creating a Node**," describes how to create new subclasses of **SoNode**. Examples show creating a new property node class, shape node class, and group node class.

- Chapter 3, "**Creating a Field**," describes how to create new subclasses of **SoField**, including single-value and multiple-value fields.

- Chapter 4, "**Creating an Action**," describes how to create new subclasses of **SoAction**.

- Chapter 5, "**Creating an Element**," describes how to create new subclasses of **SoElement**.

- Chapter 6, "**Creating an Engine**," describes how to create new subclasses of **SoEngine**, including new field converters. It also explains how notification of changes in field data propagates through the scene graph.

- Chapter 7, "**Creating a Node Kit**," describes how to create new subclasses of **SoBaseKit**.

Part II, "**Extending Interaction Classes**," has four chapters:

- Chapter 8, "**Creating Draggers and Manipulators**," describes how to create new subclasses of **SoDragger** as well as new manipulators, which are derived from other node classes such as **SoTransform**, **SoLight**, or **SoCamera**. If you are creating a new dragger, you'll need to read Chapter 7 as well, because draggers are node kits.

- Chapter 9, "**Creating a Selection Highlight Style**," describes how to create new subclasses of **SoGLRenderAction** to perform selection highlighting. If you're creating a new highlight class, you'll need to read Chapter 4, because highlight classes are derived from an action class, **SoGLRenderAction**.

- Chapter 10, "**Creating a Component**," describes how to create new components. Examples show creating a simple component derived from **SoXtRenderArea** as well as a simple viewer.

- Chapter 11, "**Creating an Event and Device**," describes how to create a new event and a new Xt device. The chapter also describes how to translate X events into Inventor events.

What You Should Know
Before Reading This Book

This book assumes you are familiar with the material presented in *The Inventor Mentor*. In addition, you need to be familiar with the C++ programming language as well as concepts related to object-oriented programming. See "Suggestions for Further Reading" for good background information.

Conventions Used in This Book

This book uses **boldface text** font for all Inventor classes, methods, and field names: **SoNode**, **SoMaterial**, **getValue()**, **setValue()**, **ambientColor**, and **center**. Parentheses indicate methods. Capital letters indicate Inventor macros: SO_NODE_ADD_FIELD(), SO_KIT_INIT_CLASS(). Code examples are in Courier font.

Programming tips are marked with their own heading and the icon shown at the right.

Key to Scene Graph Diagrams

Figure I-1 shows the symbols used in the scene graph diagrams that appear throughout this book.

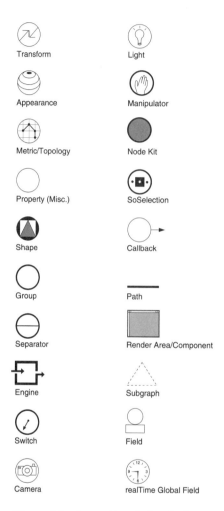

Figure I-1   Scene Graph Symbols

Suggestions for Further Reading

For basic information about programming with the Open Inventor Toolkit, see the following:

- Wernecke, Josie, *The Inventor Mentor*. Reading,Mass.:Addison-Wesley, 1994.

For a general introduction to computer graphics, see the following:

- Foley, J.D., A. van Dam, S. Feiner, and J.F. Hughes, *Computer Graphics Principles and Practice*, 2d ed. Reading, Mass.: Addison-Wesley, 1990.

- Neider, Jackie, Tom Davis, Mason Woo. *OpenGL Programming Guide*. Reading, Mass.: Addison-Wesley, 1993.

- Newman, W., and R. Sproull, *Principles of Interactive Computer Graphics*, 2d edition. New York: McGraw-Hill, 1979.

For an introduction to the C++ language, see the following:

- Lippman, Stanley, *C++ Primer*. AT&T Bell Laboratories, 1989.

- Pohl, Ira, *C++ for C Programmers*. Redwood City, Ca.: Benjamin/ Cummings Publishing Company, 1994.

- Shapiro, Jonathan, *A C++ Toolkit*. Englewood Cliffs, N.J.: Prentice Hall, 1990.

For an introduction to object-oriented programming, see the following:

- Meyer, Bertrand, *Object-Oriented Software Construction*. London: Prentice Hall International, 1988.

Acknowledgments

Following close on the heels of *The Inventor Mentor*, this book demanded a marathoner's endurance from many people. The Inventor engineering team, led by Rikk Carey, continued to provide valuable support for me. Paul Strauss wrote all sample code for the nodes, actions, fields, and elements chapters and critiqued countless drafts. Paul was the touchstone for the entire book: if a paragraph or a chapter didn't satisfy him, I knew it wasn't finished. Gavin Bell also served as a resource for the database chapters and carefully reviewed work in progress.

Discussions with Ronen Barzel, Paul Strauss, and Gavin Bell and code written by Ronen and Paul formed the backbone of the engines chapter. Paul Isaacs, the expert on node kits and manipulators, provided all examples for those chapters and even telephoned in his review comments during a Florida vacation. David Mott, the guru on highlighting, events, and devices, was also an excellent overall reviewer and critic. Alain Dumesny and David Mott wrote the components examples and made valuable suggestions for expanding the scope of that chapter. Helga Thorvaldsdóttir and Dave Immel meticulously reviewed many chapters and helped create sample code.

As we approached the finish line, the production team raced hard too. Lorrie Williams edited and formatted the material, and Laura Cooper coordinated testing and scheduling with vendors. Cheri Brown drew the line illustrations. Jackie Neider, my manager at Silicon Graphics, and the other members of the Developer Publications group—Arthur Evans, Beth Fryer, Carol Geary, Eleanor Bassler, Jed Hartman, John Stearns, Ken Jones, Liz Deeth, Patricia Creek, and Wendy Ferguson—were busy running their own marathons, but still managed to provide cheerful encouragement and sustenance (mostly in the form of chocolate).

Credit, too, goes to my husband, Steve, and my sons, Jeff and Evan, whose support at home enabled me to finish this race.

Part I

Extending Database Classes

## Chapter 1

Key Concepts

Chapters 1 through 5 are devoted to extending the set of nodes, actions, and elements in the database. Understanding how to create new nodes and actions requires some background information that was not needed in *The Inventor Mentor*. Important concepts discussed in this chapter include the *method list*, *state* and *elements*, the *stack index*, *caching*, *runtime typing*, and using extender *macros*. Most of the topics introduced in this chapter are discussed in detail in later chapters. Figure 1-1 shows a summary of key **SoEXTENDER** classes.

Adding Nodes and Actions to Inventor

If it weren't for extensibility, all actions could have been implemented simply as virtual functions on nodes. For example, GL rendering could have been a virtual function on the **SoNode** class. Adding a new node class would require implementing virtual functions for those actions that could not be inherited from the base class.

However, adding a new action would be considerably harder. It is impossible for you to add a new virtual function to the **SoNode** class or to any of the existing Inventor node classes. The only way to add a new action would be to derive classes from all nodes that would support it and to define the new method for those classes.

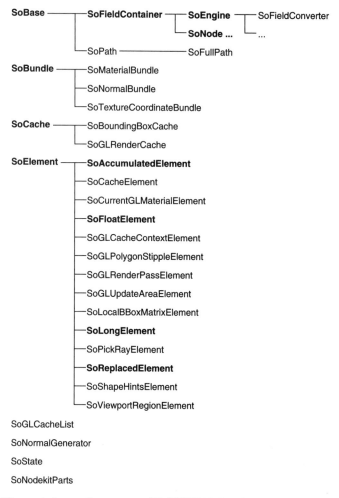

```
SoBase ─────────┬── SoFieldContainer ──┬── SoEngine ──┬── SoFieldConverter
                │                       └── SoNode ...  └── ...
                └── SoPath ─────────────── SoFullPath

SoBundle ───────┬── SoMaterialBundle
                ├── SoNormalBundle
                └── SoTextureCoordinateBundle

SoCache ────────┬── SoBoundingBoxCache
                └── SoGLRenderCache

SoElement ──────┬── SoAccumulatedElement
                ├── SoCacheElement
                ├── SoCurrentGLMaterialElement
                ├── SoFloatElement
                ├── SoGLCacheContextElement
                ├── SoGLPolygonStippleElement
                ├── SoGLRenderPassElement
                ├── SoGLUpdateAreaElement
                ├── SoLocalBBoxMatrixElement
                ├── SoLongElement
                ├── SoPickRayElement
                ├── SoReplacedElement
                ├── SoShapeHintsElement
                └── SoViewportRegionElement

SoGLCacheList

SoNormalGenerator

SoState

SoNodekitParts
```

Figure 1-1   Summary of SoEXTENDER Classes

Inventor implements actions as separate classes to solve this problem. Each action maintains a list of static methods, one for each node class (see Figure 1-2). When an action is applied to the root of a scene graph, Inventor uses the *method list* to look up the method for each node in the scene graph, based on the type identifier for the node class. See "Runtime Types" on page 18 for more information on class type identifiers.

Method list for SoGLRenderAction

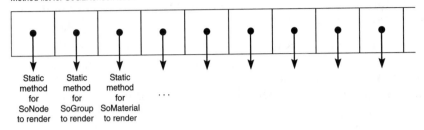

Static method for SoNode to render   Static method for SoGroup to render   Static method for SoMaterial to render   . . .

REAL MODEL (For All Built-in Actions)

Method list for SoGLRenderAction

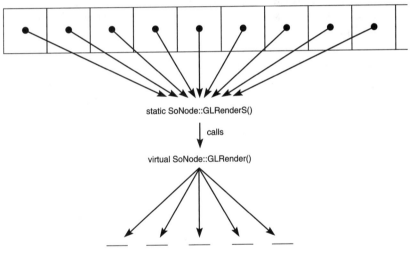

static SoNode::GLRenderS()

calls

virtual SoNode::GLRender()

Figure 1-2   Method List

For convenience, the base **SoNode** class registers static methods for all built-in Inventor actions; each of these methods calls a corresponding virtual function for that action. For example, **SoNode** registers a static method for **SoGetBoundingBoxAction** that calls the virtual **getBoundingBox()** method. All classes derived from **SoNode** can redefine **getBoundingBox()** in standard object-oriented fashion. If a class does not redefine a method, it inherits the method from its parent class

Most of the virtual methods on **SoNode** do nothing and must be redefined by the individual node classes. A few, however, such as the **SoNode** virtual methods for **search()** and **write()**, actually implement the action, since most nodes perform the action in the same way. In most cases, nodes can simply inherit these methods without redefining them.

Details on how to add a new node class are given in Chapter 2. Adding a new field class is described in Chapter 3.

If you add a new action class to Inventor, you need to set up the list of methods for the nodes that support the action (shown in Figure 1-2). This list contains one pointer to the static action method for each node class that supports the action. Adding a new action is described in Chapter 4.

Actions, State, and Elements

The Inventor database maintains a *traversal state* that is used when an action is applied to a scene graph. As described in *The Inventor Mentor*, the traversal state is a class (**SoState**) used by Inventor to store state information during execution of an action. Typically, the scene graph is traversed from top to bottom and from left to right. The traversal state is modified by the nodes encountered during this traversal. State is the way nodes in the scene graph communicate with each other. For example, shape nodes need to know whether the draw style is INVISIBLE in order to know whether to draw themselves. They use the draw-style element in the state to find out.

For simplicity and extensibility, each integral piece of information in the state is stored in a separate *element*. For example, the current diffuse color of the material is stored in an instance of the **SoDiffuseColorElement** class.

Enabling Elements

Each action class has its own notion of enabling certain elements. These elements are enabled when an instance of the action is created. By default, all elements in the state are *disabled*, which means that they can't be set or inquired. Both nodes and actions can enable the elements they require in the state for a particular action class. The list of elements to enable is set up ahead of time, typically in the **initClass()** method for the node or action before instances of either are constructed. The macro SO_ENABLE() provides a convenient way for nodes to enable elements for a particular action class. For example, the **SoPickStyle** node requires the pick-style element when picking, so its **initClass()** method enables this element in the pick action as follows:

```
SO_ENABLE(SoPickAction, SoPickStyleElement);
```

A side effect of this call is that **SoPickStyleElement** is also enabled in the **SoRayPickAction** class, which is derived from **SoPickAction**. Each action class inherits the enabled elements of its parent.

The **SoGLRenderAction** enables the **SoViewportRegionElement**, because the action is responsible for setting up this element in the state (the viewport region is specified in the action's constructor). This is how the **SoGLRenderAction** enables the **SoViewportRegionElement**:

```
enableElement(SoViewportRegionElement::getClassTypeId());
```

(Nodes typically use the SO_ENABLE() macro, and actions use the **enableElement()** method, since it's simple.) It doesn't hurt to enable an element in the state more than once (for example, a node and an action might enable the same element). If you are using the debugging library and you try to set or inquire an element that has not been enabled, an error message is printed. (See Appendix C of *The Inventor Mentor*.)

When an action is applied to a scene graph, the action builds an instance of **SoState** and passes a list of enabled elements to the state constructor. (If the list changes after an action is constructed, the action automatically rebuilds its state to include the newly enabled elements the next time the action is applied.)

Adding new element classes to Inventor is described in Chapter 5.

Setting Elements in the State

When a node is traversed, it may need to change the value of certain elements in the state. For the **SoDrawStyle** node, the code to change the current value of the **lineWidth** element looks like this:

```
if (! lineWidth.isIgnored())
   SoLineWidthElement::set(action->state, this,
                           lineWidth.getValue());
```

In this fragment, **this** is the node that is setting the value, and
lineWidth.getValue() is the new value for the element.

Each enabled element has its own stack in the state with a unique *stack
index*. Separators save and restore the state by pushing and popping these
element stacks. The top element in the stack contains the *current value* for
that element during traversal. Here is a brief summary of what happens
behind the scenes when a node sets the value of an element in the state:

1. The element class asks the state for a modifiable instance of the
    element, passing in its stack index.

2. The state looks into the appropriate stack and creates a new instance
    on top of the stack, if necessary. It first checks whether the current
    value of the element was set by a node with its Override flag set to
    TRUE. If this flag is set, it returns NULL, since you can't modify the
    value.

    If the Override flag is not set, the new top instance of the element is
    returned to the element class.

3. The element changes the value in this instance.

Figure 1-3 summarizes the relationship among nodes, actions, elements,
and the state.

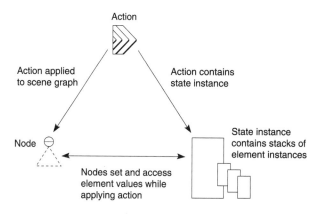

Figure 1-3   Nodes, Actions, Elements, and State

Getting Elements in the State

Each element provides a static **get()** method that returns its value from the top element in the stack. For example,

```
width = SoLineWidthElement::get(state);
```

returns the line width from the top element in the stack. Elements with multiple values provide a different sequence of **get()** methods, as described in Chapter 2.

State Elements

Supported element classes are listed here. The class name of each listed element is preceded by **So** and followed by **Element**. For brevity, the names are abbreviated in this list. Thus, the first item is **SoAmbientColorElement**.

These elements store information about the current set of materials:

AmbientColor	ambient color of current material
DiffuseColor	diffuse color of current material
EmissiveColor	emissive color of current material
Shininess	shininess value of current material
SpecularColor	specular color of current material
Transparency	transparency of current material

These elements store information about the current lighting model and light source:

LightAttenuation	amount of attenuation of light sources over distance
LightModel	current lighting model

These elements store information relevant to textures:

TextureBlendColor
　　　　　color used when blending texture

TextureCoordinateBinding
　　　　　how to bind texture coordinates to shapes

TextureCoordinate
　　　　　current set of texture coordinates

TextureImage	current texture image
TextureMatrix	current cumulative texture transformation matrix
TextureModel	how texture is applied to material component
TextureWrapS	how image wraps in *s* (horizontal) direction
TextureWrapT	how image wraps in *t* (vertical) direction

These elements contain information about how to draw and interact with shapes:

ClipPlane	current set of clipping planes
Complexity	current complexity
ComplexityType	how to interpret complexity: screen-space metric, bounding box, and so on
Coordinate	current set of coordinates
CreaseAngle	cutoff crease angle for smoothing when computing default normals
DrawStyle	current drawing style (filled, lines, and so on)
MaterialBinding	how to bind materials to shapes
NormalBinding	how to bind surface normals to shapes
Normal	current set of surface normals
PickStyle	current pick style

These elements store profile information (for 3D text and NURBS surfaces):

ProfileCoordinate	
	current coordinates used in profiles
Profile	set of current profiles

These elements store information about transformations:

BBoxModelMatrix	
	current cumulative object transformation matrix
LocalBBoxMatrix	transformation matrix from object space to local coordinate space during application of an **SoGetBoundingBoxAction**
ModelMatrix	current cumulative object transformation matrix
ProjectionMatrix	current projection matrix

Units	current factor for converting between units of measure
ViewingMatrix	current camera viewing transformation matrix

These elements are related to text objects:

FontName	name of current font
FontSize	size of current font

These elements hold information about current GL modes:

LinePattern	current dash pattern for drawing lines
LineWidth	current width for drawing lines
PointSize	current point size
ShapeHints	current shape hints

These elements hold information about viewing:

CullVolume	current culling volume
FocalDistance	current focal distance of the camera
PickRay	current ray to use for picking
ViewVolume	current viewing volume
ViewportRegion	current viewport region

These elements hold traversal information:

Cache	whether caching is active, whether cache is valid, and currently open caches (see "Caching" on page 17)
Switch	current child to traverse in switch nodes

Many of the elements named above have GL-specific versions that are used only for rendering. The following elements have *only* GL versions:

GLCacheContext	cache context
GLColorIndex	index into the current GL color map of the base color of the current surface material

CurrentGLMaterial

current state of GL materials (indices of last values sent to GL plus a flag indicating whether lighting is currently active); used to optimize the calls made to OpenGL

GLLightId integer identifier of current source (counts from 0)

GLMaterialIndex indices into the current GL material map of the ambient, diffuse, and specular components of the current surface material, as defined by GL's color index lighting model

GLRenderPass current rendering pass for multi-pass rendering (an integer)

GLTextureEnabled

whether textures are currently enabled

GLTextureQuality

current shape GLTextureQuality

GLUpdateArea rectangular area within the current viewport region that needs to be updated when rendering

Elements and Actions

Table 1-1 lists all elements and the actions for which they are enabled by default. The elements enabled for the line highlight and box highlight render actions are the same as those for the GL render action.

CB = Callback GLR = GLRender BB = BoundingBox GM = GetMatrix HE = HandleEvent P = Pick RP = RayPick S = Search	CB	GLR	BB	GM	HE	P	RP	S
AmbientColor	X	X						
BBoxModelMatrix			X					
Cache		X	X					
ClipPlane	X	X				X	X	
Complexity	X	X	X			X	X	
ComplexityType	X	X	X			X	X	
Coordinate	X	X	X			X	X	
CreaseAngle	X	X	X			X	X	
CullVolume		X						
CurrentGLMaterial		X						
DiffuseColor	X	X						
DrawStyle	X	X						
EmissiveColor	X	X						
FocalDistance	X	X	X				X	
FontName	X	X	X			X	X	
FontSize	X	X	X			X	X	
GLAmbientColor		X						
GLCacheContext		X						
GLClipPlane		X						
GLColorIndex		X						
GLCoordinate		X						

Table 1-1   Elements Enabled for Each Action

CB = Callback GLR = GLRender BB = BoundingBox GM = GetMatrix HE = HandleEvent P = Pick RP = RayPick S = Search	CB	GLR	BB	GM	HE	P	RP	S
GLDiffuseColor		X						
GLDrawStyle		X						
GLEmissiveColor		X						
GLLightId		X						
GLLightModel		X						
GLLinePattern		X						
GLLineWidth		X						
GLMaterialIndex		X						
GLModelMatrix		X						
GLNormal		X						
GLPointSize		X						
GLPolygonStipple		X						
GLProjectionMatrix		X						
GLRenderPass		X						
GLShapeHints		X						
GLShininess		X						
GLSpecularColor		X						
GLTextureBlend- Color		X						
GLTextureCoordi- nate		X						

Table 1-1 (continued)   Elements Enabled for Each Action

CB = Callback GLR = GLRender BB = BoundingBox GM = GetMatrix HE = HandleEvent P = Pick RP = RayPick S = Search	CB	GLR	BB	GM	HE	P	RP	S
GLTextureEnabled		X						
GLTextureImage		X						
GLTextureMatrix		X						
GLTextureModel		X						
GLTextureQuality		X						
GLTextureWrapS		X						
GLTextureWrapT		X						
GLUpdateArea		X						
GLViewingMatrix		X						
GLViewportRegion		X						
LightAttenuation		X						
LightModel	X	X						
LinePattern	X	X						
LineWidth	X	X						
LocalBBoxMatrix			X					
MaterialBinding	X	X				X	X	
ModelMatrix	X	X				X	X	
NormalBinding	X	X				X	X	
Normal	X	X				X	X	
PickRay							X	
PickStyle	X					X	X	

Table 1-1 (continued)   Elements Enabled for Each Action

Elements and Actions   **15**

CB = Callback GLR = GLRender BB = BoundingBox GM = GetMatrix HE = HandleEvent P = Pick RP = RayPick S = Search	CB	GLR	BB	GM	HE	P	RP	S
PointSize	X	X						
ProfileCoordinate	X	X	X			X	X	
Profile	X	X	X			X	X	
ProjectionMatrix	X	X	X				X	
ShapeHints	X	X	X			X	X	
Shininess	X	X						
SpecularColor	X	X						
Switch	X	X	X	X	X	X	X	X
TextureBlendColor	X	X						
TextureCoordinate-Binding	X	X				X	X	
TextureCoordinate	X	X				X	X	
TextureImage	X	X						
TextureMatrix	X	X				X	X	
TextureModel	X	X						
TextureWrapS	X	X						
TextureWrapT	X	X						
Transparency	X	X						
Units	X	X	X	X		X	X	

Table 1-1 (continued)   Elements Enabled for Each Action

CB = Callback GLR = GLRender BB = BoundingBox GM = GetMatrix HE = HandleEvent P = Pick RP = RayPick S = Search	CB	GLR	BB	GM	HE	P	RP	S
ViewVolume	X	X	X		X		X	
ViewingMatrix	X	X	X				X	
ViewportRegion	X	X	X	X	X	X	X	

Table 1-1 (continued)   Elements Enabled for Each Action

Caching

The Inventor Mentor offers an introduction to caching. This section provides additional background information on how the Inventor caching mechanism works. For more information, see also the discussion of **matches()** in Chapter 5.

Elements provide the mechanism in Inventor for keeping track of scene graph dependencies. When a node uses Inventor elements, information is automatically stored that enables Inventor to determine whether a given cache is still valid, or whether values in the cache or values affecting the cache have changed, requiring a new cache to be built.

In cases where an element's value is stored as a simple floating point or integer value, Inventor simply compares the value of the element in the state with the value of the element stored in the cache. If the values are the same, the cache is still valid.

In other cases, where an element's value may be composed of a large number of values, Inventor checks to see which node or nodes set the value, as follows. (The **SoCoordinateElement** is an example of an element that uses this mechanism.) Every node instance in a scene graph is automatically assigned a unique identification number, referred to as its *node ID*. This node ID is updated when any field in the node changes. Whenever a node sets an element value, its node ID is stored in the state along with the value.

When a cache is built, this node ID is also stored in the cache along with the element value. When Inventor needs to determine whether a given cache is valid, it compares the node ID in the state with the node ID in the cache. If both node IDs match, then the cache is still valid.

For elements that *accumulate* values in the state, such as transformations, a *list* of all node IDs that have modified the element is stored along with the element's value in the cache and in the state. If both lists of node IDs match, the cache is valid.

If you are creating a new node class that uses Inventor elements, caching will work automatically, since the necessary information will be stored in the state and compared appropriately with those in the cache. However, if you create a new node that depends on something that is not an element (for example, it might depend on a global variable), then you need to be sure that your new node is never cached, since it does not store the correct dependency information in the state. Use the **SoCacheElement::invalidate**() method to specify that this new node should not be cached. The more versatile solution is, of course, to use elements so that they can automatically set up the caching dependencies for you. You can derive your own element class if necessary (see Chapter 5).

Runtime Types

The **SoType** class keeps track of runtime type information in Inventor. When initialized, many classes request a unique **SoType**. You can then use this type to find out the actual class of an instance when only its base class is known, or to create an instance of a particular class, given its type or name. Useful type-related methods, which are provided by the macros for implementing most classes, include

getClassTypeId()	a static method that returns the type identifier for a specific class
getTypeId()	a virtual method that returns the type identifier for an entity (for example, a node, field, or action) whose class is unknown
isOfType()	returns TRUE if this entity (for example, node, field, or action) is of the specified type or is derived from that type

All nodes, node kits, manipulators, actions, elements, fields, engines, events, and details in Inventor must have a static method to initialize the class. This method, which must be called **initClass()**, sets up the type-identifier and file-format name information for the class. Standard Inventor classes are initialized during **SoDB::init()**, **SoInteraction::init()**, **SoNodeKit::init()**, or **SoXt::init()**. For extender classes, the **initClass()** method must be called after the database is initialized and before any instance of the class is constructed. The order for initializing is elements first, actions, then nodes.

For any new class that supports runtime typing, the **initClass()** method must be defined in the header file and implemented in the source file. Most classes have associated macros that can be used within the **initClass()** method.

Extender Macros

A number of macros are provided to make subclassing easier for you. Each chapter lists the relevant macros and where they are defined. For example, **SoNode** provides SO_NODE_INIT_CLASS() and SO_NODE_INIT_-ABSTRACT_CLASS() in the SoSubNode.h file. **SoField** provides SO_SFIELD_INIT() and SO_MFIELD_INIT() in SoSubField.h. The chapter examples illustrate how to use the macros.

Most classes provide macros for use in header files, source files, and class initialization routines. Within these general categories, macros are provided for both abstract and nonabstract classes. The include file for the macros generally is the name of the base class, prefixed by *Sub*—for example, SoSubNode.h contains the macros for defining new node classes, and SoSubAction.h contains the macros for defining new action classes.

Chapter 2

Creating a Node

This chapter explains how you can create new subclasses of **SoNode**. It discusses enabling elements in the state, constructing a node, and implementing actions for it. Chapter 1 provides important background material on these concepts, and this chapter assumes you are familiar with the material presented there.

The first part of this chapter offers an overview of the steps required to create a new node. When necessary, additional sections explain key concepts in further detail and list the relevant macros. Next, the chapter examples show how to create three new node classes:

- A property node class called **Glow**

- A shape node class called **Pyramid**

- A group node class called **Alternate**

Sections at the end of the chapter discuss the following:

- Using new node classes

- Creating abstract classes

- The **copy()** method

- The **affectsState()** method

- Creating nodes that cannot be cached

- Creating an alternate representation for a new node class

Overview

The file SoSubNode.h contains the macros for defining new node classes. The SO_NODE_HEADER() macro declares type identifier and naming variables and methods that all node classes must support. The SO_NODE_SOURCE() macro defines the static variables and methods declared in the SO_NODE_HEADER() macro. Other macros useful in creating new node classes are mentioned in the following sections.

Creating a new node requires these steps:

1. Select a name for the new node class and determine what class it is derived from.

2. Define and name each field in the node.

3. Define an **initClass()** method to initialize the type information and to ensure that the required elements are enabled in the state (see "Initializing the Node Class" on page 23).

4. Define a constructor (see "Defining the Constructor" on page 24).

5. Implement the actions supported by the node (see "Implementing Actions" on page 25).

   a. For a property node, you usually need to implement the **GLRender()** and **callback()** methods (see "Creating a Property Node" on page 28). You may also need to implement **getBoundingBox()**, **getMatrix()**, and other methods.

   b. For a shape node, you need to implement the **generate-Primitives()** method for the **SoCallbackAction** as well as the **getBoundingBox()** method. You may want to implement a specific **GLRender()** or **rayPick()** method as well (see "Creating a Shape Node" on page 32). For vertex-based shapes, you may need to implement a **generateDefaultNormals()** method (see "Generating Default Normals" on page 63).

   c. For a group node, you need to implement all actions to ensure that the children are traversed (see "Creating a Group Node" on page 49).

6. Implement a **copy()** method if the node contains any non-field instance data (see "The copy() Method" on page 62).

7. Implement an **affectsState()** method if it cannot be inherited from the parent class (see "The affectsState() Method" on page 62).

Initializing the Node Class

As discussed in Chapter 1, the **initClass()** method sets up the type identifier and file format name information for the class. The initialization macro for nodes, SO_NODE_INIT_CLASS(), does most of the work for you. One additional task for you as the node writer is to enable each of the elements in the state for each action the node supports. The following subsections provide additional information about enabling elements in the state.

Enabling Elements in the State

In the **initClass()** method, use the SO_ENABLE() macro (defined in SoAction.h) to enable the elements required by your node in the state. To use a simple example, **SoDrawStyle** enables these elements in the **SoGLRenderAction**:

```
SO_ENABLE(SoGLRenderAction, SoGLDrawStyleElement);
SO_ENABLE(SoGLRenderAction, SoGLLinePatternElement);
SO_ENABLE(SoGLRenderAction, SoGLLineWidthElement);
SO_ENABLE(SoGLRenderAction, SoGLPointSizeElement);
```

SoDrawStyle also implements the **SoCallbackAction**. It enables these elements in the **SoCallbackAction**:

```
SO_ENABLE(SoCallbackAction, SoDrawStyleElement);
SO_ENABLE(SoCallbackAction, SoLinePatternElement);
SO_ENABLE(SoCallbackAction, SoLineWidthElement);
SO_ENABLE(SoCallbackAction, SoPointSizeElement);
```

Tip: If you know that the element is already enabled by another node or action, you can skip this step. (See Table 1-1.)

Now that these elements have been enabled, their values can be set and inquired. (The debugging version of Inventor generates an error if you try to access or set an element that has not been enabled.)

Inheritance within the Element Stack

The previous example using **SoDrawStyle** elements brings up another feature of the element stack: Some elements have corresponding GL versions that are derived from them. The **SoGL** version of an element typically sends its value to OpenGL when it is set. As you might guess, **SoGLDrawStyleElement** is derived from **SoDrawStyleElement**, and

SoGLLinePatternElement is derived from **SoLinePatternElement**. The parent element class and its derived class *share* the same stack index.

If you try to enable two classes that share a stack index (for example, **SoGLDrawStyleElement** and **SoDrawStyleElement**), only the more derived class is actually enabled (in this case, **SoGLDrawStyleElement**). However, you can always use the base class static method to set or get the value for either the parent or the derived class. (You cannot, however, enable only the parent version and then try to treat it as the derived GL version.)

Defining the Constructor

The constructor defines the fields for the node and sets up their default values. If the fields contain enumerated values, their names and values are defined in the constructor as well. Use the SO_NODE_CONSTRUCTOR() macro to perform the basic work.

The SO_NODE_IS_FIRST_INSTANCE() macro returns a Boolean value that can be tested in constructors. If your class requires considerable overhead when it is initialized, you may want to perform this work only once when the first instance of the class is created. For example, the **SoCube** class sets up the coordinates and normals of the cube faces during construction of its first instance. (You could put this code in the **initClass()** method, but putting it in the constructor guarantees that someone is actually using your node class first.)

Setting Up the Node's Fields

The SO_NODE_ADD_FIELD() macro defines the fields in the node and sets up their default values. The first parameter is the name of the field. The second parameter is the default field value, in parentheses. Using **SoDrawStyle** as an example:

```
SO_NODE_ADD_FIELD(style, (SoDrawStyleElement::getDefault()));
SO_NODE_ADD_FIELD(lineWidth,
                 (SoLineWidthElement::getDefault()));
SO_NODE_ADD_FIELD(linePattern,
                 (SoLinePatternElement::getDefault()));
```

To add a field with a vector value, the syntax is as follows:

```
SO_NODE_ADD_FIELD(translation, (0.0, 0.0, 0.0));
```

Defining Enumerated Values for a Field

In the preceding example, the **style** field contains an enumerated value: FILLED, LINES, POINTS, or INVISIBLE. Use the SO_NODE_DEFINE_- ENUM_VALUE() macro to define the enumerated values. The first parameter is the type of the enumerated value. The second parameter is its value, as shown here:

```
SO_NODE_DEFINE_ENUM_VALUE(Style, FILLED);
SO_NODE_DEFINE_ENUM_VALUE(Style, LINES);
SO_NODE_DEFINE_ENUM_VALUE(Style, POINTS);
SO_NODE_DEFINE_ENUM_VALUE(Style, INVISIBLE);
```

Then, to specify that these enumerated values can be used in the **style** field of the **SoDrawStyle** node, use the SO_NODE_SET_SF_ENUM_TYPE() macro:

```
SO_NODE_SET_SF_ENUM_TYPE(style, Style);
```

Implementing Actions

Your next task is to implement each of the actions your new node supports. The **SoDrawStyle** node, as you have already seen, supports two actions, the **SoGLRenderAction** and the **SoCallbackAction**, in addition to the **SoSearchAction** and the **SoWriteAction**, which it inherits from **SoNode**.

Tip: Do not apply a new action within another action (because caching will not function properly). Also, if you are creating a new node, do not modify the node (for example, call **setValue()** on a field) within an action method.

The doAction() Method

For the GL render action, the **SoDrawStyle** node changes the values of four elements in the state based on the value of the corresponding fields. For example, if its **style** field has a value of INVISIBLE, it changes the value of the **SoGLDrawStyleElement** in the state to INVISIBLE. The corresponding code to set the element's value is

```
if (! style.isIgnored())
   SoDrawStyleElement::set(state, this,
                            (SoDrawStyleElement::Style)
                            style.getValue());
```

For the callback action, the **SoDrawStyle** node does the same thing: it sets the value of the element based on the value of the corresponding field in the node.

Since the two actions perform exactly the same tasks, this common code is put into a separate method that can be called by both the GL render and the callback actions. By convention, this shared method used by property nodes is called **doAction()** (which is a virtual method on **SoNode**). The code for the draw-style node's callback action is

```
void
SoDrawStyle::callback(SoCallbackAction *action)
(
   doAction(action);
}
```

The code for the draw-style node's GL render action is also simple (and familiar):

```
void
SoDrawStyle::GLRender(SoGLRenderAction *action)
(
   doAction(action);
}
```

To complete the story, here is the complete code for the draw-style node's **doAction()** method:

```
void
SoDrawStyle::doAction(SoAction *action)
{
   SoState    *state = action->getState();

   if (! style.isIgnored())
      SoDrawStyleElement::set(state, this,
                               (SoDrawStyleElement::Style)
                               style.getValue());
   if (! lineWidth.isIgnored())
      SoLineWidthElement::set(state, this,
                                lineWidth.getValue());
   if (! linePattern.isIgnored())
      SoLinePatternElement::set(state, this,
                                  linePattern.getValue());
```

```
    if (! pointSize.isIgnored())
        SoPointSizeElement::set(state, this,
                                pointSize.getValue());
}
```

The advantage of this scheme becomes apparent when you consider extending the set of actions (see Chapter 4). You can define a new action class and implement a static method for **SoNode** that calls **doAction()**. Then all properties that implement **doAction()** will perform the appropriate operation without needing any static methods for them.

Changing and Examining State Elements

As discussed in Chapter 1, each element class provides methods for setting and inquiring its value. The static **set()** method usually has three parameters, as shown in the previous section:

- The state from which to retrieve the element (which the element obtains from the given action)

- A pointer to the node that is changing the element's value (used for caching purposes and for checking the Override flag)

- The new value for the element

Most element classes also define a static **get()** method that returns the current value stored in an element instance. For example, to obtain the current draw style:

```
style = SoDrawStyleElement::get(action->getState());
```

Elements that have multiple values may define a different sequence of **get()** methods. For example, the material color elements and coordinate element can contain many values. In these cases, the element class defines three methods:

getInstance()	returns the top instance of the element in the state as a **const** pointer
getNum()	returns the number of values in the element
get(*n***)**	returns the *n*th value in the element

Element Bundles

Elements are designed to be small and specific, for two reasons. The first reason is that it should be possible for a node to change one aspect of the state without having to change any of the rest, including related elements. For example, the **SoBaseColor** node changes only the **SoDiffuseColorElement** without affecting any other material elements. The second reason has to do with caching. It is easy to determine when any element's value has changed, since (typically) the whole element changes at once. Therefore, determining which nodes affect a cache is a straightforward task.

However, some elements are related to each other, and it's good to deal with them together for convenience and efficiency. Classes called *bundles* provide simple interfaces to collections of related elements.

Supported Inventor bundle classes are

- SoMaterialBundle
- SoNormalBundle
- SoTextureCoordinateBundle

The **SoMaterialBundle** class accesses all elements having to do with surface materials. Methods on the bundle allow shapes to step easily through sequential materials and to send the current material to OpenGL. The **SoNormalBundle** allows you to step easily through sequential normals and provides routines for generating default normals. The **SoTextureCoordinateBundle** allows you to step through texture coordinates and provides methods for generating texture coordinates if the shape is using **SoTextureCoordinatePlane** or **SoTextureCoordinateEnvironment**.

Creating a Property Node

The easiest way to learn how to add a node class is by example. The first example creates a new property node called **Glow**, which modifies the emissive color of the current material to make objects appear to glow. It has a field called **color**, which is the color of the glow, and a float field called **brightness**, ranging from 0 to 1, indicating how much the object should glow.

For this class, we need to implement actions that deal with materials: **GLRender()** and **callback()**. We will use **doAction()** (see "The doAction() Method" on page 25), since it performs the same operation for both actions. The **doAction()** method for the **Glow** class updates the emissive color element based on the values of the **color** and **brightness** fields of the node.

The class header for our new node is shown in Example 2-1.

Example 2-1   Glow.h

```
#include <Inventor/SbColor.h>
#include <Inventor/fields/SoSFColor.h>
#include <Inventor/fields/SoSFFloat.h>
#include <Inventor/nodes/SoSubNode.h>

class Glow : public SoNode {

   SO_NODE_HEADER(Glow);

  public:
    // Fields:
    SoSFColor        color;       // Color of glow
    SoSFFloat        brightness;  // Amount of glow (0-1)

    // Initializes this class for use in scene graphs. This
    // should be called after database initialization and before
    // any instance of this node is constructed.
    static void    initClass();

    // Constructor
    Glow();

  protected:
    // These implement supported actions. The only actions that
    // deal with materials are the callback and GL render
    // actions. We will inherit all other action methods from
    // SoNode.
    virtual void   GLRender(SoGLRenderAction *action);
    virtual void   callback(SoCallbackAction *action);

    // This implements generic traversal of Glow node, used in
    // both of the above methods.
    virtual void   doAction(SoAction *action);
```

```
private:
    // Destructor. Private to keep people from trying to delete
    // nodes, rather than using the reference count mechanism.
    virtual ~Glow();

    // Holds emissive color. A pointer to this is stored in the
    // state.
    SbColor         emissiveColor;
};
```

The **Glow** node is representative of most property nodes in that it is
concerned solely with editing the current traversal state, regardless of the
action being performed. The use of the element in the example is also
typical; most elements have simple **set**() methods to store values.

The source code for the **Glow** class is shown in Example 2-2.

Example 2-2   Glow.c++

```
#include <Inventor/actions/SoCallbackAction.h>
#include <Inventor/actions/SoGLRenderAction.h>
#include <Inventor/bundles/SoMaterialBundle.h>
#include <Inventor/elements/SoEmissiveColorElement.h>
#include "Glow.h"

SO_NODE_SOURCE(Glow);

// Initializes the Glow class. This is a one-time thing that is
// done after database initialization and before any instance of
// this class is constructed.

void
Glow::initClass()
{
    // Initialize type id variables. The arguments to the macro
    // are: the name of the node class, the class this is derived
    // from, and the name registered with the type of the parent
    // class.
    SO_NODE_INIT_CLASS(Glow, SoNode, "Node");
}

// Constructor

Glow::Glow()
{
    // Do standard constructor tasks
    SO_NODE_CONSTRUCTOR(Glow);
```

```
    // Add "color" field to the field data. The default value for
    // this field is R=G=B=1, which is white.
    SO_NODE_ADD_FIELD(color, (1.0, 1.0, 1.0));

    // Add "brightness" field to the field data. The default
    // value for this field is 0.
    SO_NODE_ADD_FIELD(brightness, (0.0));
}

// Destructor

Glow::~Glow()
{
}

// Implements GL render action.

void
Glow::GLRender(SoGLRenderAction *action)
{
    // Set the elements in the state correctly. Note that we
    // prefix the call to doAction() with the class name. This
    // avoids problems if someone derives a new class from the
    // Glow node and inherits the GLRender() method; Glow's
    // doAction() will still be called in that case.
    Glow::doAction(action);

    // For efficiency, Inventor nodes make sure that the first
    // defined material is always in GL, so shapes do not have to
    // send the first material each time. (This keeps caches from
    // being dependent on material values in many cases.) The
    // SoMaterialBundle class allows us to do this easily.
    SoMaterialBundle  mb(action);
    mb.forceSend(0);
}

// Implements callback action.

void
Glow::callback(SoCallbackAction *action)
{
    // Set the elements in the state correctly.
    Glow::doAction(action);
}
```

```
// Typical action implementation - it sets the correct element
// in the action's traversal state. We assume that the element
// has been enabled.

void
Glow::doAction(SoAction *action)
{
   // Make sure the "brightness" field is not ignored. If it is,
   // then we don't need to change anything in the state.
   if (! brightness.isIgnored()) {

      // Define the emissive color as the product of the
      // "brightness" and "color" fields. "emissiveColor" is an
      // instance variable. Since material elements contain
      // pointers to the actual values, we need to store the
      // value in the instance. (We could have defined the
      // fields to contain multiple values, in which case we
      // would have to store an array of emissive colors.)
      emissiveColor = color.getValue() * brightness.getValue();

      // Set the value of the emissive color element to our one
      // new emissive color. "this" is passed in to let the
      // caching mechanism know who set this element and to
      // handle overriding. (Note that this call will have no
      // effect if another node with a TRUE Override flag set
      // the element previously.)
      SoEmissiveColorElement::set(action->getState(), this,
                                  1, &emissiveColor);
   }
}
```

Creating a Shape Node

This next example is more complicated than the property-node example, because shape nodes need to access more of the state and implement different behaviors for different actions. For example, a shape needs to draw geometry during rendering, return intersection information during picking, and compute its extent when getting a bounding box.

All shapes need to define at least two methods: **generatePrimitives()** and **getBoundingBox()**. When you define the **generatePrimitives()** method for your new class, you can inherit the **GLRender()** and **rayPick()** methods from the base class, **SoShape**, because they use the generated primitives. This feature saves time at the prototyping stage, since you need to implement only the **generatePrimitives()** method, and rendering and picking are provided at no extra cost. When you are ready for fine-tuning, you can redefine these two methods to improve performance.

Generating Primitives

When it is traversed to generate primitives for the **SoCallbackAction**, each shape generates triangles, line segments, or points. The information for each vertex of the triangle, line segment, or point is stored in an instance of **SoPrimitiveVertex**. The shape fills in the information for each vertex. Then, for each primitive generated (that is, triangle, line segment, or point), an appropriate callback function is invoked by a method on **SoShape**. For example, if the shape generates triangles, the triangle callback function is invoked for every triangle generated. Filled shapes, such as **SoCone** and **SoQuadMesh**, generate triangles (regardless of draw style), line shapes (such as **SoLineSet** and **SoIndexedLineSet**) generate line segments, and point shapes (such as **SoPointSet**) generate points.

SoPrimitiveVertex

The **SoPrimitiveVertex** contains all information for that vertex:

- Point (coordinates, in object space)
- Normal
- Texture coordinates
- Material index
- A pointer to an instance of an **SoDetail** subclass (may be NULL)

The shape's **generatePrimitives()** method sets each of these values.

The appropriate callback function can be invoked either automatically or explicitly. If you want explicit control over when the callback function is invoked, you can use the following methods provided by the **SoShape** class:

- **invokeTriangleCallbacks()**
- **invokeLineSegmentCallbacks()**
- **invokePointCallbacks()**

To take advantage of the automatic mechanism, use these three methods, provided by the **SoShape** base class as a convenience:

- **beginShape**(*action, shapeType*)
- **shapeVertex**(*&vertex*)
- **endShape**()

The *shapeType* parameter is TRIANGLE_FAN, TRIANGLE_STRIP, TRIANGLES, or POLYGON. For example, if you choose TRIANGLE_FAN, this method performs the necessary triangulation and invokes the appropriate callbacks for each successive triangle of the shape. This mechanism is similar to OpenGL's geometry calls.

Creating Details

You may want your shape to store additional information in an **SoDetail**—for example, what part of the shape each vertex belongs to. In this case, you can use an existing subclass of **SoDetail** (see *The Inventor Mentor*, Chapter 9), or you can create a new **SoDetail** subclass to hold the appropriate information. By default, the pointer to the detail in **SoPrimitiveVertex** is NULL.

If you decide to store information in an **SoDetail**, you create an instance of the subclass and store a pointer to it in the **SoPrimitiveVertex** by calling **setDetail**().

Rendering

For rendering, you may be able to inherit the **GLRender**() method from the **SoShape** class. In this case, you define a **generatePrimitives**() method as described in the previous sections. Each primitive will be generated and then rendered separately.

In other cases, you may want to write your own render method for the new shape class, especially if it would be more efficient to send the vertex information to OpenGL in some other form, such as triangle strips. The **Pyramid** node created later in this chapter implements its own **GLRender**() method. Before rendering, the shape should test whether it needs to be rendered. You can use the **SoShape::shouldGLRender**() method, which checks for INVISIBLE draw style, BOUNDING_BOX complexity, delayed transparency, and render abort.

Inventor takes care of sending the draw-style value to OpenGL (where it is handled by **glPolygonMode()**). This means that filled shapes will be drawn automatically as lines or points if the draw style indicates such. Note that if your object is composed of lines, but the draw style is POINTS, you need to handle that case explicitly. You need to check whether the draw-style element in the state is points or lines and render the shape accordingly.

Picking

For picking, you may also be able to inherit the **rayPick()** method from the **SoShape** class. In this case, you define a **generatePrimitives()** method, and the parent class **rayPick()** method tests the picking ray against each primitive that has been generated. If it intersects the primitive, it creates an **SoPickedPoint**. **SoShape** provides three virtual methods for creating details:

- **createTriangleDetail()**
- **createLineDetail()**
- **createPointDetail()**

The default methods return NULL, but your shape can override this to set up and return a detail instance.

The **Pyramid** node created later in this chapter inherits the **rayPick()** method from **SoShape** in this manner.

For some shapes, such as spheres and cylinders, it is more efficient to check whether the picking ray intersects the object without tessellating the object into primitives. In such cases, you can implement your own **rayPick()** method and use the **SoShape::shouldRayPick()** method, which first checks to see if the object is pickable.

The following excerpt from the **SoSphere** class shows how to implement your own **rayPick()** method:

```
void
SoSphere::rayPick(SoRayPickAction *action)
{
    SbVec3f             enterPoint, exitPoint, normal;
    SbVec4f             texCoord(0.0, 0.0, 0.0, 1.0);
    SoPickedPoint       *pp;
```

```
// First see if the object is pickable.
if (! shouldRayPick(action))
    return;

// Compute the picking ray in our current object space.
computeObjectSpaceRay(action);

// Create SbSphere with correct radius, centered at zero.
float       rad = (radius.isIgnored() ? 1.0 :
                    radius.getValue());
SbSphere    sph(SbVec3f(0., 0., 0.), rad);

// Intersect with pick ray. If found, set up picked point(s).
if (sph.intersect(action->getLine(), enterPoint, exitPoint)) {
    if (action->isBetweenPlanes(enterPoint) &&
        (pp = action->addIntersection(enterPoint)) != NULL) {

        normal = enterPoint;
        normal.normalize();
        pp->setObjectNormal(normal);
        // This macro computes the s and t texture coordinates
        // for the shape.
        COMPUTE_S_T(enterPoint, texCoord[0], texCoord[1]);
        pp->setObjectTextureCoords(texCoord);
    }

    if (action->isBetweenPlanes(exitPoint) &&
        (pp = action->addIntersection(exitPoint)) != NULL) {

        normal = exitPoint;
        normal.normalize();
        pp->setObjectNormal(normal);
        COMPUTE_S_T(exitPoint, texCoord[0], texCoord[1]);
        texCoord[2] = texCoord[3] = 0.0;
        pp->setObjectTextureCoords(texCoord);
    }
  }
}
```

Getting a Bounding Box

SoShape provides a **getBoundingBox()** method that your new shape class
can inherit. This method calls a virtual **computeBBox()** method, which you
need to define. (The **computeBBox()** method is also used during rendering
when bounding-box complexity is specified.)

If you are deriving a class from **SoNonIndexedShape**, you can use the **computeCoordBBox()** method within your **computeBBox()** routine. This method computes the bounding box by looking at the specified number of vertices, starting at **startIndex**. It uses the minimum and maximum coordinate values to form the diagonal for the bounding box and uses the average of the vertices as the center of the object.

If you are deriving a class from **SoIndexedShape**, you can inherit **computeBBox()** from the base **SoIndexedShape** class. This method uses all nonnegative indices in the coordinates list to find the minimum and maximum coordinate values. It uses the average of the coordinate values as the center of the object.

Pyramid Node

This example creates a **Pyramid** node, which has a square base at $y = -1$ and its apex at (0.0, 1.0, 0.0). The code presented here is similar to that used for other primitive (nonvertex-based) shapes, such as cones and cylinders. The pyramid behaves like an **SoCone**, except that it always has four sides. And, instead of a **bottomRadius** field, the **Pyramid** class has **baseWidth** and **baseDepth** fields in addition to the **parts** and **height** fields.

Some of the work for all shapes can be done by methods on the base shape class, **SoShape**. For example, **SoShape::shouldGLRender()** checks for INVISIBLE draw style when rendering. **SoShape::shouldRayPick()** checks for UNPICKABLE pick style when picking. This means that shape subclasses can concentrate on their specific behaviors.

To define a vertex-based shape subclass, you probably want to derive your class from either **SoNonIndexedShape** or **SoIndexedShape**. These classes define some methods and macros that can make your job easier.

You may notice in this example that there are macros (defined in SoSFEnum.h) that make it easy to deal with fields containing enumerated types, such as the **parts** field of our node. Similar macros are found in SoMFEnum.h and in the header files for the bit-mask fields.

The class header for the **Pyramid** node is shown in Example 2-3.

Example 2-3   Pyramid.h

```
#include <Inventor/SbLinear.h>
#include <Inventor/fields/SoSFBitMask.h>
#include <Inventor/fields/SoSFFloat.h>
#include <Inventor/nodes/SoShape.h>
// SoShape.h includes SoSubNode.h; no need to include it again.

// Pyramid texture coordinates are defined on the sides so that
// the seam is along the left rear edge, wrapping
// counterclockwise around the sides. The texture coordinates on
// the base are set up so the texture is right side up when the
// pyramid is tilted back.

class Pyramid : public SoShape {

    SO_NODE_HEADER(Pyramid);

 public:

    enum Part {                  // Pyramid parts:
       SIDES = 0x01,             // The 4 side faces
       BASE  = 0x02,             // The bottom square face
       ALL   = 0x03,             // All parts
    };

    // Fields
    SoSFBitMask    parts;        // Visible parts
    SoSFFloat      baseWidth;    // Width of base
    SoSFFloat      baseDepth;    // Depth of base
    SoSFFloat      height;       // Height, base to apex

    // Initializes this class.
    static void    initClass();

    // Constructor
    Pyramid();

    // Turns on/off a part of the pyramid. (Convenience)
    void           addPart(Part part);
    void           removePart(Part part);

    // Returns whether a given part is on or off. (Convenience)
    SbBool         hasPart(Part part) const;
```

```
protected:
     // This implements the GL rendering action. We will inherit
     // all other action behavior, including rayPick(), which is
     // defined by SoShape to pick against all of the triangles
     // created by generatePrimitives.
     virtual void  GLRender(SoGLRenderAction *action);

     // Generates triangles representing a pyramid.
     virtual void  generatePrimitives(SoAction *action);

     // This computes the bounding box and center of a pyramid. It
     // is used by SoShape for the SoGetBoundingBoxAction and also
     // to compute the correct box to render or pick when
     // complexity is BOUNDING_BOX. Note that we do not have to
     // define a getBoundingBox() method, since SoShape already
     // takes care of that (using this method).
     virtual void  computeBBox(SoAction *action,
                               SbBox3f &box, SbVec3f &center);
private:
     // Face normals. These are static because they are computed
     // once and are shared by all instances.
     static SbVec3f frontNormal, rearNormal;
     static SbVec3f leftNormal,  rightNormal;
     static SbVec3f baseNormal;

     // Destructor
     virtual ~Pyramid();

     // Computes and returns half-width, half-height, and
     // half-depth based on current field values.
     void          getSize(float &halfWidth,
                           float &halfHeight,
                           float &halfDepth) const;
};
```

The source code for the Pyramid node is shown in Example 2-4.

Example 2-4   Pyramid.c++

```
#include <GL/gl.h>
#include <Inventor/SbBox.h>
#include <Inventor/SoPickedPoint.h>
#include <Inventor/SoPrimitiveVertex.h>
#include <Inventor/actions/SoGLRenderAction.h>
#include <Inventor/bundles/SoMaterialBundle.h>
#include <Inventor/elements/SoGLTextureCoordinateElement.h>
#include <Inventor/elements/SoGLTextureEnabledElement.h>
```

```
#include <Inventor/elements/SoLightModelElement.h>
#include <Inventor/elements/SoMaterialBindingElement.h>
#include <Inventor/elements/SoModelMatrixElement.h>
#include <Inventor/misc/SoState.h>
#include "Pyramid.h"

// Shorthand macro for testing whether the current parts field
// value (parts) includes a given part (part).
#define HAS_PART(parts, part) (((parts) & (part)) != 0)

SO_NODE_SOURCE(Pyramid);

// Normals to four side faces and to base.
SbVec3f Pyramid::frontNormal, Pyramid::rearNormal;
SbVec3f Pyramid::leftNormal,  Pyramid::rightNormal;
SbVec3f Pyramid::baseNormal;

// This initializes the Pyramid class.

void
Pyramid::initClass()
{
   // Initialize type id variables.
   SO_NODE_INIT_CLASS(Pyramid, SoShape, "Shape");
}

// Constructor

Pyramid::Pyramid()
{
   SO_NODE_CONSTRUCTOR(Pyramid);
   SO_NODE_ADD_FIELD(parts,      (ALL));
   SO_NODE_ADD_FIELD(baseWidth, (2.0));
   SO_NODE_ADD_FIELD(baseDepth, (2.0));
   SO_NODE_ADD_FIELD(height,     (2.0));

   // Set up static values and strings for the "parts"
   // enumerated type field. This allows the SoSFEnum class to
   // read values for this field. For example, the first line
   // below says that the first value (index 0) has the value
   // SIDES (defined in the header file) and is represented in
   // the file format by the string "SIDES".
   SO_NODE_DEFINE_ENUM_VALUE(Part, SIDES);
   SO_NODE_DEFINE_ENUM_VALUE(Part, BASE);
   SO_NODE_DEFINE_ENUM_VALUE(Part, ALL);
```

```
    // Copy static information for "parts" enumerated type field
    // into this instance.
    SO_NODE_SET_SF_ENUM_TYPE(parts, Part);

    // If this is the first time the constructor is called, set
    // up the static normals.
    if (SO_NODE_IS_FIRST_INSTANCE()) {
       float invRoot5      = 1.0 / sqrt(5.0);
       float invRoot5Twice = 2.0 * invRoot5;

       frontNormal.setValue(0.0, invRoot5,  invRoot5Twice);
       rearNormal.setValue( 0.0, invRoot5, -invRoot5Twice);
       leftNormal.setValue( -invRoot5Twice, invRoot5, 0.0);
       rightNormal.setValue( invRoot5Twice, invRoot5, 0.0);
       baseNormal.setValue(0.0, -1.0, 0.0);
    }
}

// Destructor

Pyramid::~Pyramid()
{
}

// Turns on a part of the pyramid. (Convenience function.)

void
Pyramid::addPart(Part part)
{
    parts.setValue(parts.getValue() | part);
}

// Turns off a part of the pyramid. (Convenience function.)

void
Pyramid::removePart(Part part)
{
    parts.setValue(parts.getValue() & ~part);
}
```

```
// Returns whether a given part is on or off. (Convenience
// function.)

SbBool
Pyramid::hasPart(Part part) const
{
   return HAS_PART(parts.getValue(), part);
}


// Implements the SoGLRenderAction for the Pyramid node.

void
Pyramid::GLRender(SoGLRenderAction *action)
{
   // Access the state from the action.
   SoState  *state = action->getState();

   // See which parts are enabled.
   int curParts = (parts.isIgnored() ? ALL : parts.getValue());

   // First see if the object is visible and should be rendered
   // now. This is a method on SoShape that checks for INVISIBLE
   // draw style, BOUNDING_BOX complexity, and delayed
   // transparency.
   if (! shouldGLRender(action))
     return;

   // Make sure things are set up correctly for a solid object.
   // We are solid if all parts are on. beginSolidShape() is a
   // method on SoShape that sets up backface culling and other
   // optimizations.
   if (curParts == ALL)
     beginSolidShape(action);

   // Change the current GL matrix to draw the pyramid with the
   // correct size. This is easier than modifying all of the
   // coordinates and normals of the pyramid. (For extra
   // efficiency, you can check if the field values are all set
   // to default values - if so, then you can skip this step.)
   // Scale world if necessary.
   float         halfWidth, halfHeight, halfDepth;
   getSize(halfWidth, halfHeight, halfDepth);
   glPushMatrix();
   glScalef(halfWidth, halfHeight, halfDepth);
```

```
    // See if texturing is enabled. If so, we will have to
    // send explicit texture coordinates. The "doTextures" flag
    // will indicate if we care about textures at all.
    SbBool doTextures =
       (SoGLTextureEnabledElement::get(state) &&
        SoTextureCoordinateElement::getType(state) !=
        SoTextureCoordinateElement::NONE);

    // Determine if we need to send normals. Normals are
    // necessary if we are not doing BASE_COLOR lighting.
    SbBool sendNormals =
       (SoLightModelElement::get(state) !=
        SoLightModelElement::BASE_COLOR);

    // Determine if there's a material bound per part.
    SoMaterialBindingElement::Binding binding =
       SoMaterialBindingElement::get(state);
    SbBool materialPerPart =
       (binding == SoMaterialBindingElement::PER_PART ||
        binding == SoMaterialBindingElement::PER_PART_INDEXED);

    // Make sure first material is sent if necessary. We'll use
    // the SoMaterialBundle class because it makes things very
    // easy.
    SoMaterialBundle mb(action);
    mb.sendFirst();

    // Render the parts of the pyramid. We don't have to worry
    // about whether to render filled regions, lines, or points,
    // since that is already taken care of. We are also ignoring
    // complexity, which we could use to render a more
    // finely-tessellated version of the pyramid.

    // We'll use this macro to make the code easier. It uses the
    // "point" variable to store the vertex point to send.
    SbVec3f  point;

#define SEND_VERTEX(x, y, z, s, t)\
    point.setValue(x, y, z);               \
    if (doTextures)                        \
       glTexCoord2f(s, t);                 \
    glVertex3fv(point.getValue())

    if (HAS_PART(curParts, SIDES)) {
```

```
// Draw each side separately, so that normals are correct.
// If sendNormals is TRUE, send face normals with the
// polygons. Make sure the vertex order obeys the
// right-hand rule.

glBegin(GL_TRIANGLES);

    // Front face: left front, right front, apex
    if (sendNormals)
      glNormal3fv(frontNormal.getValue());
    SEND_VERTEX(-1.0, -1.0,  1.0, .25,  0.0);
    SEND_VERTEX( 1.0, -1.0,  1.0, .50,  0.0);
    SEND_VERTEX( 0.0,  1.0,  0.0, .325, 1.0);

    // Right face: right front, right rear, apex
    if (sendNormals)
      glNormal3fv(rightNormal.getValue());
    SEND_VERTEX( 1.0, -1.0,  1.0, .50,  0.0);
    SEND_VERTEX( 1.0, -1.0, -1.0, .75,  0.0);
    SEND_VERTEX( 0.0,  1.0,  0.0, .625, 1.0);

    // Rear face: right rear, left rear, apex
    if (sendNormals)
      glNormal3fv(rearNormal.getValue());
    SEND_VERTEX( 1.0, -1.0, -1.0, .75,  0.0);
    SEND_VERTEX(-1.0, -1.0, -1.0, 1.0,  0.0);
    SEND_VERTEX( 0.0,  1.0,  0.0, .875, 1.0);

    // Left face: left rear, left front, apex
    if (sendNormals)
      glNormal3fv(leftNormal.getValue());
    SEND_VERTEX(-1.0, -1.0, -1.0, 0.0,  0.0);
    SEND_VERTEX(-1.0, -1.0,  1.0, .25,  0.0);
    SEND_VERTEX( 0.0,  1.0,  0.0, .125, 1.0);

  glEnd();
}

if (HAS_PART(curParts, BASE)) {

  // Send the next material if it varies per part.
  if (materialPerPart)
    mb.send(1, FALSE);

  if (sendNormals)
    glNormal3fv(baseNormal.getValue());
```

```
   // Base: left rear, right rear, right front, left front
   glBegin(GL_QUADS);
   SEND_VERTEX(-1.0, -1.0, -1.0, 0.0,  0.0);
   SEND_VERTEX( 1.0, -1.0, -1.0, 1.0,  0.0);
   SEND_VERTEX( 1.0, -1.0,  1.0, 1.0,  1.0);
   SEND_VERTEX(-1.0, -1.0,  1.0, 0.0,  1.0);
   glEnd();
}

// Restore the GL matrix.
glPopMatrix();

// Terminate the effects of rendering a solid shape if
// necessary.
if (curParts == ALL)
   endSolidShape(action);
}

// Generates triangles representing a pyramid.

void
Pyramid::generatePrimitives(SoAction *action)
{
   // The pyramid will generate 6 triangles: 1 for each side
   // and 2 for the base. (Again, we are ignoring complexity.)
   // This variable is used to store each vertex.
   SoPrimitiveVertex   pv;

   // Access the state from the action.
   SoState   *state = action->getState();

   // See which parts are enabled.
   int curParts = (parts.isIgnored() ? ALL : parts.getValue());

   // We need the size to adjust the coordinates.
   float halfWidth, halfHeight, halfDepth;
   getSize(halfWidth, halfHeight, halfDepth);

   // See if we have to use a texture coordinate function,
   // rather than generating explicit texture coordinates.
   SbBool useTexFunc =
     (SoTextureCoordinateElement::getType(state) ==
      SoTextureCoordinateElement::FUNCTION);
```

```
// If we need to generate texture coordinates with a
// function, we'll need an SoGLTextureCoordinateElement.
// Otherwise, we'll set up the coordinates directly.
const SoTextureCoordinateElement *tce;
SbVec4f texCoord;
if (useTexFunc)
  tce = SoTextureCoordinateElement::getInstance(state);
else {
  texCoord[2] = 0.0;
  texCoord[3] = 1.0;
}

// Determine if there's a material bound per part.
SoMaterialBindingElement::Binding binding =
  SoMaterialBindingElement::get(state);
SbBool materialPerPart =
  (binding == SoMaterialBindingElement::PER_PART ||
   binding == SoMaterialBindingElement::PER_PART_INDEXED);

// We'll use this macro to make the code easier. It uses the
// "point" variable to store the primitive vertex's point.
SbVec3f  point;

#define GEN_VERTEX(pv, x, y, z, s, t, normal)    \
    point.setValue(halfWidth  * x,               \
              halfHeight * y,                    \
              halfDepth  * z);                   \
    if (useTexFunc)                              \
      texCoord = tce->get(point, normal);        \
    else {                                       \
      texCoord[0] = s;                           \
      texCoord[1] = t;                           \
    }                                            \
    pv.setPoint(point);                          \
    pv.setNormal(normal);                        \
    pv.setTextureCoords(texCoord);               \
    shapeVertex(&pv)

  if (HAS_PART(curParts, SIDES)) {

    // We will generate 4 triangles for the sides of the
    // pyramid. We can use the beginShape() / shapeVertex() /
    // endShape() convenience functions on SoShape to make the
    // triangle generation easier and clearer. (The
    // shapeVertex() call is built into the macro.)
```

```
    // Note that there is no detail information for the
    // Pyramid. If there were, we would create an instance of
    // the correct subclass of SoDetail (such as
    // PyramidDetail) and call pv.setDetail(&detail); once.

    beginShape(action, TRIANGLES);

    // Front face: left front, right front, apex
    GEN_VERTEX(pv, -1.0, -1.0,  1.0, .25,  0.0, frontNormal);
    GEN_VERTEX(pv,  1.0, -1.0,  1.0, .50,  0.0, frontNormal);
    GEN_VERTEX(pv,  0.0,  1.0,  0.0, .325, 1.0, frontNormal);

    // Right face: right front, right rear, apex
    GEN_VERTEX(pv,  1.0, -1.0,  1.0, .50,  0.0, rightNormal);
    GEN_VERTEX(pv,  1.0, -1.0, -1.0, .75,  0.0, rightNormal);
    GEN_VERTEX(pv,  0.0,  1.0,  0.0, .625, 1.0, rightNormal);

    // Rear face: right rear, left rear, apex
    GEN_VERTEX(pv,  1.0, -1.0, -1.0, .75,  0.0, rearNormal);
    GEN_VERTEX(pv, -1.0, -1.0, -1.0, 1.0,  0.0, rearNormal);
    GEN_VERTEX(pv,  0.0,  1.0,  0.0, .875, 1.0, rearNormal);

    // Left face: left rear, left front, apex
    GEN_VERTEX(pv, -1.0, -1.0, -1.0, 0.0,  0.0, leftNormal);
    GEN_VERTEX(pv, -1.0, -1.0,  1.0, .25,  0.0, leftNormal);
    GEN_VERTEX(pv,  0.0,  1.0,  0.0, .125, 1.0, leftNormal);

    endShape();
}

if (HAS_PART(curParts, BASE)) {

    // Increment the material index in the vertex if
    // necessary. (The index is set to 0 by default.)
    if (materialPerPart)
      pv.setMaterialIndex(1);
    // We will generate two triangles for the base, as a
    // triangle strip.
    beginShape(action, TRIANGLE_STRIP);
```

```
    // Base: left front, left rear, right front, right rear
    GEN_VERTEX(pv, -1.0, -1.0,  1.0, 0.0,  1.0, baseNormal);
    GEN_VERTEX(pv, -1.0, -1.0, -1.0, 0.0,  0.0, baseNormal);
    GEN_VERTEX(pv,  1.0, -1.0,  1.0, 1.0,  1.0, baseNormal);
    GEN_VERTEX(pv,  1.0, -1.0, -1.0, 1.0,  0.0, baseNormal);

    endShape();
  }
}

// Computes the bounding box and center of a pyramid.

void
Pyramid::computeBBox(SoAction *, SbBox3f &box, SbVec3f &center)
{
  // Figure out what parts are active.
  int curParts = (parts.isIgnored() ? ALL : parts.getValue());

  // If no parts are active, set the bounding box to be tiny.
  if (curParts == 0)
    box.setBounds(0.0, 0.0, 0.0, 0.0, 0.0, 0.0);

  else {
    // These points define the min and max extents of the box.
    SbVec3f min, max;

    // Compute the half-width, half-height, and half-depth of
    // the pyramid. We'll use this info to set the min and max
    // points.
    float   halfWidth, halfHeight, halfDepth;
    getSize(halfWidth, halfHeight, halfDepth);

    min.setValue(-halfWidth, -halfHeight, -halfDepth);

    // The maximum point depends on whether the SIDES are
    // active. If not, only the base is present.
    if (HAS_PART(curParts, SIDES))
      max.setValue(halfWidth, halfHeight, halfDepth);
    else
      max.setValue(halfWidth, -halfHeight, halfDepth);

    // Set the box to bound the two extreme points.
    box.setBounds(min, max);
  }
```

```
    // This defines the "natural center" of the pyramid. We could
    // define it to be the center of the base, if we want, but
    // let's just make it the center of the bounding box.
    center.setValue(0.0, 0.0, 0.0);
}

// Computes and returns half-width, half-height, and half-depth
// based on current field values.

void
Pyramid::getSize(float &halfWidth,
             float &halfHeight,
             float &halfDepth) const
{
    halfWidth  = (baseWidth.isIgnored() ? 1.0 :
                    baseWidth.getValue() / 2.0);
    halfHeight = (height.isIgnored()    ? 1.0 :
                    height.getValue()    / 2.0);
    halfDepth  = (baseDepth.isIgnored() ? 1.0 :
                    baseDepth.getValue() / 2.0);
}
```

Tip: The easiest way to make sure your **generatePrimitives**() method is ❖
working is to use it for rendering, by temporarily commenting out your
shape's **GLRender**() method (if it has one).

Creating a Group Node

This example illustrates how to create a group node subclass. (It is unlikely,
however, that you'll need to create a new group class.) Our example class,
Alternate, traverses every other child (that is, child 0, then child 2, and so
on). Since, like the base **SoGroup** class, it has no fields, this example also
illustrates how to create a node with no fields.

If you do create a new group class, you will probably need to define a new
traversal behavior for it. You may be able to inherit some of the traversal
behavior from the parent class. Most groups define a protected
traverseChildren() method that implements their "typical" traversal
behavior. Your new group can probably inherit the **read**() and **write**()
methods from **SoGroup**.

Child List

SoGroup, and all classes derived from it, store their children in an instance of **SoChildList**. This extender class provides useful methods for group classes, including the **traverse()** method, which has three forms:

traverse(*action*)   traverses all children in the child list

traverse(*action, firstChild, lastChild*)
> traverses the children from first child to last child, inclusive

traverse(*action, childIndex*)
> traverses one child with the specified index

Hidden Children

If you want your new node to have children, but you don't want to grant public access to the child list, you can implement the node to have *hidden children*. Node kits are an example of groups within the Inventor library that have hidden children. Because node kits have a specific internal structure, access to the children needs to be restricted. If you want the node to have hidden children, it should not be derived from **SoGroup**, which has public children only.

SoNode provides a virtual **getChildren()** method that returns NULL by default. To implement a new node with hidden children, you need to do the following:

1. Maintain an **SoChildList** for the node. This list can be a hierarchy of nodes.

2. Implement a **getChildren()** method that returns a pointer to the child list. (**SoPath** uses **getChildren()** to maintain paths.)

Using the Path Code

Recall that an action can be applied to a node, a single path, or a path list. Before a group can traverse its children, it needs to know what the action has been applied to. The **getPathCode()** method of **SoAction** returns an enumerated value that indicates whether the action is being applied to a path and, if so, where this group node is in relation to the path or paths. The values returned by **getPathCode()** are as follows:

NO_PATH	the action is not being applied to a path (that is, the action is applied to a node)
BELOW_PATH	this node is at or below the last node in the path chain
OFF_PATH	this node is not on the path chain (the node is to the left of the path; it needs to be traversed if it affects the nodes in the path)
IN_PATH	the node is in the chain of the path (but is not the last node)

Figure 2-1 shows five group nodes. Assume the render action is being applied to the path shown. Groups A and C are considered IN_PATH. Group B is OFF_PATH, and Groups D and E are BELOW_PATH.

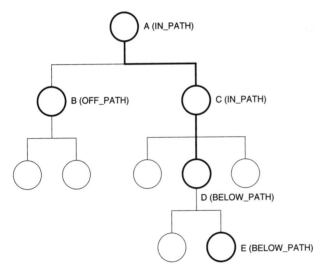

Figure 2-1   Using the Path Code for Groups

For **SoGroup**, if the group's path code is NO_PATH, BELOW_PATH, or OFF_PATH, it traverses all of its children. (Even if a node is OFF_PATH, you need to traverse it because it affects the nodes in the path to its right. Note, though, that if an **SoSeparator** is OFF_PATH, you do not need to traverse it because it will not have any effect on the path.) If a node is IN_PATH, you may not need to traverse all children in the group, since children to the right of the action path do not affect the nodes in the path. In this case, **getPathCode()** returns the indices of the children that need to be traversed. The **traverseChildren()** method for **SoGroup** looks like this:

```
void
SoGroup::traverseChildren(SoAction *action)
{
   int         numIndices;
   const   int   *indices;

   if (action->getPathCode(numIndices, indices)
      == SoAction::IN_PATH)
      children.traverse(action, 0, indices[numIndices - 1]);
         // traverse all children up to and including the last
         // child to traverse

   else
      children.traverse(action); // traverse all children
}
```

The GL render, callback, handle event, pick, and search methods for
SoGroup all use **traverseChildren()**. The write method for **SoGroup**, which
can be inherited by most subclasses, tests each node in the group before
writing it out. The get matrix method does not use **traverseChildren()**
because it doesn't need to traverse as much. If the path code for a group is
NO_PATH or BELOW_PATH, it does not traverse the children. Here is the
code for **SoGroup::getMatrix()**:

```
void
SoGroup::getMatrix(SoGetMatrixAction *action)
{
   int         numIndices;
   const int   *indices;

   switch (action->getPathCode(numIndices, indices)) {
      case SoAction::NO_PATH:
      case SoAction::BELOW_PATH:
         break;
      case SoAction::IN_PATH:
         children.traverse(action, 0, indices[numIndices - 1]);
         break;
      case SoAction::OFF_PATH:
         children.traverse(action);
         break;
   }
}
```

If a node is IN_PATH, the **getMatrix()** method traverses all the children in
the group up to and including the last child in the action path (but not the
children to the right of the path). If a node is OFF_PATH, the **getMatrix()**

method traverses all the children in the group, since they can affect what is in the path.

What Happens If an Action Is Terminated?

Some actions, such as the GL render, handle event, and search actions, can terminate prematurely—for example, when the node to search for has been found. The **SoAction** class has a flag that indicates whether the action has terminated. The **SoChildList** class checks this flag automatically, so this termination is built into the **SoChildList::traverse()** methods, and the group traversal methods do not need to check the flag.

The new **Alternate** class can inherit the read and write methods from **SoGroup**. We just have to define the traversal behavior for the other actions. Most of the other actions can be handled by the **traverseChildren()** method.

Alternate Node

The class header for the **Alternate** node is shown in Example 2-5.

Example 2-5   Alternate.h

```
#include <Inventor/nodes/SoGroup.h>
// SoGroup.h includes SoSubNode.h; no need to include it again.

class Alternate : public SoGroup {

   SO_NODE_HEADER(Alternate);

 public:
   // Initializes this class.
   static void   initClass();

   // Default constructor
   Alternate();

   // Constructor that takes approximate number of children as
   // a hint
   Alternate::Alternate(int numChildren);
```

```
protected:
   // Generic traversal of children for any action.
   virtual void   doAction(SoAction *action);

   // These implement supported actions.
   virtual void   getBoundingBox(SoGetBoundingBoxAction *action);
   virtual void   GLRender(SoGLRenderAction *action);
   virtual void   handleEvent(SoHandleEventAction *action);
   virtual void   pick(SoPickAction *action);
   virtual void   getMatrix(SoGetMatrixAction *action);
   virtual void   search(SoSearchAction *action);

private:
   // Destructor
   virtual ~Alternate();
};
```

The **Alternate** class source code is shown in Example 2-6.

Example 2-6   Alternate.c++

```
#include <Inventor/misc/SoChildList.h>
#include <Inventor/actions/SoGLRenderAction.h>
#include <Inventor/actions/SoGetBoundingBoxAction.h>
#include <Inventor/actions/SoGetMatrixAction.h>
#include <Inventor/actions/SoHandleEventAction.h>
#include <Inventor/actions/SoPickAction.h>
#include <Inventor/actions/SoSearchAction.h>
#include "Alternate.h"

SO_NODE_SOURCE(Alternate);

// This initializes the Alternate class.

void
Alternate::initClass()
{
   // Initialize type id variables
   SO_NODE_INIT_CLASS(Alternate, SoGroup, "Group");
}

// Constructor
Alternate::Alternate()
{
   SO_NODE_CONSTRUCTOR(Alternate);
}
```

```
// Constructor that takes approximate number of children.

Alternate::Alternate(int numChildren) : SoGroup(numChildren)
{
    SO_NODE_CONSTRUCTOR(Alternate);
}

// Destructor

Alternate::~Alternate()
{
}

// Each of these implements an action by calling the standard
// traversal method. Note that (as in the Glow node source) we
// prefix the call to doAction() with the name of the class, to
// avoid problems with derived classes.

void
Alternate::getBoundingBox(SoGetBoundingBoxAction *action)
{
    Alternate::doAction(action);
}

void
Alternate::GLRender(SoGLRenderAction *action)
{
    Alternate::doAction(action);
}

void
Alternate::handleEvent(SoHandleEventAction *action)
{
    Alternate::doAction(action);
}

void
Alternate::pick(SoPickAction *action)
{
    Alternate::doAction(action);
}
```

```
// This implements the traversal for the SoGetMatrixAction,
// which is handled a little differently: it does not traverse
// below the root node or tail of the path it is applied to.
// Therefore, we need to compute the matrix only if this group
// is in the middle of the current path chain or is off the path
// chain (since the only way this could be true is if the group
// is under a group that affects the chain).

void
Alternate::getMatrix(SoGetMatrixAction *action)
{
    int         numIndices;
    const int   *indices;

    // Use SoAction::getPathCode() to determine where this group
    // is in relation to the path being applied to (if any).
    switch (action->getPathCode(numIndices, indices)) {

      case SoAction::NO_PATH:
      case SoAction::BELOW_PATH:
        // If there's no path, or we're off the end, do nothing.
        break;

      case SoAction::OFF_PATH:
      case SoAction::IN_PATH:
        // If we are in the path chain or we affect nodes in the
        // path chain, traverse the children.
        Alternate::doAction(action);
        break;
    }
}

// This implements the traversal for the SoSearchAction, which
// is also a little different. The search action is set to
// either traverse all nodes in the graph or just those that
// would be traversed during normal traversal. We need to check
// that flag before traversing our children.

void
Alternate::search(SoSearchAction *action)
{
    // If the action is searching everything, then traverse all
    // of our children as SoGroup would.
    if (action->isSearchingAll())
      SoGroup::search(action);
```

```
    else {
      // First, make sure this node is found if we are searching
      // for Alternate (or group) nodes.
      SoNode::search(action);

      // Traverse the children in our usual way.
      Alternate::doAction(action);
    }
}

// This implements typical action traversal for an Alternate
// node, skipping every other child.

void
Alternate::doAction(SoAction *action)
{
    int          numIndices;
    const int    *indices;

    // This will be set to the index of the last (rightmost)
    // child to traverse.
    int          lastChildIndex;

    // If this node is in a path, see which of our children are
    // in paths, and traverse up to and including the rightmost
    // of these nodes (the last one in the "indices" array).
    if (action->getPathCode(numIndices, indices) ==
       SoAction::IN_PATH)
      lastChildIndex = indices[numIndices - 1];

    // Otherwise, consider all of the children.
    else
      lastChildIndex = getNumChildren() - 1;

    // Now we are ready to traverse the children, skipping every
    // other one. For the SoGetBoundingBoxAction, however, we
    // have to do some extra work in between each pair of
    // children - we have to make sure the center points get
    // averaged correctly.
    if (action->isOfType(
          SoGetBoundingBoxAction::getClassTypeId())) {
      SoGetBoundingBoxAction *bba =
        (SoGetBoundingBoxAction *) action;
      SbVec3f  totalCenter(0.0, 0.0, 0.0);
      int      numCenters = 0;
```

```
      for (int i = 0; i <= lastChildIndex; i += 2) {
        children->traverse(bba, i);

        // If the traversal set a center point in the action,
        // add it to the total and reset for the next child.
        if (bba->isCenterSet()) {
          totalCenter += bba->getCenter();
          numCenters++;
          bba->resetCenter();
        }
      }
      // Now, set the center to be the average. Since the
      // centers were already transformed, there's no need to
      // transform the average.
      if (numCenters != 0)
        bba->setCenter(totalCenter / numCenters, FALSE);
    }

    // For all other actions, just traverse every other child.
    else
      for (int i = 0; i <= lastChildIndex; i += 2)
        children->traverse(action, i);
  }
```

Using New Node Classes

Node classes you have created must be initialized in every application that uses them. Example 2-7 shows how this is done, using the **Glow**, **Pyramid**, and **Alternate** node classes defined in the previous examples. The program reads a file (newNodes.iv, shown in Example 2-8) that has a scene graph containing instances of these nodes. It writes the scene graph to standard output and then opens an examiner viewer to display the graph.

You can see from this example that extender node classes should be initialized after standard classes, which are initialized by **SoDB::init()**. In this program, **SoDB::init()** is called by **SoXt::init()**. Also, base classes must be initialized before any classes derived from them, since the initialization macros for a node class refer to the parent class.

Notice in Example 2-8 that the **Pyramid** and **Glow** nodes, because they are not built into the Inventor library, write out their field names and types. (The **Alternate** class has no fields.) See the discussion of the file format for new (unknown) nodes in *The Inventor Mentor*, Chapter 11.

The **isBuiltIn** flag is a protected variable in **SoFieldContainer**, from which **SoNode** is derived. If this flag is FALSE, field types are written out along with the field values. By default, this flag is FALSE, but all Inventor classes set it to TRUE. If you are building a toolkit that uses Inventor and want your new classes to appear the same as Inventor classes, be sure to set this flag to TRUE.

Example 2-7   NewNodes.c++

```
#include <Inventor/SoDB.h>
#include <Inventor/SoInput.h>
#include <Inventor/Xt/SoXt.h>
#include <Inventor/Xt/viewers/SoXtExaminerViewer.h>
#include <Inventor/actions/SoWriteAction.h>
#include <Inventor/nodes/SoSeparator.h>

// Header files for new node classes
#include "Glow.h"
#include "Pyramid.h"
#include "Alternate.h"

main(int, char **argv)
{
    SoInput      myInput;
    SoSeparator  *root;

    // Initialize Inventor and Xt
    Widget myWindow = SoXt::init(argv[0]);
    if (myWindow == NULL) exit(1);

    // Initialize the new node classes
    Glow::initClass();
    Pyramid::initClass();
    Alternate::initClass();

    if (! myInput.openFile("newNodes.iv")) {
      fprintf(stderr, "Can't open \"newNodes.iv\"\n");
      return 1;
    }

    root = SoDB::readAll(&myInput);
    if (root == NULL) {
      printf("File \"newNodes.iv\" contains bad data\n");
      return 2;
    }
```

```
    root->ref();

    // Write the graph to stdout
    SoWriteAction wa;
    wa.apply(root);

    // Render it
    SoXtExaminerViewer *myViewer =
      new SoXtExaminerViewer(myWindow);
    myViewer->setSceneGraph(root);
    myViewer->setTitle("NewNodes");
    myViewer->show();
    myViewer->viewAll();

    SoXt::show(myWindow);
    SoXt::mainLoop();
}
```

Example 2-8   newNodes.iv

```
#Inventor V2.0 ascii

#
# Input file for "newNodes" example program
#

Separator {

   Separator {
     Transform {
       translation 0 -1.1 0
     }
     Cube {
       width      10
       height     .1
       depth      10
     }
   }

   Material {
     diffuseColor   .3 .6 .9
     shininess      .5
   }

   # Skip every other child
   Alternate {
     fields        []
```

```
Pyramid {
   fields          [SFBitMask parts,
                    SFFloat    baseWidth,
                    SFFloat    baseDepth,
                    SFFloat    height ]
}

Cube {}            # This child is skipped

Separator {
  Glow {
     fields        [SFColor color,
                    SFFloat brightness ]
     brightness    .6
     color         1 .3 .3
  }
  Transform {
     translation 3 .6 0
  }
  Pyramid {
     fields        [SFBitMask parts,
                    SFFloat    baseWidth,
                    SFFloat    baseDepth,
                    SFFloat    height ]
     height        3.2
  }
}

Sphere {}          # This child is skipped
  }
}
}
```

Creating an Abstract Node Class

Creating an abstract node class is slightly different from creating a
nonabstract one. Examples of abstract node classes are **SoCamera**, **SoLight**,
and **SoShape**.

First, abstract classes should use the ABSTRACT versions of the macros
described in SoSubNode.h. For example, the **SoLight** class makes this call in
its **initClass()** method:

```
SO_NODE_INIT_ABSTRACT_CLASS(SoLight, "Light", SoNode);
```

Second, the constructor for an abstract class should be protected, meaning
that it is impossible to create an instance of it.

The copy() Method

The **copy()** method defined for **SoNode** creates a copy of an instance of a node. If your node has no data other than fields and public children, then the **copy()** methods defined for **SoNode** and **SoGroup** should suffice.

However, if you have extra instance data in your node that needs to be copied, you will have to override the copy method. For example, if our **Pyramid** node class defined earlier contained a private integer member variable called **count** (for some private reason), the **copy()** method would look like this:

```
SoNode *
Pyramid::copy(SbBool copyConnections) const
{
   // Use the standard version of the copy method to create a
   // copy of this instance, including its field data
   Pyramid *newPyramid = (Pyramid *)
                     SoNode::copy(copyConnections);

   // Copy the "count" field explicitly
   newPyramid->count = count;

   return newPyramid;
}
```

The affectsState() Method

The **affectsState()** method on **SoNode** indicates whether a node has a net effect on the state. (For example, **SoSeparator** changes the state, but it restores the state, so there's no net effect.) The default value for this method is TRUE, but some node classes such as **SoSeparator**, **SoShape**, **SoArray**, and **SoMultipleCopy** define it to be FALSE. When you define a new node class, you may need to redefine its **affectsState()** method if it differs from that of the parent class.

Uncacheable Nodes

You may create a new node whose effects should not be cached during rendering or bounding-box computation. For example, the **SoCallback** node allows a user to change the effect of the callback function, such as drawing a cube instead of a sphere, without ever making an Inventor call.

Uncacheable nodes such as **SoCallback** should call

```
SoCacheElement::invalidate(state)
```

which aborts construction of the current cache. This call can be made during the render or bounding box action (the two actions that support caching). The **invalidate()** method also turns off auto-caching on any **SoSeparator** nodes over the uncacheable node.

Creating an Alternate Representation

When you create a new node, you probably also want to create an alternate representation for it that can be written to a file. For example, a good alternate representation for the **Glow** node would be an **SoMaterial** node with all fields ignored except for **emissiveColor**. The alternate representation is in the form of a field called **alternateRep**, of type **SoSFNode**. If your node is later read into an Inventor application that is not linked with this new node, Inventor will be able to render the node using this alternate representation even though the node has not been initialized with the database. (See Chapter 11 in *The Inventor Mentor* on reading in extender nodes and engines.)

Within your program, when a change is made to the original node, you may want the alternate representation to change as well. In this case, override the **write()** method on **SoNode** to update the alternate representation, and then have it call the **write()** method of the base class.

Generating Default Normals

If you define your own vertex-based shape class and the parent class does not generate default normals, you need to generate default normals for rendering with the Phong lighting model and for generating primitives. **SoVertexShape** provides the **generateDefaultNormals()** method, which you can override for use when normal binding is DEFAULT. Although the specifics depend on the shape itself, **SoNormalBundle** provides methods to facilitate this process.

❖ **Tip:** If you define a node class that creates a node sensor attached to itself or a field sensor attached to one of its fields, you'll need to redefine **readInstance()** so that the sensor doesn't fire when the node is read from a file. Your **readInstance()** method needs to detach the sensor, call the **readInstance()** method of the parent class, and then reattach the sensor. Node kits provide the **setUpConnections()** method to make and break these connections (see Chapter 7).

## Chapter 3

Creating a Field

If the set of field classes supported by Inventor does not suit your needs when defining a node or engine class, you may have to create your own field subclass. This chapter describes creating single-value and multiple-value fields. If you create a new field and you need automatic type conversion so that it can be connected to a field of a different type, you can build an engine that is a subclass of **SoFieldConverter**. Creating new field converters is explained in Chapter 6.

The chapter examples show creating two field classes:

- A single-value field called **SFDouble**

- A multiple-value field called **MFDouble**

Overview

The file SoSubField.h contains the macros for defining new field classes. If you do create a field class, you will probably need to use only a few of these macros. The more commonly used ones are documented in this chapter.

Creating a new field requires these steps:

1. Select a name for the new field class, determine whether it is derived from **SoSField** or **SoMField** (or a subclass), and determine the type of the field value (for example, **float**, **SbVec3f**).

2. Define an **initClass()** method to initialize type information. This step is required for both single-value and multiple-value fields (see "Initializing the Field Class" on page 66).

3. Implement the reading and writing methods for the field.

   a. For single-value fields, implement **readValue()** and **writeValue()** methods (see "Creating a Single-Value Field" on page 66).

   b. For multiple-value fields, implement **read1Value()** and **write1Value()** methods. You may also want to implement a **getNumValuesPerLine()** method for a multiple-value field. This method is used by the ASCII file format and tells how many values fit on one line when the field is written out (see "Creating a Multiple-Value Field" on page 69).

4. If it is useful, you can optionally define other methods for setting and accessing values in the field. For example, **SoSFVec3f** allows you to set the value from three floats or from an array of three floats, and so on.

Initializing the Field Class

The **initClass()** method in the source file sets up runtime type information for the field class. For single-value fields, use the SO_SFIELD_INIT() macro. For multiple-value fields, use SO_MFIELD_INIT(). See Chapter 1 for a brief description of runtime type-checking in Open Inventor.

Creating a Single-Value Field

This section shows how to create a single-value field class, **SFDouble**, that contains a double-precision real number.

The header file for this class uses the SO_SFIELD_HEADER() macro to declare all required member variables and functions for a single-value field. This macro declares the methods and variables for field classes that are derived from **SoSFField**. The first argument to the macro is the name of the new field. The second argument is the type of the value stored in the field, and the third is the type that can be passed to or returned from a function. For **double**, a primitive type, these two arguments are identical. For more complicated field types, this last type is typically a reference to the field value; for example,

```
const SbVec3f &
```

for a field holding an **SbVec3f**.

If your new field class is derived from another single-value field (rather than from an abstract class), use the SO_SFIELD_DERIVED_HEADER() macro.

Example 3-1 shows the header file for the **SFDouble** class.

Example 3-1   SFDouble.h

```
#include <Inventor/fields/SoSubField.h>

class SFDouble : public SoSField {

    // Declares all required member variables and functions for a
    // single-value field
    SO_SFIELD_HEADER(SFDouble, double, double);

  public:
    // Initializes field class, setting up runtime type info
    static void    initClass();
};
```

The source file for the **SFDouble** field class uses the SO_SFIELD_SOURCE() macro to define all required member variables and functions for the single-value field. It uses the SO_SFIELD_INIT() macro to initialize the field class and set up runtime type information.

SO_SFIELD_SOURCE() defines all methods that are declared in SO_SFIELD_HEADER(). SO_SFIELD_DERIVED_SOURCE() defines all methods that are declared in SO_SFIELD_DERIVED_HEADER(). (Even if you did not use the standard macros in your class header because you wanted to implement methods differently, you may still be able to use these macros in your source file. See SoSubField.h for details.)

Two methods for reading and writing the new field are also included. The **SoInput** class defines several **read()** methods that read a primitive type from the current input. One of these methods reads a number of type **double**, so we can use that method here to read into the **value** member variable defined in SO_SFIELD_HEADER(). The **read()** methods return FALSE on error, which is just what we want. Similarly, the **SoOutput** class has several **write()** methods. The new class uses the one that writes out a **double**.

Example 3-2 shows the source file for the **SFDouble** class.

Example 3-2   SFDouble.c++

```
#include "SFDouble.h"

// Defines all required member variables and functions for a
// single-value field
SO_SFIELD_SOURCE(SFDouble, double, double);

// Initializes the class, setting up runtime type info.

void
SFDouble::initClass()
{
   // This macro takes the name of the class and the name of the
   // parent class
   SO_SFIELD_INIT_CLASS(SFDouble, SoSField);
}


// This reads the value of a double-precision field from a
// file. It returns FALSE if the value could not be read
// successfully.


SbBool
SFDouble::readValue(SoInput *in)
{
   // Read a double from the input
   return in->read(value);
}


// This writes the value of a double-precision field to a
// file.

void
SFDouble::writeValue(SoOutput *out) const
{
   // Write a double
   out->write(value);
}
```

For more complex field-value types, you must be careful when writing
values; you have to see if the output format is binary before writing spaces

or other ASCII formatting. For example, the method to write the value of an
SoSFVec3f field looks like this:

```
void
SoSFVec3f::writeValue(SoOutput *out) const
{
    // Write first component of vector
    out->write(value[0]);

    // If not writing binary format, output a space between
    // values
    if (! out->isBinary())
        out->write(' ');

    // Repeat for other components of vector
    out->write(value[1]);
    if (! out->isBinary())
        out->write(' ');
    out->write(value[2]);
}
```

Creating a Multiple-Value Field

This section shows how to create a multiple-value field class, **MFDouble**,
that contains any number of double-precision real numbers.

Example 3-3 shows the header file for the **MFDouble** class. It uses the
SO_MFIELD_HEADER() macro, which is typically the only macro you need
to use in an **SoMField** subclass header, unless you wish to change value
handling or construction/destruction.

Use the SO_MFIELD_DERIVED_HEADER() macro to declare the methods
and variables for fields that are derived from other multiple-value fields
(rather than from an abstract class).

Example 3-3   MFDouble.h

```
#include <Inventor/fields/SoSubField.h>

class MFDouble : public SoMField {

    // This macro is just like the one for single-value fields.
    SO_MFIELD_HEADER(MFDouble, double, double);
```

```
public:
    static void     initClass();

private:
    // This returns the number of ASCII values to write per
    // output line. It can be used to produce more compact
    // output files for fields containing small value types.
    virtual int    getNumValuesPerLine() const;
};
```

The SO_MFIELD_SOURCE() macro defines all methods that are declared in SO_MFIELD_HEADER(). This macro includes several other macros that you may find useful even if you don't want to use all of them.

SO_MFIELD_SOURCE_MALLOC(), used in Example 3-4, is an alternate version of SO_MFIELD_SOURCE(). The difference is that this macro implements value storage management using **malloc()**, **realloc()**, and **free()**, while SO_MFIELD_SOURCE() uses the **new** and **delete** operators. While SO_MFIELD_SOURCE_MALLOC() produces faster and more efficient code than the other source macro, it should be used only for field classes whose values have no constructors or destructors (since they would never be called). For example, the **SoMFShort** class uses this macro, since values of type **short** are not C++ instances, and therefore do not have any constructors or destructors. The **MFDouble** field contains a basic type (a **double**) that does not need a constructor, so we are free to use this alternate (and more efficient) macro.

SO_MFIELD_DERIVED_SOURCE() defines all methods that are declared in SO_MFIELD_DERIVED_HEADER(). Use these macros if you are deriving a field from another field.

Example 3-4 shows the source file for the **MFDouble** class.

Example 3-4   MFDouble.c++

```
#include "MFDouble.h"

// Defines all required member variables and functions for a
// multiple-value field. We use the version that allocates field
// value storage with malloc(), since there is no constructor to
// call for our values.
SO_MFIELD_SOURCE_MALLOC(MFDouble, double, double);
```

```
// Initializes the class, setting up runtime type info.

void
MFDouble::initClass()
{
    // This macro takes the name of the class and the name of the
    // parent class
    SO_MFIELD_INIT_CLASS(MFDouble, SoMField);
}

// This reads one value of the double-precision field from a
// file. It is passed the index of the value to read; we can
// assume that the field already contains enough room to hold
// this value. It returns FALSE if the value could not be read
// successfully.

SbBool
MFDouble::read1Value(SoInput *in, int index)
{
    // Read a double from the input
    return in->read(values[index]);
}

// This writes one value of a double-precision field to a
// file.

void
MFDouble::write1Value(SoOutput *out, int index) const
{
    // Write a double
    out->write(values[index]);
}

// Returns number of ASCII values to write out per line.

int
MFDouble::getNumValuesPerLine() const
{
    // We can probably fit 4 doubles per line pretty easily.
    return 4;
}
```

## Chapter 4

Creating an Action

In this chapter, you'll learn how to create a subclass of **SoAction**. Make sure you understand the material in Chapters 1 and 2 before reading this chapter.

The chapter examples show creating and using an action class called **GetVolumeAction**.

Overview

The file SoSubAction.h contains the macros for defining new action classes. The SO_ACTION_HEADER() macro declares type identifier and naming variables and methods that all action classes must support. The SO_ACTION_SOURCE() macro defines the static variables and methods declared in the SO_ACTION_HEADER() macro.

Creating a new action requires these steps:

1. Select a name for the new action class and determine what class it is derived from.

2. Define an **initClass()** method to initialize the runtime type information for the class (see "Initializing the Action Class" on page 74).

   a. Enable elements in the state that are used by nodes when the action is applied to them (see "Enabling Elements in the State" on page 74).

b. Register a static method for each node class that supports this action (see "Registering Static Methods" on page 75).

3. Write the constructor for the action (see "Defining the Constructor" on page 75).

4. Write the destructor for the action (see "Defining the Destructor" on page 75).

5. If necessary, override the **beginTraversal()** method to implement a different traversal behavior or to perform special initialization before traversal. The **apply()** methods all call **beginTraversal()** (see "Traversal Behavior" on page 76).

6. Implement the methods that you registered in step 2b of this list (see "Implementing Static Methods" on page 76).

❖ **Tip:** An easy way to create a new action is to derive it from the callback action. The callback action provides generic traversal of the scene graph and enables all standard elements. Note that deriving a new action class requires more work than simply registering callback functions with the callback action. In many cases, this latter approach will suffice.

Initializing the Action Class

All action classes must have a static method to initialize the class (just like node classes). In this method, typically called **initClass()**, the type identifier information for the class is set up. This method must be called for all action classes to set up the method list correctly before an instance of the action can be created. The required work of this method is done by the SO_ACTION_INIT_CLASS() macro.

Enabling Elements in the State

Your action may also need to enable certain elements in the state. For example, the **SoRayPickAction** enables the **SoPickRayElement** in its initClass() routine:

```
enableElement(SoPickRayElement::getClassTypeId());
```

Recall from Chapter 2 that you can also enable elements in node class initialization methods using the SO_ENABLE() macro. All elements enabled by a parent action class are automatically enabled in a derived class.

Registering Static Methods

In addition, you need to explicitly register a static method for each supported node class with the method list for your new action. At a minimum, register a method for **SoNode**, which can be inherited by other nodes. Use the SO_ACTION_ADD_METHOD() macro to register methods with the method list. For example:

```
SO_ACTION_ADD_METHOD(SoCube, cubeVolume);
```

See "Implementing Static Methods" on page 76 for information on implementing new static methods.

Defining the Constructor

Use the SO_ACTION_CONSTRUCTOR() to perform the basic work for you. For example:

```
GetVolumeAction::GetVolumeAction()
{
    SO_ACTION_CONSTRUCTOR(GetVolumeAction);
}
```

Defining the Destructor

There is no macro for defining a destructor. Use the destructor to free up anything you created in the constructor or in any other methods for the class. For example:

```
SoWriteAction::~SoWriteAction()
{
    // Get rid of the SoOutput if we created it in the
    // constructor
    if (createdOutput)
        delete output;
}
```

Traversal Behavior

The **apply()** method on **SoAction** always calls **beginTraversal()** to begin traversal of the graph. The default behavior of **beginTraversal()** is simply to call **SoAction::traverse()**. If you need to initialize the action every time it is applied, you can implement a **beginTraversal()** method for your action class. For example, the **SoGetBoundingBoxAction** sets the bounding box to be empty each time before it begins traversing the scene graph. Afterwards, it calls **SoAction::traverse()**. Note that **beginTraversal()** is passed a node, which is either the root of the graph the action is being applied to or the head of a path. Regardless of whether the action is applied to a node, a path, or a path list, the **traverse()** method handles the traversal appropriately.

For certain classes, you may also want to perform certain operations after traversal, or you may want to change the traversal behavior itself. For example, the render action performs multiple passes for antialiasing.

Implementing Static Methods

Chapter 2 provides important background material on implementing static methods and on **doAction()**. If you are creating a new node class, the static methods are typically included in the new node class. If you are creating a new action class, the static methods are included in the new action class. In the end, the new class (whether node or action) registers these static methods with the action class.

First, for **SoNode**, you will usually want to register the **nullAction()** method (defined on **SoAction**). This method will be used for any node classes that do not have a specific method registered for them.

For the node classes that actually do something for your action, you need to implement a static method. You'll probably choose one of two approaches:

- Implement a new method for the class to handle the method in its unique way.

- Implement a simple method that calls the **doAction()** method for that class if you want it to perform the action in its typical manner (for example, group nodes traverse their children in a specified order, property nodes affect elements in the state, and so on).

In our example class, the **GetVolumeAction** registers the **nullAction()** method for **SoNode**. This method, defined on **SoAction**, will be inherited by nodes that do not implement their own **GetVolumeAction**:

```
SO_ACTION_ADD_METHOD(SoNode, nullAction);
```

GetVolumeAction implements specific methods for the **SoCube** and **SoSphere** classes. For purposes of example, only the cube and sphere classes implement the **GetVolumeAction**. If you were actually creating and using such an action, you would probably want to be able to obtain the volume of any shape.

For **GetVolumeAction**, the group and relevant property classes (such as the coordinate, transformation, and complexity classes) all call **doAction()**, since they perform their "typical" action behavior:

```
void
GetVolumeAction::callDoAction(SoAction *action, SoNode *node)
{
    node->doAction(action);
}
```

Creating a New Action

The example presented here defines **GetVolumeAction**, an action class that computes the volume of shapes. Each shape adds its volume (in world space) to the volume collected so far.

Since the standard shape classes know nothing about **GetVolumeAction**, we have to register the appropriate methods for them with the method list. This is illustrated in the example by adding methods for the **SoCube** and **SoSphere** classes to compute volume.

When you create a new action, you have to decide which elements to enable. You must go through the list of elements and decide which ones have a bearing on the action being performed. Since the **GetVolumeAction** is concerned solely with geometry and coordinate spaces, we enable only elements that are relevant to these properties. We ignore material, textures, and other appearance properties. Note that we also enable **SoSwitchElement**, since it is vital to correct traversal of graphs with switch nodes; all actions doing traversal should enable this element.

Example 4-1 shows the header file for the **GetVolumeAction** class.

Example 4-1   GetVolumeAction.h

```
#include <Inventor/actions/SoSubAction.h>

class GetVolumeAction : public SoAction {

    SO_ACTION_HEADER(GetVolumeAction);

  public:
    // Initializes this action class for use with scene graphs
    static void     initClass();

    // Constructor and destructor
    GetVolumeAction();
    virtual ~GetVolumeAction();

    // Returns computed volume after action is applied
    float           getVolume() const { return volume; }

  protected:
    // Initiates action on graph
    virtual void    beginTraversal(SoNode *node);

  private:
    float           volume;        // Computed volume

    // These are the methods that are used to apply the action
    // to various node classes. The third method is registered
    // for all relevant non-shape nodes. The calling sequence for
    // these methods is that used for all methods in the global
    // action table.
    static void     cubeVolume(SoAction *, SoNode *);
    static void     sphereVolume(SoAction *, SoNode *);
    static void     callDoAction(SoAction *, SoNode *);

    // This adds the given object-space volume to the total. It
    // first converts the volume to world space, using the
    // current model matrix.
    void            addVolume(float objectSpaceArea);
};
```

Example 4-2 shows the source code for the **GetVolumeAction** class.

Example 4-2   GetVolumeAction.c++

```
#include <Inventor/elements/SoComplexityElement.h>
#include <Inventor/elements/SoComplexityTypeElement.h>
#include <Inventor/elements/SoCoordinateElement.h>
#include <Inventor/elements/SoElements.h>
#include <Inventor/elements/SoFontNameElement.h>
#include <Inventor/elements/SoFontSizeElement.h>
#include <Inventor/elements/SoModelMatrixElement.h>
#include <Inventor/elements/SoProfileCoordinateElement.h>
#include <Inventor/elements/SoProfileElement.h>
#include <Inventor/elements/SoSwitchElement.h>
#include <Inventor/elements/SoUnitsElement.h>
#include <Inventor/elements/SoViewVolumeElement.h>
#include <Inventor/elements/SoViewingMatrixElement.h>
#include <Inventor/elements/SoViewportRegionElement.h>
#include <Inventor/nodes/SoCamera.h>
#include <Inventor/nodes/SoComplexity.h>
#include <Inventor/nodes/SoCoordinate3.h>
#include <Inventor/nodes/SoCoordinate4.h>
#include <Inventor/nodes/SoCube.h>
#include <Inventor/nodes/SoFont.h>
#include <Inventor/nodes/SoGroup.h>
#include <Inventor/nodes/SoProfile.h>
#include <Inventor/nodes/SoProfileCoordinate2.h>
#include <Inventor/nodes/SoProfileCoordinate3.h>
#include <Inventor/nodes/SoSphere.h>
#include <Inventor/nodes/SoTransformation.h>
#include "GetVolumeAction.h"

SO_ACTION_SOURCE(GetVolumeAction);

// Initializes the GetVolumeAction class. This is a one-time
// thing that is done after database initialization and before
// any instance of this class is constructed.

void
GetVolumeAction::initClass()
{
   // Initialize the runtime type variables
   SO_ACTION_INIT_CLASS(GetVolumeAction, SoAction);
```

```
// Enable elements that are involved in volume computation.
// Most of these deal with geometrix properties
// (coordinates, profiles) or transformations (model matrix,
// units). Some are needed for certain groups (switches,
// level-of-detail) to function correctly.
SO_ENABLE(GetVolumeAction, SoModelMatrixElement);
SO_ENABLE(GetVolumeAction, SoComplexityElement);
SO_ENABLE(GetVolumeAction, SoComplexityTypeElement);
SO_ENABLE(GetVolumeAction, SoCoordinateElement);
SO_ENABLE(GetVolumeAction, SoFontNameElement);
SO_ENABLE(GetVolumeAction, SoFontSizeElement);
SO_ENABLE(GetVolumeAction, SoProfileCoordinateElement);
SO_ENABLE(GetVolumeAction, SoProfileElement);
SO_ENABLE(GetVolumeAction, SoSwitchElement);
SO_ENABLE(GetVolumeAction, SoUnitsElement);
SO_ENABLE(GetVolumeAction, SoViewVolumeElement);
SO_ENABLE(GetVolumeAction, SoViewingMatrixElement);
SO_ENABLE(GetVolumeAction, SoViewportRegionElement);

// Now we need to register methods to implement this action
// for various node classes. We have created implementations
// for two specific shape nodes, SoCube and SoSphere, so we
// can register specific methods for those two classes. We
// also want to make sure that group classes traverse their
// children correctly for this action, so we will use a
// method that calls doAction() to handle groups. Finally,
// we need to make sure that relevant property nodes set up
// the state correctly; we can use the same method that
// calls doAction() for these classes, as well. We will use
// the SO_ACTION_ADD_METHOD() macro to make this easier.

// This registers a method to call for SoNode, so it will be
// used for any node class that does not have a more
// specific method registered for it. This makes sure that
// there is always a method to call for any node. The
// "nullAction" method is defined on SoAction for use in
// cases like this.
SO_ACTION_ADD_METHOD(SoNode, nullAction);

// These register methods for the two shapes that can
// really handle the action
SO_ACTION_ADD_METHOD(SoCube, cubeVolume);
SO_ACTION_ADD_METHOD(SoSphere, sphereVolume);
```

```
        // Register the method that calls doAction() for all group
        // classes and for relevant properties (transformations,
        // coordinates, profiles, and so on).
        SO_ACTION_ADD_METHOD(SoCamera,               callDoAction);
        SO_ACTION_ADD_METHOD(SoComplexity,           callDoAction);
        SO_ACTION_ADD_METHOD(SoCoordinate3,          callDoAction);
        SO_ACTION_ADD_METHOD(SoCoordinate4,          callDoAction);
        SO_ACTION_ADD_METHOD(SoFont,                 callDoAction);
        SO_ACTION_ADD_METHOD(SoGroup,                callDoAction);
        SO_ACTION_ADD_METHOD(SoProfile,              callDoAction);
        SO_ACTION_ADD_METHOD(SoProfileCoordinate2,   callDoAction);
        SO_ACTION_ADD_METHOD(SoProfileCoordinate3,   callDoAction);
        SO_ACTION_ADD_METHOD(SoTransformation,       callDoAction);
}

// Constructor

GetVolumeAction::GetVolumeAction()
{
        SO_ACTION_CONSTRUCTOR(GetVolumeAction);
}

// Destructor. Does nothing.

GetVolumeAction::~GetVolumeAction()
{
}

// Initiates action on a graph. This is called when the action
// is applied to a node, a path, or a path list. It gives us a
// chance to initialize things before beginning traversal.

void
GetVolumeAction::beginTraversal(SoNode *node)
{
        // Initialize volume to 0
        volume = 0.0;

        // Begin traversal at the given root node.
        traverse(node);
}
```

```
// This method implements the action for an SoCube node.

void
GetVolumeAction::cubeVolume(SoAction *action, SoNode *node)
{
    // The action is really an instance of GetVolumeAction
    GetVolumeAction *volumeAct = (GetVolumeAction *) action;

    // And the node pointer is really a cube:
    const SoCube    *cube = (const SoCube *) node;

    // Find the dimensions of the cube
    float width    = (cube->width.isIgnored()  ? 2.0 :
                        cube->width.getValue());
    float height   = (cube->height.isIgnored() ? 2.0 :
                        cube->height.getValue());
    float depth    = (cube->depth.isIgnored()  ? 2.0 :
                        cube->depth.getValue());

    // ...and the volume
    float cubeVol = width * height * depth;

    // Add the volume to the accumulated volume in the action
    volumeAct->addVolume(cubeVol);
}

// This method implements the action for an SoSphere node.

void
GetVolumeAction::sphereVolume(SoAction *action, SoNode *node)
{
    // The action is really an instance of GetVolumeAction
    GetVolumeAction *volumeAct = (GetVolumeAction *) action;

    // And the node pointer is really a sphere:
    const SoSphere  *sphere = (const SoSphere *) node;

    // Find the radius of the sphere
    float radius = (sphere->radius.isIgnored() ? 1.0 :
                        sphere->radius.getValue());

    // Compute the volume using our favorite formula that we all
    // remember from our math classes, right?
    float sphereVol = 4./3. * M_PI * radius * radius * radius;
```

```
    // Add the volume to the accumulated volume in the action
    volumeAct->addVolume(sphereVol);
}

// This method implements the action for all of the relevant
// non-shape node classes.

void
GetVolumeAction::callDoAction(SoAction *action, SoNode *node)
{
    node->doAction(action);
}

// This adds the given object-space volume to the total, first
// converting it to world space using the current model matrix.

void
GetVolumeAction::addVolume(float objectSpaceVolume)
{
    // Find the current modeling matrix
    const SbMatrix &modelMatrix =
      SoModelMatrixElement::get(state);

    // The determinant of the upper-left 3x3 of this matrix is
    // the conversion factor we need to go from object-space
    // volume to world space. Pretty cool, indeed.
    float objectToWorldFactor = modelMatrix.det3();

    // Add in the converted volume to our current volume
    volume += objectToWorldFactor * objectSpaceVolume;
}
```

Using New Action Classes

Like nodes, action classes must be initialized before any instances can be constructed. Also note that before you can add a method to the method list, you must initialize both the action class and the node class involved.

Example 4-3 reads in a scene graph from the file volume.iv and applies the **GetVolumeAction** action to it, printing the resulting volume.

Example 4-3   PrintVolume.c++

```c++
#include <Inventor/SoDB.h>
#include <Inventor/SoInput.h>
#include <Inventor/SoInteraction.h>
#include <Inventor/nodes/SoSeparator.h>

// Header file for new action class
#include "GetVolumeAction.h"

main()
{
   // Initialize Inventor
   SoInteraction::init();

   // Initialize the new action class
   GetVolumeAction::initClass();

   // Open the file and read the scene
   SoInput     myInput;
   SoSeparator  *root;
   if (! myInput.openFile("volume.iv")) {
     fprintf(stderr, "Can't open \"volume.iv\" for reading\n");
     return 1;
   }
   root = SoDB::readAll(&myInput);
   if (root == NULL) {
     printf("Couldn't read scene from \"volume.iv\"\n");
     return 2;
   }
   root->ref();

   // Compute the volume: apply a GetVolumeAction to the root
   GetVolumeAction va;
   va.apply(root);

   // Print the result
   printf("Total volume = %g\n", va.getVolume());

   return 0;
}
```

Chapter 5

Creating an Element

If you want to create nodes that have effects not covered by the set of standard Inventor elements, you may need to create a new element class. Be sure you are familiar with the information in Chapters 1, 2, and 4 before you read this chapter.

The first part of this chapter offers an overview of the steps required to create a new element class. When necessary, additional sections explain key concepts in further detail and list relevant macros. The chapter example shows creating a new element, the **temperature** element, which is derived from **SoFloatElement**.

Overview

The file SoSubElement.h contains the macros for defining new element classes. The SO_ELEMENT_HEADER() macro declares type identifier and naming variables and methods that all element classes must support. The SO_ELEMENT_SOURCE() macro defines the static variables and methods declared in the SO_ELEMENT_HEADER() macro. Other macros useful in creating new element classes are mentioned in the following sections.

Creating a new element requires these steps:

1. Select a name for the new element class and determine what class it is derived from (see "Deriving a Class from an Existing Element" on page 86).

2. Implement an **initClass()** method to initialize the type information (see "The initClass() Method" on page 89).

3. Implement a destructor. Elements don't have constructors (see "Destructor" on page 89).

4. Implement an **init()** method (see "The init() Method" on page 90).

5. Implement **set()** and **get()** methods to modify and access current values (see "The set() and get() Methods" on page 90).

6. Implement a **print()** method for debugging purposes (see "The print() Method" on page 90).

7. Depending on what your class is derived from and the nature of your element, you may need to implement the following methods:

   a. **matches()** and **copyMatchInfo()** (see "Additional Methods" on page 90).

   b. **push()** and **pop()** (see "Pushing and Popping Elements" on page 95).

   c. **setElt()** (see "Additional Methods" on page 90).

Deriving a Class from an Existing Element

Elements are used for storing information in the Inventor traversal state. Writing a new element goes hand-in-hand with writing a new node, since nodes set and get element values. As explained in Chapter 1, elements provide the mechanism for caching in Inventor. They also provide the pushing and popping facility used by separators. Later sections in this chapter supply details on both topics.

Before an element class can be used, it must be *initialized* using one of the macros provided (see "Creating a New Element" on page 96). The element must also be *enabled* in the method list of each action for which it is required. (Nodes and actions enable the elements in an action's state.)

As shown in Figure 5-1, most elements are derived from one of four abstract base classes: **SoFloatElement**, **SoLongElement**, **SoReplacedElement**, or **SoAccumulatedElement**. Most elements fall into the **SoReplacedElement** category. The diffuse-color and specular-color elements are examples of elements that fall into this category, because their value replaces the previous value (and it is not a simple floating-point or integer value). A few elements, such as transformations and profiles, accumulate values.

SoElement
- **SoAccumulatedElement**
  - SoClipPlaneElement —— SoGLClipPlaneElement
  - SoModelMatrixElement
    - SoBBoxModelMatrixElement
    - SoGLModelMatrixElement
  - SoProfileElement
  - SoTextureMatrixElement —— SoGLTextureMatrixElement
- SoCacheElement
- SoCurrentGLMaterialElement
- **SoFloatElement**
  - SoComplexityElement
  - SoCreaseAngleElement
  - SoFocalDistanceElement
  - SoFontSizeElement
  - SoGLTextureQualityElement
  - SoLineWidthElement —— SoGLLineWidthElement
  - SoPointSizeElement —— SoGLPointSizeElement
- SoGLCacheContextElement
- SoGLPolygonStippleElement
- SoGLRenderPassElement
- SoGLUpdateAreaElement
- SoLocalBBoxMatrixElement
- **SoLongElement**
  - SoComplexityTypeElement
  - SoDrawStyleElement —— SoGLDrawStyleElement
  - SoGLLightIdElement
  - SoGLTextureEnabledElement
  - SoLightModelElement —— SoGLLightModelElement
  - SoLinePatternElement —— SoGLLinePatternElement
  - SoMaterialBindingElement
  - SoNormalBindingElement
  - SoPickStyleElement
  - SoSwitchElement
  (continued)

Figure 5-1   Element Class Tree (Part 1 of 2)

SoElement

SoLongElement ─────────── SoTextureCoordinateBindingElement
(continued)

SoTextureModelElement ───────── SoGLTextureModelElement

SoTextureWrapSElement ───────── SoGLTextureWrapSElement

SoTextureWrapTElement ───────── SoGLTextureWrapTElement

SoPickRayElement   SoUnitsElement

SoReplacedElement ─────────── SoAmbientColorElement ───────── SoGLAmbientColorElement

SoCoordinateElement ───────── SoGLCoordinateElement

SoCullVolumeElement

SoDiffuseColorElement───────── SoGLDiffuseColorElement

SoEmissiveColorElement ───────── SoGLEmissiveColorElement

SoFontNameElement

SoGLColorIndexElement

SoGLMaterialIndexElement

SoLightAttenuationElement

SoNormalElement ───────── SoGLNormalElement

SoProfileCoordinateElement

SoProjectionMatrixElement ───────── SoGLProjectionMatrixElement

SoShininessElement ───────── SoGLShininessElement

SoSpecularColorElement ───────── SoGLSpecularColorElement

SoTextureBlendColorElement───────SoGLTextureBlendColorElement

SoTextureCoordinateElement ───── SoGLTextureCoordinateElement

SoTextureImageElement───────── SoGLTextureImageElement

SoTransparencyElement

SoViewVolumeElement

SoViewingMatrixElement ───────── SoGLViewingMatrixElement

SoShapeHintsElement ───────── SoGLShapeHintsElement

SoViewportRegionElement ───────── SoGLViewportRegionElement

Figure 5-2   Element Class Tree (Part 2 of 2)

In addition, some elements have a derived element class that is used to cause the side effects required for OpenGL. An example is **SoDrawStyleElement**, from which **SoGLDrawStyleElement** is derived. "Special Behavior for Derived Elements" on page 94 discusses the use of these element class pairs.

The first question to ask when creating a new element class is: What class can I derive my new element from? The answer depends partly on the kind of information stored in the element. If it can be stored as a single floating-point value (such as complexity or font size), derive your new class from **SoFloatElement**. If it can be stored as an integer (such as drawing style, an enumerated value), derive your new class from **SoLongElement**. You will probably be able to inherit many of the base class methods in these cases.

If your new element contains other types of values, you may be able to derive it from **SoReplacedElement**. If the current value of the element accumulates with previous values, you can derive it from **SoAccumulated-Element**. Later sections in this chapter describe in detail how these classes differ from each other.

The initClass() Method

The **initClass()** method sets up runtime type checking for the class. Use SO_ELEMENT_INIT_CLASS() in the initialization method for non-abstract classes. Use SO_ELEMENT_INIT_ABSTRACT_CLASS() in the initialization method for abstract classes.

Destructor

The destructor for the element is of the standard format:

```
SoModelMatrixElement::~SoModelMatrixElement()
```

If your element requires special cleanup—for example, because it allocates memory space that needs to be freed—the destructor should also perform that work.

At this point, you might be thinking, "What about the element constructor? Don't I need to write one?" Actually, you don't. The constructor for an element is built into the header, and you do not have access to it. There are only two times when an element instance is created:

- When the first instance of an element is created and put on the stack by the state
- When a new element instance is pushed onto the stack

In the first case, the virtual **init()** method is used after creating the first instance of the element. In the second case, the virtual **push()** method is used after creating each subsequent instance of the element. You can override the virtual **init()** and **push()** methods if your element class requires its own default value or other special behavior.

The init() Method

The **init()** method is called to initialize the very first instance of the element class used in a state instance and to set up its default values. The state creates the element and calls **init()** on it. Since all other instances are created by pushing, this method is called only once for each state instance.

The set() and get() Methods

All elements also need **set()** and **get()** methods that are used by the nodes to modify and access current values. There may also be a static method that returns the default value(s) for the element.

The print() Method

The **print()** method prints out an element's values, primarily for debugging purposes. This method, called by **SoState::print()**, is useful in tracking down problems during graph traversal.

Additional Methods

You may need to implement additional methods for certain element classes. Detailed information on **matches()** and **copyMatchInfo()** is presented in "Special Considerations for Caching" on page 91. The **setElt()** method is discussed in "Special Behavior for Derived Elements" on page 94. The **push()** and **pop()** methods are discussed in "Pushing and Popping Elements" on page 95.

matches()	called to determine whether an element matches another element. This method is used to compare states for cache validity. **copyMatchInfo()** is used to create a copy of an element to be added to a cache.
setElt()	a virtual method that is called by an element's static **set()** method in some cases. For details, read "Special Behavior for Derived Elements" on page 94.
push()	used in a few cases to set up a new element instance that is a copy of the one just below it in the stack. Elements that contain two or more pieces of data and elements that implement side effects (often for OpenGL rendering) need to implement a **push()** method. The default **push()** method does nothing, since most elements contain only one piece of data and the value is typically set immediately after a push. Subclasses of **SoAccumulatedElement** must define their own **push()** method to copy values from the next instance in the stack, since the new instance accumulates values on top of the old ones. Use the **SoElement** method **getNextInStack()**.
pop()	the counterpart to **push()**. The default method does nothing. You need to implement a **pop()** method if your element has side effects. For example, when the **SoGLDrawStyleElement** pops, it restores the previous value by sending it to OpenGL. Other examples are the GL matrix elements, which call **glPopMatrix()** when they pop (see "Pushing and Popping Elements" on page 95).

Special Considerations for Caching

Elements do all of the work for caching in Inventor. If you are creating a node or an action that uses existing elements, you don't need to worry about caching. However, if you are creating a new element, you need to provide the necessary information so that caching continues to work. (You might want to reread "Caching" in Chapter 1 before continuing with this section.)

A cache is essentially a faster representation of the data you're trying to generate or compute in Inventor. What the cache contains depends on the action. A GL render cache contains an OpenGL display list. A bounding-box cache contains the bounding box itself. Using the cache speeds up subsequent traversal of the scene graph. In addition, the cache contains a list of the elements outside the cache that the information inside the cache depends on. For efficiency, the cache does not make an exact copy of each element it depends on. Instead, it copies only enough information to determine later on whether the cache is still valid.

The form of this information depends on the element. For some elements, such as those derived from **SoFloatElement** or **SoLongElement**, the *value* of the element is compared. For others, the *node ID* of the node that set the element's value is compared. For elements such as those derived from **SoAccumulatedElement**, the *list of node IDs* for all nodes that affect the instance of the element is compared. The **copyMatchInfo()** method should copy just enough information so that **matches()** can work properly.

Inventor uses an element's **copyMatchInfo()** method to copy the comparison data for the element into the cache. Then, to determine whether a cache is valid, Inventor compares each element in the cache with the corresponding element in the state by calling the element's **matches()** method.

You can inherit the **matches()** and **copyMatchInfo()** methods from the base classes, or for efficiency, you can write routines that are tailored to your new element class. The following sections explain in more detail how those routines work for the base classes.

SoFloatElement and SoLongElement

In many cases, you need to store only the *value* of the element in the cache. It doesn't matter which node has set the value. If the value of the element in the cache matches the value of the element in the state, the cache is still valid. The **matches()** and **copyMatchInfo()** methods for the **SoFloatElement** and **SoLongElement** classes function in this way.

SoReplacedElement

SoReplacedElement redefines the **getElement()** method of **SoElement** to store the node ID of the node that is about to set the value in the element. (Recall that a node's ID is unique and changes whenever the node changes.) **SoReplacedElement** also redefines **matches()** to compare the node IDs and return TRUE if the node IDs of the two elements match, as follows:

```
SbBool
SoReplacedElement::matches(const SoElement *elt) const
{
    return (nodeId == ((const SoReplacedElement *)
            elt)->nodeId);
}
```

An example of such an element is the coordinate element, which stores multiple coordinate values. Rather than compare all the values, this element simply compares the node IDs. The **copyMatchInfo()** method for this class copies only the node ID, since that is the information used to determine if the cache matches the state:

```
SoElement *
SoReplacedElement::copyMatchInfo() const
{
    SoReplacedElement *result =
        (SoReplacedElement *)getTypeId().createInstance();

    result->nodeId = nodeId;

    return result;
}
```

SoAccumulatedElement

Elements that accumulate values need to keep a list of node IDs for all nodes that affect an instance of the element. To determine whether a cache is valid for an accumulated element, the node ID list for the element in the cache is compared with the node ID list for the element in the state.

The **SoAccumulatedElement** class redefines the **matches()** method to compare lists of node IDs. If they plan to use the standard **matches()** method, subclasses of **SoAccumulatedElement** need to use the following methods provided by this parent class to keep the list of node IDs up to date:

clearNodeIds()	clears the list of node IDs
addNodeId()	adds the ID of the given node to the current list
setNodeId()	sets the node ID list to only the node ID of the given node

Special Behavior for Derived Elements

In Inventor, elements that do not have a derived class have only a static **set()** method. Elements with derived classes for their GL versions often have both a static **set()** method and a **setElt()** method. Using this mechanism, nodes can deal with the generic base class for elements without dealing individually with each subclass. For example, a node's **doAction()** method can simply call **SoDrawStyleElement::set** rather than calling **SoGLDrawStyleElement::set**. If you are deriving an element from an existing element class, or if you are creating a new hierarchy of element classes, the **setElt()** mechanism described here may prove useful.

Suppose you are writing a new renderer and need some elements to perform additional work. In this case, you can derive an element from the existing element. You write a virtual **setElt()** method for your new derived class that sets the element to its correct value and performs the desired side effects. The rest is C++ magic, as follows:

1. The static **set()** method of the base class calls its virtual **setElt()** method.

2. If there is no derived class, the **setElt()** method of the base class is called. If there is a derived class, the **setElt()** method of the derived class is called to set the element value.

In Open Inventor, this mechanism is used for the GL rendering version of certain elements. Let's take a closer look at the plain vanilla and GL versions of the draw-style element to illustrate this process. As noted in "Deriving a Class from an Existing Element" on page 86, the GL version is used to perform side effects required for GL rendering. The base class, **SoDrawStyleElement**, provides a static **set()** method that calls a virtual **setElt()** on the modifiable instance of the element:

```
// Sets draw style in element accessed from state.

void
SoDrawStyleElement::set(SoState *state, SoNode *node, Style
                        style)
```

```
{
    SoDrawStyleElement *elt;

    // Get an instance we can change (pushing if necessary)
    elt = (SoDrawStyleElement *)
              getElement(state, classStackIndex,node);

    if (elt != NULL)
        elt->setElt(style);        // virtual setElt()--see below
}
```

The virtual **setElt()** is defined in the base class as follows:

```
SoLongElement::setElt( long value )
{
    data = value;
}
```

The derived GL class, **SoGLDrawStyleElement**, redefines the virtual **setElt()** method to do two things:

- It sets the value in the Inventor instance of the element.

- It makes the proper calls to OpenGL (**glPolygonMode**()) to reflect the current state.

The code for the **setElt()** method in **SoGLDrawStyleElement** is as follows:

```
// Sets draw style in element.
void
SoGLDrawStyleElement::setElt(long value)
if (data != value) {
    data = value;
    send();        // The send() method calls glPolygonMode().
}
```

At the same time, **SoGLDrawStyleElement** inherits the static **set()** method from the parent class, **SoDrawStyleElement**. Note that you can derive other classes from **SoDrawStyleElement** in a similar way to support other rendering actions.

Pushing and Popping Elements

You need to implement a **push()** method for your new element if the pushed copy of the element uses the previous element in some way. For example, accumulated elements such as the **SoProfileElement** need the previous element because they append values to the previous values. Their **push()** method copies the values from the previous element in the stack into the new element on the stack so that the current value can be appended to it. You also need to implement a **push()** method if your element requires some side effect when its value is set. For example, some matrix elements call **glPushMatrix()** inside their **push()** routine. You do not need to implement a **push()** method for most replaced elements (unless they have side effects), since their new value wipes out the previous value.

The **push()** method is called when you call **set()** on an element for the first time after the state is pushed (for example, underneath a separator). You may need to implement a corresponding **pop()** method whenever you implement a **push()** method for an element.

If your **pop()** method has side effects, those side effects need to be included in a cache for the separator that performs the pop; otherwise, the separator cannot restore the state properly. Include this line in an element's **pop()** method to tell all open caches they need to depend on this element when validating a cache:

```
capture(state);
```

For example, suppose the scene graph contains a draw-style node with a value of FILLED. A separator node to the right of this draw-style node contains a draw-style node with a value of LINES and a cube. Assume caching is turned on at the separator node. The separator's cache contains instructions for setting the draw-style to LINES and drawing the cube. When the state is restored, the draw-style element's **pop()** method causes the draw-style to be restored to its previous value (FILLED). If that previous value changes, this separator's cache is no longer valid.

Creating a New Element

This example creates an element called **TemperatureElement** that holds the current temperature of shapes during traversal. This element is derived from the **SoFloatElement** class.

Example 5-1 shows the header file for the **TemperatureElement**.

Example 5-1   TemperatureElement.h

```
#include <Inventor/elements/SoFloatElement.h>

class TemperatureElement : public SoFloatElement {
```

```
   SO_ELEMENT_HEADER(TemperatureElement);

public:
   // Initializes the TemperatureElement class
   static void     initClass();

   // Initializes element
   virtual void    init(SoState *state);

   // Sets the current temperature in the state to the given
   // temperature (in degrees Fahrenheit)
   static void     set(SoState *state, SoNode *node, float temp);

   // Returns the current temperature from the state
   static float    get(SoState *state);

   // Returns the default temperature
   static float    getDefault()          { return 98.6; }

private:
   virtual ~TemperatureElement();
};
```

Example 5-2 shows the source code for the **TemperatureElement**.

Example 5-2   TemperatureElement.c++

```
#include "TemperatureElement.h"

SO_ELEMENT_SOURCE(TemperatureElement);

// Initializes the TemperatureElement class.

void
TemperatureElement::initClass()
{
   SO_ELEMENT_INIT_CLASS(TemperatureElement, SoFloatElement);
}

// Destructor

TemperatureElement::~TemperatureElement()
{
}
```

```
// Initializes the first instance used in an action's state.

void
TemperatureElement::init(SoState *)
{
   data = getDefault();
}

// Sets the current temperature in the state.

void
TemperatureElement::set(SoState *state, SoNode *node,
                  float temp)
{
   // Use the corresponding method on SoFloatElement to set the
   // value in the top instance in the state
   SoFloatElement::set(classStackIndex, state, node, temp);
}

// Returns the current temperature from the state.

float
TemperatureElement::get(SoState *state)
{
   // Use the corresponding method on SoFloatElement to get the
   // value from the top instance in the state
   return SoFloatElement::get(classStackIndex, state);
}
```

## Chapter 6

Creating an Engine

This chapter describes how to create new subclasses of **SoEngine**. New concepts introduced in this chapter include how notification of changes in field data propagates through the scene graph and how to block notification if desired. Be sure you are familiar with Chapter 13 in *The Inventor Mentor* before you continue in this chapter.

The first part of this chapter offers an overview of the steps required to create a new engine. When necessary, additional sections explain key concepts in further detail and list the relevant macros. Chapter examples show how to create six engine classes:

- A simple engine called **MultFloatVec3f**

- An engine with multiple inputs called **SoComposeVec2f**

- An engine with multiple outputs called **SoDecomposeVec2f**

- An engine that simulates fanning in of multiple connections called **FanIn**

- An engine that controls propagation of its output value called **Ticker**

- A field converter engine called **ConvertSFShortToSFFloat**

Overview

As described in *The Inventor Mentor*, all engines have at least one input and one output. The inputs are derived from **SoField** (either **SoSF** or **SoMF** fields). Outputs are of type **SoEngineOutput**. In addition, each engine has an **evaluate()** method, which uses the current input values and produces new output values. The file SoSubEngine.h contains the macros for defining new engine classes. The SO_ENGINE_HEADER() macro declares type identifier and naming variables and methods that all engine classes must support. The macro defines the static variables and methods declared in the SO_ENGINE_HEADER() macro. Other macros useful in creating new engine classes are mentioned in the following sections.

Creating a new engine requires these steps:

1. Select a name for the new engine class and determine what class it is derived from.

2. Define and name each input and output of the engine (see "Defining Inputs and Outputs" on page 101).

3. Define an **initClass()** method to initialize the type information (see "Initializing the Engine Class" on page 101).

4. Define a constructor (see "Defining the Constructor" on page 101).

5. Define a destructor.

6. Implement an **evaluate()** method for the engine class (see "Notification and Evaluation" on page 110).

7. If necessary, implement an **inputChanged()** method (see "Creating a Fan-in Engine" on page 114 and "Creating a Second-Ticker Engine" on page 116).

8. Implement a **copy()** method if the engine contains any nonfield instance data (see Chapter 2, "Creating a Node," for more information on implementing a **copy()** method).

Defining Inputs and Outputs

Declare the inputs and outputs for the engine in the header file. For example:

```
SoSFTrigger on;
SoSFTrigger off;
SoSFTrigger toggle;
SoEngineOutput isOn;   // (SoSFBool)
SoEngineOutput isOff; // (SoSFBool)
```

Note that, by convention, each output is commented with the field type for that output. The output type isn't formally specified in the header file, though. It's set up in the constructor in the source file.

Also be sure to include the files for the field classes used by the inputs of your new engine.

Initializing the Engine Class

Implement an **initClass()** method, as described in Chapter 1, "Runtime Types" on page 18. The **initClass()** method sets up the type identifier and file format name information for the class. This method must be called before the engine can be used in an application. Use the SO_ENGINE_INIT_CLASS() macro within the **initClass()** method. For example:

```
void
FanIn::initClass()
{
    SO_ENGINE_INIT_CLASS(FanIn, SoEngine, "Engine");
}
```

Defining the Constructor

Implement the constructor for the class. Begin with the macro SO_ENGINE_CONSTRUCTOR(). Then use the macros SO_ENGINE_ADD_INPUT() and SO_ENGINE_ADD_OUTPUT() to add the engine inputs and outputs and to set default values for the outputs. Perform any other class-specific initialization, if needed. For example:

```
SoOnOff::SoOnOff()
  {
    SO_ENGINE_CONSTRUCTOR(SoOnOff);
    SO_ENGINE_ADD_INPUT(on, ());     // no default value for
                                     // trigger fields
    SO_ENGINE_ADD_INPUT(off, ());    // no default value
    SO_ENGINE_ADD_INPUT(toggle, ()); // no default value
    SO_ENGINE_ADD_OUTPUT(isOn, SoSFBool);
    SO_ENGINE_ADD_OUTPUT(isOff, SoSFBool);
    state = FALSE;                   // engine is off by default
  }
```

Notice that this is where the outputs are bound to a particular field type.

Implementing an evaluate() Method

The **evaluate()** method is responsible for taking the input values and producing output values. The input values are read using the standard field **getValue()** routines. You can use the SO_ENGINE_OUTPUT() macro to set the values in the engine's outputs.

Note: SO_ENGINE_OUTPUT() is used for setting values in outputs. Do not perform any calculation inside this macro. Side effects are not allowed, because this macro loops through each connection. You can, however, call SO_ENGINE_OUTPUT() multiple times, once for each output, as shown in the **SoComposeVec2f** class (Examples 6-3 and 6-4).

Creating a Simple Engine

The following examples illustrate the basic steps outlined in "Overview" on page 100. Example 6-1 shows the header file for a simple engine, **MultFloatVec3f**, which multiplies a float value (**SoSFFloat**) by a vector value (**SoSFVec3f**) and produces an output of type **SoSFVec3f**. Example 6-2 shows the source file for this class.

❖ **Tip:** The **SoCalculator** engine provides a built-in way of doing this type of simple arithmetic.

Example 6-1   MultFloatVec3f.h

```
#include <Inventor/engines/SoSubEngine.h>
#include <Inventor/fields/SoSFFloat.h>
#include <Inventor/fields/SoSFVec3f.h>

class MultFloatVec3f : public SoEngine {

   SO_ENGINE_HEADER(MultFloatVec3f);

 public:

    // Input fields: a scalar (float) and a vector
    SoSFFloat        scalar;
    SoSFVec3f        vector;

    // The output is a vector
    SoEngineOutput  product;   // (SoSFVec3f) product

    // Initializes this class for use in scene graphs. This
    // should be called after database initialization and before
    // any instance of this engine is constructed.
    static void initClass();

    // Constructor
    MultFloatVec3f();

 private:
    // Destructor. Since engines are never deleted explicitly,
    // this can be private.
    virtual ~MultFloatVec3f();

    // Evaluation method
    virtual void evaluate();
};
```

Example 6-2   MultFloatVec3f.c++

```
#include "MultFloatVec3f.h"

SO_ENGINE_SOURCE(MultFloatVec3f);

// Initializes the MultFloatVec3f class. This is a one-time
// thing that is done after database initialization and before
// any instance of this class is constructed.
```

```
void
MultFloatVec3f::initClass()
{
   // Initialize type id variables. The arguments to the macro
   // are: the name of the engine class, the class this is
   // derived from, and the name registered with the type
   // of the parent class.
   SO_ENGINE_INIT_CLASS(MultFloatVec3f, SoEngine, "Engine");
}

// Constructor

MultFloatVec3f::MultFloatVec3f()
{
   // Do standard constructor stuff
   SO_ENGINE_CONSTRUCTOR(MultFloatVec3f);

   // Define input fields and their default values
   SO_ENGINE_ADD_INPUT(scalar,  (0.0));
   SO_ENGINE_ADD_INPUT(vector,  (0.0, 0.0, 0.0));

   // Define the output, specifying its type
   SO_ENGINE_ADD_OUTPUT(product, SoSFVec3f);
}

// Destructor. Does nothing.

MultFloatVec3f::~MultFloatVec3f()
{
}

// This is the evaluation routine.

void
MultFloatVec3f::evaluate()
{
   // Compute the product of the input fields
   SbVec3f  prod = scalar.getValue() * vector.getValue();

   // "Send" the value to the output. In effect, we are setting
   // the value in all fields to which this output is connected.
   SO_ENGINE_OUTPUT(product, SoSFVec3f, setValue(prod));
}
```

Dealing with Multiple-Value Fields

This second engine has a slightly more complex **evaluate()** method. Before creating the output, it determines the longest input field, and replicates the last value in short fields that need to be filled out to match the number of values in the longest field. The SO_ENGINE_OUTPUT() macro is used to set the number of values in the fields connected from the output, as well as to set the values.

Creating an Engine with Multiple Inputs

Examples 6-3 and 6-4 show the header and source files for **SoComposeVec2f**. This engine has two inputs, **x** and **y**, of type **SoMFFloat**, and one output, an **SoEngineOutput** of type **SoMFVec2f**.

This engine illustrates a general policy for handling multiple-value inputs that is followed by all arithmetic engines in Inventor. This policy is useful for engines that process multiple-value inputs as "parallel" independent data sets, but it is not required. Because the **x** and **y** inputs of the **SoComposeVec2f** engine are multiple-value fields, they can each contain any number of values. Figure 6-1 illustrates a case where the last value of **y** is replicated to fill out the field with values to match up with the number of values provided in **x**.

```
INPUTS                  OUTPUT SoMFVec2f

x   a b c d
    ↓ ↓ ↓ ↓             a,e   b,f   c,f   d,f
y   e f (f) (f)
```

Figure 6-1   Replicating Values in Fields with Fewer Values

Note that the constructor sets the default value for both input fields to 0.0.

Example 6-3   SoComposeVec2f.h

```
#include <Inventor/engines/SoSubEngine.h>
#include <Inventor/fields/SoMFFloat.h>
#include <Inventor/fields/SoMFVec2f.h>

class SoComposeVec2f : public SoEngine {

   SO_ENGINE_HEADER(SoComposeVec2f);
```

```
public:

  // Inputs:
  SoMFFloat        x;
  SoMFFloat        y;

  // Output:
  SoEngineOutput  vector;  // (SoMFVec2f)

  // Initialization
  static void initClass();

  // Constructor
  SoComposeVec2f();

 private:
  // Destructor
  virtual ~SoComposeVec2f();

  // Evaluation method
  virtual void evaluate();
};
```

Example 6-4   SoComposeVec2f.c++

```
#include "SoComposeVec2f.h"

SO_ENGINE_SOURCE(SoComposeVec2f);

// Initializes the SoComposeVec2f class.

void
SoComposeVec2f::initClass()
{
    SO_ENGINE_INIT_CLASS(SoComposeVec2f, SoEngine, "Engine");
}

// Constructor

SoComposeVec2f::SoComposeVec2f()
{
   // Do standard constructor tasks
   SO_ENGINE_CONSTRUCTOR(SoComposeVec2f);
```

```
   // Define input fields and their default values
   SO_ENGINE_ADD_INPUT(x,   (0.0));
   SO_ENGINE_ADD_INPUT(y,   (0.0));

   // Define the output, specifying its type
   SO_ENGINE_ADD_OUTPUT(vector, SoMFVec2f);
}

// Destructor. Does nothing.
SoComposeVec2f::~SoComposeVec2f()
{
}

// This is the evaluation routine.
void
SoComposeVec2f::evaluate()
{
   // Figure out how many input values we have
   int numX = x.getNum();
   int numY = y.getNum();

   // We will output as many values as there are in the input
   // with the greater number of values
   int numToOutput = (numX > numY ? numX : numY);

   // Make sure that all of the fields connected from the output
   // have enough room for the results. The SoMField::setNum()
   // method does this.
   SO_ENGINE_OUTPUT(vector, SoMFVec2f, setNum(numToOutput));

   // Now output the vectors composed from the input values
   float xValue, yValue;
   int    i;
   for (i = 0; i < numToOutput; i++) {

      // If there are different numbers of values in the input
      // fields, repeat the last value as necessary.
      xValue = (i < numX ? x[i] : x[numX - 1]);
      yValue = (i < numY ? y[i] : y[numY - 1]);

      // Set the vector value in the indexed slot in all
      // connected fields
      SO_ENGINE_OUTPUT(vector, SoMFVec2f,
                       set1Value(i, xValue, yValue));

   }
}
```

Creating an Engine with Multiple Outputs

This engine class shows creating an engine with more than one output. Examples 6-5 and 6-6 illustrate an engine that decomposes a vector into its individual float values. The **evaluate()** method uses the **getNum()** method to determine how many input values there are. Then it uses the **SoMField::setNum()** method to ensure that the fields connected from this engine have enough room for the results, as in the previous example.

Example 6-5   SoDecomposeVec2f.h

```
#include <Inventor/engines/SoSubEngine.h>
#include <Inventor/fields/SoMFFloat.h>
#include <Inventor/fields/SoMFVec2f.h>

class SoDecomposeVec2f : public SoEngine {

   SO_ENGINE_HEADER(SoDecomposeVec2f);

 public:

    // Input:
    SoMFVec2f        vector;

    // Outputs:
    SoEngineOutput  x;      // (SoMFFloat)
    SoEngineOutput  y;      // (SoMFFloat)

    // Initialization
    static void initClass();

    // Constructor
    SoDecomposeVec2f();

 private:
    // Destructor
    virtual ~SoDecomposeVec2f();

    // Evaluation method
    virtual void evaluate();
};
```

Example 6-6   SoDecomposeVec2f.c++

```cpp
#include "SoDecomposeVec2f.h"

SO_ENGINE_SOURCE(SoDecomposeVec2f);

// Initializes the SoDecomposeVec2f class.

void
SoDecomposeVec2f::initClass()
{
    SO_ENGINE_INIT_CLASS(SoDecomposeVec2f, SoEngine, "Engine");
}

// Constructor

SoDecomposeVec2f::SoDecomposeVec2f()
{
    // Do standard constructor tasks
    SO_ENGINE_CONSTRUCTOR(SoDecomposeVec2f);

    // Define input field and its default value
    SO_ENGINE_ADD_INPUT(vector,  (0.0, 0.0));

    // Define the outputs, specifying their types
    SO_ENGINE_ADD_OUTPUT(x, SoMFFloat);
    SO_ENGINE_ADD_OUTPUT(y, SoMFFloat);
}

// Destructor. Does nothing.

SoDecomposeVec2f::~SoDecomposeVec2f()
{
}

// This is the evaluation routine.

void
SoDecomposeVec2f::evaluate()
{
    // Figure out how many input values we have
    int numToOutput = vector.getNum();

    // Make sure that all of the fields connected from the
    // outputs have enough room for the results. The
    // SoMField::setNum() method does this.
    SO_ENGINE_OUTPUT(x, SoMFFloat, setNum(numToOutput));
```

```
    SO_ENGINE_OUTPUT(y, SoMFFloat, setNum(numToOutput));

    // Now output the values extracted from the input vectors
    for (int i = 0; i < numToOutput; i++) {
      SO_ENGINE_OUTPUT(x, SoMFFloat, set1Value(i, vector[i][0]));
      SO_ENGINE_OUTPUT(y, SoMFFloat, set1Value(i, vector[i][1]));
    }
}
```

Notification and Evaluation

If you are creating new engine classes, you may need to understand the following details on how changed values are propagated through an Inventor scene graph and engine network. Because evaluation can be slow, Inventor uses "lazy" evaluation for data in its engine network. Engines are evaluated only when their values are needed, and they are not reevaluated unnecessarily. For some engines, you might want to know whether a certain input has changed, and then take some action based on that knowledge. In such cases, you write an **inputChanged()** method for the engine. This section provides important background information on how and when an engine calls its **inputChanged()** and **evaluate()** methods. It also includes several examples of engines that implement an **inputChanged()** method.

Whenever a change is made to a field, notification propagates through the scene graph that the values dependent on this new value must be reevaluated. However, the evaluation does not occur until the value is requested through a call to getValue() (or getNum(), [ ], or getValues()). In other words, notification of a changed value is *pushed* through the scene graph. Any values needing reevaluation are marked as needing evaluation. Since no evaluation is performed at this time, notification is an efficient process.

Evaluation, by contrast, can be a slow process, depending on the nature of the engines. For this reason, evaluation is *pulled* through the scene graph on demand. Whenever a **getValue()** is called, if the field is connected to other fields or engines, those connections are traced, and fields marked as needing evaluation are evaluated before the new value is sent to its destination.

For example, consider the scene graph and engine network shown in Figure 6-2.

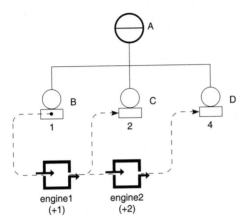

Figure 6-2   A Simple Engine Network

This scene graph contains four nodes: A, B, C, and D. Nodes B, C, and D contain fields that are connected to engines. For simplicity, assume that Nodes B, C, and D contain only one field, and Engines 1 and 2 have one input and one output each. Engine 1 adds 1 to its input and copies the result to its output. Engine 2 adds 2 to its input and copies the result to its output. The engines are connected to the nodes as shown in the diagram. If you change the value of the field in Node B from 1 to 3, the following things occur:

1. Node B notifies A that its field has changed. If the scene graph is contained within a render area, A, in turn, notifies the redraw sensor.

2. Node B notifies Engine 1 that its field needs to be evaluated. Then Engine 1's **inputChanged()** method is called.

3. Engine 1 notifies the field in Node C, which is marked as needing evaluation. C notifies A, which notifies the redraw sensor.

4. Engine 2's field is marked as needing evaluation, then its **inputChanged()** method is called.

5. Engine 2 notifies Node D, which is marked as needing evaluation. D notifies A, which notifies the redraw sensor.

Steps 1 through 5 illustrate the *push* model of notification.

At this point, the value in Node B has changed to 3, but the value of the field in Node C is still 2, and the value of the field in Node D is still 4. When a **getValue()** is called on the field in Node D, the fields and engines that have been marked as needing evaluation are evaluated, and the new values propagate through the scene graph. At this point, the value of the field in Node C becomes 4, and the value of the field in Node D becomes 6.

If a **getValue()** is called on the field in Node C instead of Node D, however, Node D remains out of date, because its value was not needed.

An output, like a field connection, can be enabled and disabled. If an output is disabled, notification is not propagated through it, and none of the fields connected to it are marked as needing evaluation.

What Inventor Does behind the Scenes

Table 6-1 summarizes the process of notification and evaluation. Column 3 of the table provides some additional information about what Inventor does behind the scenes. Whenever **setValue()** or anything that changes a field is called by the application, Inventor automatically calls the engine's **inputChanged()** method. Similarly, whenever **getValue()** or any accessor of a field is called by the application, Inventor calls the engine's **evaluate()** method.

Note that the only time an engine knows when its input has changed is when Inventor calls its **inputChanged()** method. This notification is guaranteed to happen every time a **setValue()** occurs on one of the engine's inputs. Also, note that **inputChanged()** is always called before **evaluate()**. In fact, **inputChanged()** could be called several times before **evaluate()** is called (if several **setValue()** calls occur before a **getValue()** call occurs).

Program Calls	Effect	Inventor Calls
setValue()	Notification of the change is propagated through the scene graph	inputChanged()
getValue()	Updated values are pulled through the scene graph as each evaluate() method produces new output values	evaluate()

Table 6-1   Sequence for Notification and Evaluation

Blocking Notification

An engine can implement the **inputChanged()** method so that it blocks notification under certain conditions. An **SoGate** engine provides an example of blocking notification. When its **enable** field is set to FALSE (the default), notification of the **setValue()** calls does not propagate through it to the rest of the scene graph. However, if the **trigger** field is touched, the following occurs:

- Inventor automatically calls **inputChanged()**. The **inputChanged()** method for the gate engines sets the **enable** field to TRUE.

When **getValue()** is called on a gate engine's output, the following occurs:

- Inventor automatically calls **evaluate()** on the gate engine. The gate engines' **evaluate()** method outputs one value and sets the **enable** field to FALSE.

Here is the code for the gate engines' **inputChanged()** and **evaluate()** methods:

```
void
SoGate::inputChanged(SoField *whichInput)
{
   if (whichInput == &enable)
      output.enable(enable.getValue());
   else if (whichInput == &trigger)
      output.enable(TRUE);
}

void
SoGate::evaluate()
{
   trigger.getValue(); // Clears notification
   SO_ENGINE_OUTPUT(output, type,
                    setValues(0, input.getNum(),
                    input.getValues(0)));
   // Get rid of any extra values in output
   SO_ENGINE_OUTPUT(output, type, setNum(input.getNum()));
   output.enable(enable.getValue());
}
```

Note: Do not call **setValue()** within an **inputChanged()** method. You can call **getValue()** within **inputChanged()**, but be aware that doing this could slow down notification because **getValue()** causes Inventor to pause and pull new values through the scene graph.

Creating a Fan-in Engine

The following engine provides a simple example of how an **inputChanged()** method is used to take different actions based on which input was touched. This engine accepts up to four inputs and produces one output (simulating fan-in of connections, which is not allowed directly). It simply copies the most recently touched input to the output. Example 6-7 shows the header file for the fan-in engine. Example 6-8 shows the source file for this class.

Example 6-7   FanIn.h

```
#include <Inventor/engines/SoSubEngine.h>
#include <Inventor/fields/SoSFFloat.h>

// This engine class takes up to four inputs (input0 through
// input3) and outputs the most recently changed one to the
// output.

class FanIn : public SoEngine {

 public:

    SO_ENGINE_HEADER(FanIn);

    // Inputs:
    SoSFFloat       input0;
    SoSFFloat       input1;
    SoSFFloat       input2;
    SoSFFloat       input3;

    // Output:
    SoEngineOutput  output;   // (SoSFFloat)

    // Initialization
    static void initClass();

    // Constructor
    FanIn();

 private:
    // This saves a pointer to the field that changed most
    // recently
    SoSFFloat       *lastChangedField;
```

```
    // Destructor
    virtual ~FanIn();

    // This is called when an input value changes - we will use
    // it to figure out which input was changed most recently
    virtual void inputChanged(SoField *whichField);

    // Evaluation method
    virtual void evaluate();
};
```

Example 6-8   FanIn.c++

```
#include "FanIn.h"

SO_ENGINE_SOURCE(FanIn);

// Initializes the FanIn class.

void
FanIn::initClass()
{
    SO_ENGINE_INIT_CLASS(FanIn, SoEngine, "Engine");
}

// Constructor

FanIn::FanIn()
{
    // Do standard constructor stuff
    SO_ENGINE_CONSTRUCTOR(FanIn);

    // Define input fields and their default values
    SO_ENGINE_ADD_INPUT(input0,  (0.0));
    SO_ENGINE_ADD_INPUT(input1,  (0.0));
    SO_ENGINE_ADD_INPUT(input2,  (0.0));
    SO_ENGINE_ADD_INPUT(input3,  (0.0));

    // Define the output, specifying its type
    SO_ENGINE_ADD_OUTPUT(output, SoSFFloat);

    // Initialize the pointer that indicates which field changed
    // most recently
    lastChangedField = NULL;
}
```

```
// Destructor. Does nothing.

FanIn::~FanIn()
{
}

// This is called when one of our input fields changes. We will
// use it to determine which input value to output.

void
FanIn::inputChanged(SoField *whichField)
{
   // Save a pointer to the field that changed; cast it to an
   // SoSFFloat, since that's the only input field type we have
   lastChangedField = (SoSFFloat *) whichField;
}

// This is the evaluation routine.

void
FanIn::evaluate()
{
   // If evaluate() is called, we must have been notified at
   // some point of a change (including a new connection), so
   // our lastChangedField should never be NULL here. Check it
   // anyway, just for completeness
   if (lastChangedField == NULL) {
     fprintf(stderr, "Uh-oh, there's a NULL lastChangedField"
             "in FanIn::evaluate()!\n");
     return;
   }

   // Output the value from the last changed field
   float   value = lastChangedField->getValue();
   SO_ENGINE_OUTPUT(output, SoSFFloat, setValue(value));
}
```

Creating a Second-Ticker Engine

As we saw with the gate engines, it's often convenient to enable and disable
outputs in an **inputChanged()** method in order to control propagation of
notification. The following engine illustrates how disabling outputs can be
useful. This engine has one input, **timeIn**, and one output, **timeOut**. It
outputs the time once a second and blocks notification in between "ticks."

This engine could be used if you want to render a scene only once a second. Because the **realTime** global field changes 60 times per second, you could use this engine to block notification in between. Example 6-9 shows the header file for the Ticker engine. Example 6-10 shows the source file for this class.

Note: Be careful when disabling outputs. If all outputs are disabled, **evaluate()** is never called.

Example 6-9   Ticker.h

```
#include <Inventor/engines/SoSubEngine.h>
#include <Inventor/fields/SoSFTime.h>

class Ticker : public SoEngine {

 public:

   SO_ENGINE_HEADER(Ticker);

   // Input:
   SoSFTime        timeIn;

   // Output:
   SoEngineOutput  timeOut;   // (SoSFTime)

   // Initialization
   static void initClass();

   // Constructor
   Ticker();

 private:
   // This saves the number of seconds of the last time this
   // engine was notified of a change
   double          lastSeconds;

   // Destructor
   virtual ~Ticker();

   // This is called when our input value changes - we will use
   // it to see if we need to output a new time value.
   virtual void inputChanged(SoField *whichField);

   // Evaluation method
   virtual void evaluate();
};
```

Example 6-10 Ticker.c++

```
#include <Inventor/SoDB.h>
#include "Ticker.h"

SO_ENGINE_SOURCE(Ticker);

// Initializes the Ticker class.

void
Ticker::initClass()
{
   SO_ENGINE_INIT_CLASS(Ticker, SoEngine, "Engine");
}

// Constructor

Ticker::Ticker()
{
   // Do standard constructor stuff
   SO_ENGINE_CONSTRUCTOR(Ticker);

   // Define input field and its default value
   SO_ENGINE_ADD_INPUT(timeIn,  (SbTime::zero()));

   // Define the output, specifying its type
   SO_ENGINE_ADD_OUTPUT(timeOut, SoSFTime);

   // Initialize the variable that stores the number of seconds
   // of the last time the input changed
   lastSeconds = -1.0;

   // Connect to the global "realTime" field by default. This
   // way, users do not have to make this connection explicitly,
   // and can change it if they want.
   timeIn.connectFrom(SoDB::getGlobalField("realTime"));
}

// Destructor. Does nothing.

Ticker::~Ticker()
{
}
```

```
// This is called when one of our input fields changes. We will
// use it to determine whether to produce any output. Since we
// have only 1 input field, we don't have to see which field
// changed.

void
Ticker::inputChanged(SoField *)
{

    // Get the current input time and get rid of any fractional
    // part, using the math library's floor() function
    SbTime    currentTime = timeIn.getValue();
    double    currentSeconds = floor(currentTime.getValue());

    // If the new number of seconds is different from the last
    // one we stored, enable the output. The next time this
    // engine is evaluated, the time will be output.
    if (currentSeconds != lastSeconds)
      timeOut.enable(TRUE);

    // Otherwise, make sure the output is disabled, since we
    // don't want to output any values until we cross the next
    // second barrier.
    else
      timeOut.enable(FALSE);
}

// This is the evaluation routine.

void
Ticker::evaluate()
{
    // Output the current number of seconds
    SbTime    currentTime(lastSeconds);
    SO_ENGINE_OUTPUT(timeOut, SoSFTime, setValue(currentTime));
}
```

Creating a New Field Converter

Whenever a connection is made between fields, inputs, or outputs and the
types aren't the same, Inventor tries to insert an engine to convert from the
source type to the destination type. Inventor maintains a table that lists the
class of engine that converts between a given pair of types.

You can define new converters and add them to the table, either to support additional conversions between built-in field types, or to support conversions to or from new fields you have created (see Chapter 3). For convenience, a single class of engine can support several different types of conversions (for example, a single engine may be able to convert from a rational number field to a float, a short, or a long). When Inventor creates an instance of the field converter, it tells it the source and destination field types.

Overview

Creating a field converter is similar to creating other types of engines, with a few additional steps. The following checklist summarizes things you need to do when you create a new field converter.

1. Select a name for the new field converter class and determine what class it is derived from.

2. Define and name each input and output for the engine, as for a standard engine.

3. Define the constructor, destructor, and **evaluate()** method, as for a standard engine.

4. Declare two required virtual methods:

   virtual SoField ***getInput**(SoType *type*);

   virtual SoEngineOutput ***getOutput**(SoType *type*);

   These methods are called by Inventor to obtain the input and output it will connect to and from for a particular conversion.

Initializing the Field Converter Class

Implement the **initClass()** method. For each conversion that the engine supports, after the SO_ENGINE_INIT_CLASS() macro, call

SoDB::addConverter(*typeIdOfSourceField*, *typeIdOfDestinationField*,
YourEngine::**getClassTypeId**());

The evaluate() Method

If the converter has multiple inputs or outputs, its **evaluate**() method can check **input.isConnected**() and **output.getNumConnections**() to find out which conversion needs to be done. Or, the **getInput**() and **getOutput**() methods can save their parameters in instance variables and the **evaluate**() method can check them.

The getInput() and getOutput() Methods

The **getInput**() and **getOutput**() methods check the passed type and return the appropriate input or output. It is guaranteed that Inventor will never call these methods except for pairs of types registered with **SoDB::addConverter**().

Sample Field Converter

Example 6-11 shows the header file for a new field converter, **ConvertSFShortToSFFloat**. Example 6-12 shows the source code for this class.

Example 6-11   ConvertSFShortToSFFloat.h

```
#include <Inventor/engines/SoFieldConverter.h>
#include <Inventor/fields/SoSFShort.h>
#include <Inventor/fields/SoSFFloat.h>

class ConvertSFShortToSFFloat : public SoFieldConverter {

  public:

    SO_ENGINE_HEADER(ConvertSFShortToSFFloat);

    // Input:
    SoSFShort        input;

    // Output:
    SoEngineOutput   output;  // (SoSFFloat)

    // Initialization
    static void initClass();
```

```
      // Constructor
      ConvertSFShortToSFFloat();

    private:
      // Destructor
      virtual ~ConvertSFShortToSFFloat();

      // Evaluation method
      virtual void evaluate();

      // These must be defined for a field converter. They return
      // the input and output connections of the given types. In
      // our case, we have only one input and one output, so we
      // know that those will be the given types.
      virtual SoField *        getInput(SoType type);
      virtual SoEngineOutput * getOutput(SoType type);
};
```

Example 6-12 ConvertSFShortToSFFloat.c++

```
#include <Inventor/SoDB.h>
#include "ConvertSFShortToSFFloat.h"

SO_ENGINE_SOURCE(ConvertSFShortToSFFloat);

// Initializes the ConvertSFShortToSFFloat class.

void
ConvertSFShortToSFFloat::initClass()
{
    SO_ENGINE_INIT_CLASS(ConvertSFShortToSFFloat,
                         SoFieldConverter, "FieldConverter");

    // Register this converter's type with the Inventor database
    // to convert from a field (or engine output) of type
    // SoSFShort to a field of type SoSFFloat.
    // We only call this once, since this engine offers only one
    // type conversion.
    SoDB::addConverter(SoSFShort::getClassTypeId(),
                       SoSFFloat::getClassTypeId(),
                       getClassTypeId());
}
```

```
// Constructor

ConvertSFShortToSFFloat::ConvertSFShortToSFFloat()
{
    // Do standard constructor tasks
    SO_ENGINE_CONSTRUCTOR(ConvertSFShortToSFFloat);

    // Define input field and its default value
    SO_ENGINE_ADD_INPUT(input,  (0));

    // Define the output, specifying its type
    SO_ENGINE_ADD_OUTPUT(output, SoSFFloat);
}

// Destructor. Does nothing.

ConvertSFShortToSFFloat::~ConvertSFShortToSFFloat()
{
}

// This is the evaluation routine.

void
ConvertSFShortToSFFloat::evaluate()
{
    // Get the input value as a short, convert it to a float, and
    // output it
    float    value = (float) input.getValue();
    SO_ENGINE_OUTPUT(output, SoSFFloat, setValue(value));
}

// This returns the input field for the given type. Since we
// have only one input field, we don't have to check the type.

SoField *
ConvertSFShortToSFFloat::getInput(SoType)
{
    return &input;
}

// This does the same for the output.

SoEngineOutput *
ConvertSFShortToSFFloat::getOutput(SoType)
{
    return &output;
}
```

## Chapter 7

Creating a Node Kit

This chapter describes how to create a node-kit class. The examples show how to create a new subclass and how to customize the node-kit catalog. Creating a node kit is essentially the same as creating a node, except you use special node-kit macros found in SoSubKit.h. In addition, you use special macros for defining the node-kit catalog.

Before reading this chapter, be sure to read Chapter 14 in *The Inventor Mentor*, as well as Chapter 2 in this book.

The first part of this chapter offers an overview of the steps required to create a new node kit. When necessary, additional sections explain key concepts in further detail and list the relevant macros. The chapter examples show how to create three node-kit classes:

- **SoAppearanceKit**, a node kit in the Inventor library, which is a simple grouping of properties

- **PyramidKit**, a node kit that uses an existing node-kit class and changes one of its parts

- **JumpingJackKit**, a node kit that adds new parts to the parent class, including a built-in event callback that moves the parts when the user selects the object with the mouse

Overview

Node kits are nodes that organize their children into a particular structure. This structure is defined by *parts* in a *catalog*. To define a new node-kit class, the main task is to create a catalog for the class (in addition to the standard tasks for deriving a "regular" node). Once a catalog is established, the rest of the functionality, such as **setPart()**, **getPart()**, and **createPathToPart()**, is provided by the base class for all node kits, **SoBaseKit**.

SoBaseKit is a direct descendant of **SoNode**. Therefore, when creating new node kits, you follow the standard procedure for creating and using new classes of nodes, except that you use the node-kit macros in the file SoSubKit.h. (Since you have to derive from at least **SoBaseKit**, you never need to include this file directly.) The SO_KIT_HEADER() macro declares type identifier and naming variables and methods that all node-kit classes must support. It also defines the private variable **nodekitCatalog** and a protected virtual method for retrieving it, **getNodekitCatalog()**. It defines the static method **getClassNodekitCatalog()** as well. The SO_KIT_SOURCE() macro defines the static variables and methods declared in the SO_KIT_HEADER() macro. Other macros useful in creating new node-kit classes are mentioned in the following sections.

Beyond this, most of the work for making a node kit focuses on creating the node-kit catalog. This catalog is a static variable and is therefore shared by all instances of the class. Whenever a user requests that a part should be added or retrieved (through **getPart()**, **setPart()**, and so on), the node-kit catalog is consulted. The node-kit catalog for any given class is created once when the first instance of that class is created.

Creating a new node kit requires these steps:

1. Select a name for the new node-kit class and determine what class it is derived from.

2. If the node kit has fields, define and name each field.

3. Design each part in the catalog. Use the SO_KIT_CATALOG_ENTRY_HEADER() macro to declare a name for the part in the header file (see "Defining and Naming Catalog Entries" on page 127). The parts themselves are described in the constructor.

4. Define an **initClass()** method to initialize the type information (see "Initializing the Node-Kit Class" on page 127).

5. Define a constructor (see "Defining the Constructor" on page 127).

6. Implement actions, if necessary. Typically, you won't need to implement additional actions for a node kit. You may, however, want to redefine the **setDefaultOnNonWritingFields()** method (see "Writing Information About Parts" on page 138).

7. Implement a **copy()** method if the node kit contains any non-field instance data (see Chapter 2).

8. Implement an **affectsState()** method if this method cannot be inherited from the parent class (see Chapter 2).

Defining and Naming Catalog Entries

In the header file, use the macro SO_KIT_CATALOG_ENTRY_HEADER() for each part in the catalog. For example:

```
SO_KIT_CATALOG_ENTRY_HEADER(lightModel);
SO_KIT_CATALOG_ENTRY_HEADER(environment);
SO_KIT_CATALOG_ENTRY_HEADER(drawStyle);
```

Note: This macro creates a protected **SoSFNode** field for each part in the node kit. Since the nodes are stored this way, we can use the field mechanisms to write the parts out by name. Node kit parts are hidden children and are written out differently from public children. They are written out as the part name, followed by the node being used.

Initializing the Node-Kit Class

In the **initClass()** routine for your class, use the macro SO_KIT_INIT_CLASS(). For example:

```
JumpingJackKit::initClass()
{
    SO_KIT_INIT_CLASS(JumpingJackKit, SoBaseKit, "BaseKit");
}
```

Defining the Constructor

In the constructor for the node-kit class, you define the new parts for the node-kit catalog and create the node-kit parts list for each instance (as well as performing the standard node subclass construction). Some parts may be created in the constructor as well.

A series of macros is used to define a node-kit catalog. They are described in "Defining a Node-Kit Part" on page 135. Initially, the catalog is the same as that of the parent class and is set up with the macro

SO_KIT_CONSTRUCTOR()

Next, you can modify the catalog by adding new parts. A new part is entered in the catalog using one of three macros:

SO_KIT_ADD_CATALOG_ENTRY()

SO_KIT_ADD_CATALOG_ABSTRACT_ENTRY()

SO_KIT_ADD_CATALOG_LIST_ENTRY()

Attributes of existing parts may be modified using these macros:

SO_KIT_ADD_LIST_ITEM_TYPE()

SO_KIT_CHANGE_ENTRY_TYPE()

SO_KIT_CHANGE_NULL_BY_DEFAULT()

The node-kit parts list is created by the macro SO_KIT_INIT_INSTANCE(). The parts list is a protected member containing pointers to all the existing parts in this instance of the node kit. This macro also creates any parts that are created by default, such as the "shape" part in the **SoShapeKit** (a cube) and the "light" part in the **SoLightKit** (a directional light).

The **setUpConnections()** method can be redefined by the class. If so, it is called at the end of the constructor. This method attaches or detaches sensors, callback functions, and field connections. It is called at the beginning and end of **SoBaseKit::readInstance()** and at the beginning and end of **SoBaseKit::copy()**. For each of these operations, it turns the sensors and field connections off, performs the operation, and then turns the sensors and field connections on again. See Chapter 8 for an example of using **setUpConnections()**.

About Parts

This section describes the parameters that define a part. "Case Study: The Parts of SoSeparatorKit" on page 132 shows the values for these parameters as they are used in the catalog for **SoSeparatorKit**.

Anatomy of a Part

Node-kit catalogs are made up of parts in a particular arrangement. A part is completely described by the following parameters:

SbName
: *name*
This parameter is the name used to refer to this part, such as "shape," "material," "leg," and so on. The part corresponding to the node kit itself is always given the name "this" in its own catalog.

SoType
: *type*
This parameter is the node type identifier for this part, such as **SoTransform::getClassTypeId()**. The *type* may be the type of an abstract node. It is checked whenever a user attempts to get or set a part. For example, if a user calls

```
setPart("partName", newNode),
```

the **setPart()** method first checks that **newNode** belongs to a class derived from *type*. The node is only installed as "partName" if it passes this type-checking test.

SoType
: *defaultType*
This parameter is used only when the node kit needs to build a part, but that part's *type* is the type of an abstract node. For example, in **SoShapeKit**, the part "shape" has a *type* equal to that of **SoShape** (an abstract class), but the *defaultType* is **SoCube**. If the user calls **getPart()**, but the part has not yet been created, then the kit creates and returns an **SoCube** (the *defaultType*). However, when calling **setPart()**, any node of a type derived from **SoShape** (the value of *type*) is permissible.

SbBool
: *nullByDefault*
This parameter specifies whether a part is NULL by default. If FALSE, the part is always created by the SO_KIT_INIT_INSTANCE() macro for the node kit that uses this catalog.

SbBool
: *isLeaf*
This parameter is not explicitly set by you as the designer of the node kit. It is calculated automatically as you add parts to the node-kit catalog. If *isLeaf* is TRUE,

then the part has no children within the catalog. So in the **SoAppearanceKit** shown in Figure 7-5, all parts except for "this" would have *isLeaf* set to TRUE.

Leaf parts are the only ones in the catalog that the end user of the node kit can retrieve through calls like **getPart()** and **createPathToPart()**. All other parts are considered internal to the node kit. (Of course, not every leaf part can be returned. See *isPublic* on page 131.)

Note that a part can still have children in a *scene graph* without having children within the catalog. For example, any public leaf part in the catalog whose type is derived from **SoGroup** can be retrieved with **getPart()**. Following this, children can be added. The result is that in the *scene graph*, this part is not a leaf node. But it is still a leaf part in the catalog.

Some parts, such as the "childList" part in **SoSeparatorKit**, are *list parts*. A list part is always of type **SoNodeKitList**, a special type of group node, and the node kit ensures that only certain types of nodes are added to it as children. So, in a scene graph, it may very well have children. But in the catalog, it does not.

Finally, imagine using an **SoAppearanceKit** as a leaf part in a higher level node kit such as an **SoSeparatorKit**. Children may be added to the "appearance" part through calls such as:

```
myKit->setPart("appearance.material", myMtl)
```

This could add a child to the part "appearance," but the appearance part would remain a leaf part in the catalog.

SbName   *parentName*
This parameter is the name of the catalog part that is the parent of this part. The *parentName* of the part "this" is always the empty string ("").

SbName   *rightSiblingName*
This parameter is the name of the catalog part that is the right sibling of this part. If a part does not have any right siblings in the catalog, then the *rightSiblingName* is the empty string ("").

SbBool	*isList* If this parameter is TRUE, then the part is treated as a list and will be an **SoNodeKitList** node. The children of this part are restricted to certain classes of nodes. Whenever you add a child to a node-kit list, it checks to see if that child is of the correct type. If the type is not allowed, the child is not added. Use the standard methods for adding, removing, replacing, and inserting children in the node-kit list.
SoType	*listContainerType* This parameter has meaning only if *isList* is TRUE. The **SoNodeKitList** keeps a hidden child of type **SoGroup** below itself and above its children. This extra node is the container node, and its type is given by the *listContainerType* parameter. The container node can be any **SoGroup** (for example, separator, switch, or group).
SbPList	*listItemTypes* This parameter has meaning only if *isList* is TRUE. It is a list of the types permitted as children of the part. For example,

```
addChild("myList", newChild)
```

works only if *newChild* is derived from one of the types in the *listItemTypes* for the part "myList."

SbBool	*isPublic* This parameter indicates whether a user can request this part. If *isPublic* is TRUE, then the part can be accessed. Otherwise, it is considered internal to the node kit. Note that if the part is not a leaf part, then *isPublic* is always FALSE.

For example, consider the hypothetical **PublicSpherePrivateSphereKit** illustrated in Figure 7-1. If "privateAppearance" were a private part of type **SoAppearanceKit**, then the user could *not* call

```
setPart("privateAppearance.material", newNode)
```

because both "privateAppearance" and its material part are considered private.

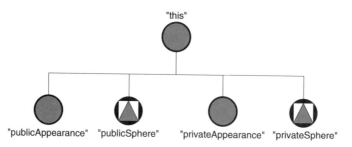

Figure 7-1   Hypothetical PublicSpherePrivateSphereKit

Case Study: The Parts of SoSeparatorKit

Figure 7-2 and Tables 7-1 through 7-3 show the parts of **SoSeparatorKit**. This kit is the base class for **SoShapeKit** and **SoWrapperKit**. Both subclasses inherit the parts in the **SoSeparatorKit**'s catalog. The parts in this catalog are as follows:

"callbackList"   a list part that can contain either **SoCallback** or **SoEventCallback** nodes. If you want to make your instance of an **SoSeparatorKit** respond to events, you can create callback nodes and add them to this list. This part is inherited from **SoBaseKit**.

"topSeparator"   a separator node that is required to prevent the property nodes from influencing nodes outside the node kit.

The "pickStyle," "appearance," "units," "transform," and "texture2Transform" parts are all composed of property nodes. Note that "appearance" is, in turn, a node kit.

"childList"   a list of **SoSeparatorKits**. By using the "childList" and the "transform" parts, you can create motion hierarchies.

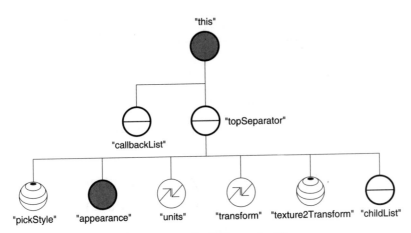

Figure 7-2   Catalog Diagram for SoSeparatorKit

name	type	defaultType
"this"	SoSeparatorKit	same
"callbackList"	SoNodeKitList	same
"topSeparator"	SoSeparator	same
"pickStyle"	SoPickStyle	same
"appearance"	SoAppearanceKit	same
"units"	SoUnits	same
"transform"	SoTransform	same
"texture2Transform"	SoTexture2Transform	same
"childList"	SoNodeKitList	same

Table 7-1   Type Parameters of SoSeparatorKit Parts

name	isLeaf	parentName	rightSibling
"this"	FALSE	" "	" "
"callbackList"	TRUE	"this"	"topSeparator"
"topSeparator"	FALSE	"this"	" "
"pickStyle"	TRUE	"topSeparator"	"appearance"
"appearance"	TRUE	"topSeparator"	"units"
"units"	TRUE	"topSeparator"	"transform"
"transform"	TRUE	"topSeparator"	"texture2Transform"
"texture2Transform"	TRUE	"topSeparator"	"childList"
"childList"	TRUE	"topSeparator"	" "

Table 7-2 Catalog Layout Parameters of SoSeparatorKit Parts

name	isList	listContainer-Type	listItemTypes	isPublic
"this"	FALSE	--	--	FALSE
"callbackList"	TRUE	SoSeparator	SoCallback and SoEventCallback	TRUE
"topSeparator"	FALSE	--	--	FALSE
"pickStyle"	FALSE	--	--	TRUE
"appearance"	FALSE	--	--	TRUE
"units"	FALSE	--	--	TRUE
"transform"	FALSE	--	--	TRUE
"texture2-Transform"	FALSE	--	--	TRUE
"childList"	TRUE	SoSeparator	SoSeparatorKit	TRUE

Table 7-3 Behavior Parameters of SoSeparatorKit Parts

Defining a Node-Kit Part

As mentioned in "Overview" on page 126, node-kit catalogs are defined within the constructor. Three macros assist you in defining new parts for the node-kit catalog:

SO_KIT_ADD_CATALOG_ENTRY()
>   adds a part to the catalog

SO_KIT_ADD_CATALOG_ABSTRACT_ENTRY()
>   adds a part that is an abstract type to the catalog

SO_KIT_ADD_CATALOG_LIST_ENTRY()
>   adds a list part to the catalog

Adding a Catalog Entry

To add new parts to a catalog, use the following macro:

SO_KIT_ADD_CATALOG_ENTRY(*name, className, nullByDefault,*
>   *parentName, rightSiblingName, isPublicPart*)

If your new part is a list part, or if the type is going to be an abstract type, see "Adding a List Entry" on page 136 or "Adding an Entry of Abstract Type" on page 137. Note that the *rightSiblingName* may change if entries are added to the catalog. If you add another part later, it is possible that the *rightSiblingName* will change. Figures 7-3 and 7-4 illustrate this.

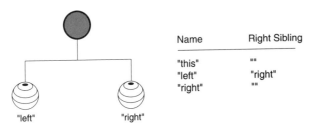

Name	Right Sibling
"this"	""
"left"	"right"
"right"	""

Figure 7-3   Right Sibling Names Before Adding the "middle" Part

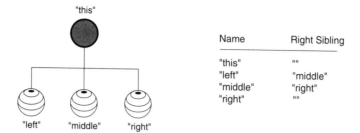

Name	Right Sibling
"this"	""
"left"	"middle"
"middle"	"right"
"right"	""

Figure 7-4   Right Sibling Names After Adding the "middle" Part

Suppose you want to add a part as the middle child in Figure 7-3. If the new part is a public label node that is NULL by default, you use the following macro:

```
SO_KIT_ADD_CATALOG_ENTRY(middle, SoLabel, TRUE, this,
                  right, TRUE);
```

Notice that part names are not quoted in macros. Figure 7-4 shows how the right sibling names change after this part has been added to the node kit.

Adding a List Entry

If the part you wish to add is a list part, use the following macro, which adds the argument *listItemClassName*. This parameter is used for type-checking when the user attempts to add new nodes as children of the list parts.

SO_KIT_ADD_CATALOG_LIST_ENTRY(*name, listContainerClassName,*
nullByDefault, parentName,
rightName, listItemClassName,
isPublicPart)

If you want your list to accept more than one type of node, then use the macro SO_KIT_ADD_LIST_ITEM_TYPE(), described in "Adding a Type to a List Entry" on page 138. Note that the list container class name must be a subclass of **SoGroup**.

The "childList" part of **SoSeparatorKit** is a list of other **SoSeparatorKits**. The part itself is an **SoNodeKitListPart** node, and it is the rightmost part in the catalog below "topSeparator." The container is an **SoSeparator** node.

The following code adds "childList" to the catalog:

```
SO_KIT_ADD_CATALOG_LIST_ENTRY(childList, SoSeparator, TRUE,
                              topSeparator,  , SoSeparatorKit,
                              TRUE);
```

Adding an Entry of Abstract Type

If you wish to add a part of abstract type, you also need to provide the parameter *defaultType*, to be used when the kit has to construct the part on demand. This macro adds one parameter to the regular part-creation macro. Its syntax is

SO_KIT_ADD_CATALOG_ABSTRACT_ENTRY(*name, className,*
                  defaultClassName, nullByDefault, parentName,
                  rightName, isPublicPart)

For example, suppose you want to add an abstract part "anyKit" as the rightmost child of "this." This part can be any node kit, but the *defaultType* is an appearance kit. To create this part:

```
SO_KIT_ADD_CATALOG_ABSTRACT_ENTRY(anyKit, SoBaseKit,
                  SoAppearanceKit, TRUE, this, , TRUE);
```

Changing a Defined Part

Three macros assist you in changing parts that have already been defined in the node kit (either in this class or in a parent class):

SO_KIT_CHANGE_ENTRY_TYPE()
        changes the type or default type of a part inherited from the parent class

SO_KIT_ADD_LIST_ITEM_TYPE()
        adds a type to the list of accepted child types (for list types only)

SO_KIT_CHANGE_NULL_BY_DEFAULT()
        changes whether a part is NULL by default. If TRUE, the part is NULL by default. If FALSE, the part is always created during the SO_KIT_INIT_INSTANCE() macro for the node kit that uses this catalog.

Changing the Type of a Part

If you wish to change the *type* or *defaultType* of a part that is inherited from the parent class, use the following macro. If you change the *type*, the new type must be a subclass of the inherited type. This is useful if the part has an abstract type in the parent class, but you wish to narrow this parameter in the child class. If you change the *defaultType*, any subclass of *type* is allowable. The syntax of this macro is

SO_KIT_CHANGE_ENTRY_TYPE(*name, newClassName,*
newDefaultClassName)

In this chapter, **PyramidKit** changes the *type* of the "shape" part from **SoShape** to **Pyramid**, and it changes the *defaultType* from **SoCube** to **Pyramid**:

```
SO_KIT_CHANGE_ENTRY_TYPE(shape, Pyramid, Pyramid);
```

Adding a Type to a List Entry

When you want a list part to accept more than one type of node as a child, use this macro to add to the *listItemTypes*:

SO_KIT_ADD_LIST_ITEM_TYPE(*name, newClass*)

For example, if you wanted "childList" to also accept **SoCube** nodes, you'd add:

```
SO_KIT_ADD_LIST_ITEM_TYPE(childList, SoCube);
```

Writing Information About Parts

If you don't want a part to be written out, you can override the **setDefaultOnNonWritingFields**() method to call the base class version first. Then, for any part you don't want written out, call

partName.**setDefault**(TRUE);

Be aware, though, that the part may write out anyway under certain conditions. For example, if the part lies on a path that is being written to a file, the part will write out regardless of this setting.

SoAppearanceKit

SoAppearanceKit is a subclass of **SoBaseKit**, provided as part of the standard Inventor library. It is a collection of all property nodes that affect the appearance of a rendered shape. Eight parts are added as direct children of the node kit. A diagram of the catalog's structure is shown in Figure 7-5.

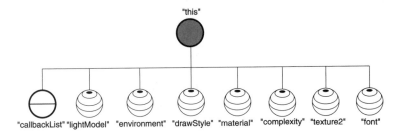

Figure 7-5   Catalog Diagram for SoAppearanceKit

Examples 7-1 and 7-2 show the complete header and source files for the **SoAppearanceKit** class. For brevity's sake, comments are omitted.

Example 7-1   SoAppearanceKit.h

```
#include <Inventor/nodekits/SoBaseKit.h>

class SoAppearanceKit : public SoBaseKit {

    SO_KIT_HEADER(SoAppearanceKit);

    // Defines fields for the new parts in the catalog
    SO_KIT_CATALOG_ENTRY_HEADER(lightModel);
    SO_KIT_CATALOG_ENTRY_HEADER(environment);
    SO_KIT_CATALOG_ENTRY_HEADER(drawStyle);
    SO_KIT_CATALOG_ENTRY_HEADER(material);
    SO_KIT_CATALOG_ENTRY_HEADER(complexity);
    SO_KIT_CATALOG_ENTRY_HEADER(texture2);
    SO_KIT_CATALOG_ENTRY_HEADER(font);

  public:
    // Constructor
    SoAppearanceKit();

  SoINTERNAL public:
    static void initClass();
```

```
private:

  // Destructor
  virtual ~SoAppearanceKit();
};
```

Example 7-2   SoAppearanceKit.c++
```c++
#include <Inventor/SoDB.h>
#include <Inventor/nodekits/SoAppearanceKit.h>
#include <Inventor/nodes/SoLightModel.h>
#include <Inventor/nodes/SoEnvironment.h>
#include <Inventor/nodes/SoDrawStyle.h>
#include <Inventor/nodes/SoMaterial.h>
#include <Inventor/nodes/SoComplexity.h>
#include <Inventor/nodes/SoTexture2.h>
#include <Inventor/nodes/SoFont.h>

SO_KIT_SOURCE(SoAppearanceKit);

void
SoAppearanceKit::initClass()
{
   SO_KIT_INIT_CLASS(SoAppearanceKit, SoBaseKit, "BaseKit");
}

//    Constructor
SoAppearanceKit::SoAppearanceKit()
{
   SO_KIT_CONSTRUCTOR(SoAppearanceKit);

   isBuiltIn = TRUE;

   // Initialize children catalog and add entries to it
   // These are the macros you use to make a catalog.
   // Use combinations of ...ADD_CATALOG_ENTRY
   // and ...ADD_CATALOG_LIST_ENTRY.  See SoSubKit.h for more
   // info on syntax of these macros.
   SO_KIT_ADD_CATALOG_ENTRY(lightModel,  SoLightModel, TRUE,
                            this, ,TRUE );
   SO_KIT_ADD_CATALOG_ENTRY(environment, SoEnvironment,TRUE,
                            this, ,TRUE );
   SO_KIT_ADD_CATALOG_ENTRY(drawStyle,   SoDrawStyle,  TRUE,
                            this, ,TRUE );
   SO_KIT_ADD_CATALOG_ENTRY(material,    SoMaterial,   TRUE,
                            this, ,TRUE );
```

```
    SO_KIT_ADD_CATALOG_ENTRY(complexity,  SoComplexity, TRUE,
                             this, ,TRUE );
    SO_KIT_ADD_CATALOG_ENTRY(texture2,   SoTexture2,   TRUE,
                             this, ,TRUE );

    SO_KIT_ADD_CATALOG_ENTRY(font, SoFont, TRUE, this, ,TRUE );

    SO_KIT_INIT_INSTANCE();
}

// Destructor (necessary since inline destructor is too
// complex)

// Use: public

SoAppearanceKit::~SoAppearanceKit()
{
}
```

PyramidKit

The next two examples show **PyramidKit**, a new subclass of **SoShapeKit**
that uses the **Pyramid** node created in Chapter 2. By making it a subclass of
SoShapeKit, this new kit inherits all the parts, such as "appearance,"
"transform," and "units," used by all the other shape kits. This class changes
the *type* and *defaultType* of one of the parts in the parent class, **SoShapeKit**.

Example 7-3 shows the header file for **PyramidKit**. Example 7-4 shows the
source code for this new node-kit class.

Example 7-3   PyramidKit.h

```
#include <Inventor/nodekits/SoShapeKit.h>

class PyramidKit : public SoShapeKit {
   SO_KIT_HEADER(PyramidKit);
  public:
   PyramidKit();
   static void initClass();
  private:
   virtual ~PyramidKit();
};
```

Example 7-4   PyramidKit.c++

```
#include <Inventor/SoDB.h>

// Include files for new classes
#include "Pyramid.h"
#include "PyramidKit.h"

SO_KIT_SOURCE(PyramidKit);

void
PyramidKit::initClass()
{
   SO_KIT_INIT_CLASS(PyramidKit, SoShapeKit, "ShapeKit");
}

PyramidKit::PyramidKit()
{
   SO_KIT_CONSTRUCTOR(PyramidKit);

   // Change the 'shape' part to be a Pyramid node.
   SO_KIT_CHANGE_ENTRY_TYPE(shape, Pyramid, Pyramid );

   SO_KIT_INIT_INSTANCE();

}

PyramidKit::~PyramidKit()
{
}
```

JumpingJackKit

This section describes one more new class of node kit, **JumpingJackKit**. It is a stick figure of a man that responds to mouse events by moving his arms and legs back and forth. Figure 7-6 shows a diagram of Jack's catalog.

All parts of the body ("head," "body," "leftArm," "rightArm," "leftLeg," "rightLeg") are of type **SoShapeKit**, so that users can replace them with any shape they want.

An **SoEventCallback** node is added as a child of the "callbackList" part. When the mouse goes down over Jack, this node's callback animates the body by editing the transforms of the arm and leg body parts.

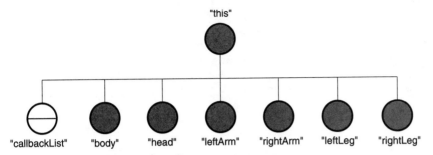

"this"

"callbackList"   "body"   "head"   "leftArm"   "rightArm"   "leftLeg"   "rightLeg"

Figure 7-6   Catalog Diagram for JumpingJackKit

Example 7-5 shows the header file for **JumpingJackKit.**

Example 7-5   JumpingJackKit.h

```
#include <Inventor/nodekits/SoBaseKit.h>

class SoEventCallback;

class JumpingJackKit : public SoBaseKit {

   SO_KIT_HEADER(JumpingJackKit);

   SO_KIT_CATALOG_ENTRY_HEADER(body);
   SO_KIT_CATALOG_ENTRY_HEADER(head);
   SO_KIT_CATALOG_ENTRY_HEADER(leftArm);
   SO_KIT_CATALOG_ENTRY_HEADER(rightArm);
   SO_KIT_CATALOG_ENTRY_HEADER(leftLeg);
   SO_KIT_CATALOG_ENTRY_HEADER(rightLeg);

 public:
   JumpingJackKit();

     // Overrides default method. All the parts are shapeKits,
     // so this node will not affect the state.
     virtual SbBool affectsState() const;

   static void initClass();

 private:

   // Constructor calls to build and set up parts.
   void createInitialJack();
```

```
    // An SoEventCallback will be inserted into the
    // "callbackList" (inherited from SoBaseKit) as the part
    // "callbackList[0]". This routine jumpJackJump() will be
    // set as the callback function for that part. It is this
    // routine which changes the angles in the joints.
    static void jumpJackJump(void *userData,
      SoEventCallback *eventCB);

    virtual ~JumpingJackKit();
};
```

The constructor for **JumpingJackKit** calls **createInitialJack()**. This routine, shown in Example 7-6, constructs the man, moves the parts to a starting position, and creates an **SoEventCallback** node, which it installs as "callbackList[0]." The constructor also creates the node-kit catalog and performs other standard construction tasks.

The callback is called "jumpJackJump." Basically, it sees if the mouse-down event occurred over the object. If so, then the limbs are rotated.

Example 7-6   JumpingJackKit.c++

```
#include <Inventor/SoPickedPoint.h>
#include <Inventor/events/SoMouseButtonEvent.h>
#include <Inventor/nodekits/SoShapeKit.h>
#include <Inventor/nodes/SoCube.h>
#include <Inventor/nodes/SoCylinder.h>
#include <Inventor/nodes/SoEventCallback.h>
#include <Inventor/nodes/SoSphere.h>
#include <Inventor/nodes/SoTransform.h>

#include "JumpingJackKit.h"

SO_KIT_SOURCE(JumpingJackKit);

void
JumpingJackKit::initClass()
{
    SO_KIT_INIT_CLASS(JumpingJackKit,SoBaseKit, "BaseKit");
}

JumpingJackKit::JumpingJackKit()
{
    SO_KIT_CONSTRUCTOR(JumpingJackKit);
```

```
    // Add the body parts to the catalog...
    SO_KIT_ADD_CATALOG_ENTRY(body, SoShapeKit,
                             TRUE, this,, TRUE);
    SO_KIT_ADD_CATALOG_ENTRY(head, SoShapeKit,
                             TRUE, this,, TRUE);
    SO_KIT_ADD_CATALOG_ENTRY(leftArm, SoShapeKit,
                             TRUE, this,, TRUE);
    SO_KIT_ADD_CATALOG_ENTRY(rightArm, SoShapeKit,
                             TRUE, this,, TRUE);
    SO_KIT_ADD_CATALOG_ENTRY(leftLeg, SoShapeKit,
                             TRUE, this,, TRUE);
    SO_KIT_ADD_CATALOG_ENTRY(rightLeg, SoShapeKit,
                             TRUE, this,, TRUE);

    SO_KIT_INIT_INSTANCE();

    createInitialJack();
}

JumpingJackKit::~JumpingJackKit()
{
}

// This kit is made up entirely of SoShapeKits.
// Since SoShapeKits do not affect state, neither does this.
SbBool
JumpingJackKit::affectsState() const
{
    return FALSE;
}

// Set up parts for default configuration of the jumping jack
void
JumpingJackKit::createInitialJack()
{
    // Create the head.
    SoSphere *headSphere = new SoSphere;
    setPart("head.shape", headSphere);

    // Create the body.
    SoCube *bodyCube = new SoCube;
    setPart("body.shape", bodyCube);
```

```
      // Create the limbs
      SoCylinder *limbCylinder = new SoCylinder;
      setPart("leftLeg.shape",  limbCylinder);
      setPart("leftArm.shape",  limbCylinder);
      setPart("rightLeg.shape", limbCylinder);
      setPart("rightArm.shape", limbCylinder);

      // Place the body and head
      set("body.transform", "scaleFactor 1 2 1");
      set("head.transform", "translation 0 3 0");

      // Place the limbs
      set("leftArm.transform",  "scaleFactor 0.5 1.5 0.5");
      set("leftLeg.transform",  "scaleFactor 0.5 1.5 0.5");
      set("rightArm.transform", "scaleFactor 0.5 1.5 0.5");
      set("rightLeg.transform", "scaleFactor 0.5 1.5 0.5");
      set("leftArm.transform",  "center 0 1 0");
      set("leftLeg.transform",  "center 0 1 0");
      set("rightArm.transform", "center 0 1 0");
      set("rightLeg.transform", "center 0 1 0");
      set("leftArm.transform",  "translation -1  1   0.5");
      set("leftLeg.transform",  "translation -1 -2.5 0.5");
      set("rightArm.transform", "translation  1  1   0.5");
      set("rightLeg.transform", "translation  1 -2.5 0.5");

      // Create the Event Callback to make jack jump.
      // When it receives a mouse button event, it will
      // call the method jumpJackJump.
      SoEventCallback *myEventCB = new SoEventCallback;
      myEventCB->addEventCallback(
            SoMouseButtonEvent::getClassTypeId(),
            JumpingJackKit::jumpJackJump, this);
      setPart("callbackList[0]", myEventCB);
}

// Animates the jumping jack (called by the "eventCallback[0]"
// part when a left mouse button press occurs).
void
JumpingJackKit::jumpJackJump(void *userData,
                             SoEventCallback *myEventCB)
{
   const SoEvent *myEvent = myEventCB->getEvent();

   // See if it's a left mouse down event
   if (SO_MOUSE_PRESS_EVENT(myEvent, BUTTON1)) {
     JumpingJackKit *myJack = (JumpingJackKit *) userData;
```

```
// See if the jumping jack was picked.
const SoPickedPoint *myPickedPoint;
myPickedPoint = myEventCB->getPickedPoint();
if (myPickedPoint && myPickedPoint->getPath() &&
    myPickedPoint->getPath()->containsNode(myJack)) {

   // The jumping jack was picked. Make it jump!
   SoTransform *myXf;
   SbVec3f zAxis(0,0,1);
   SbRotation noRot = SbRotation::identity();

   myXf = SO_GET_PART(myJack,
                      "leftArm.transform",SoTransform);
   if (myXf->rotation.getValue() == noRot)
     myXf->rotation.setValue(zAxis ,-1.6);
   else
     myXf->rotation.setValue(noRot);

   myXf = SO_GET_PART(myJack,
                      "leftLeg.transform",SoTransform);
   if (myXf->rotation.getValue() == noRot)
     myXf->rotation.setValue(zAxis ,-1.2);
   else
     myXf->rotation.setValue(noRot);
   myXf = SO_GET_PART(myJack,
                      "rightArm.transform",SoTransform);
   if (myXf->rotation.getValue() == noRot)
     myXf->rotation.setValue(zAxis , 1.6);
   else
     myXf->rotation.setValue(noRot);

   myXf = SO_GET_PART(myJack,
                      "rightLeg.transform",SoTransform);
   if (myXf->rotation.getValue() == noRot)
     myXf->rotation.setValue(zAxis , 1.2);
   else
     myXf->rotation.setValue(noRot);
   myEventCB->setHandled();
  }
 }
}
```

Example 7-7 shows a short program to create a jumping jack that responds to user events. Notice how it calls **initClass()** for **JumpingJackKit** before it creates an instance of this new node-kit class.

Example 7-7   JumpingJackTest.c++

```cpp
#include <Inventor/Xt/SoXt.h>
#include <Inventor/Xt/viewers/SoXtExaminerViewer.h>

// Header files for new node class
#include "JumpingJackKit.h"

main(int, char **argv)
{
   // Initialize Inventor and Xt
   Widget myWindow = SoXt::init(argv[0]);
   if (myWindow == NULL) exit(1);

   // Initialize the new node class
   JumpingJackKit::initClass();

   JumpingJackKit *jackyBaby = new JumpingJackKit;
   jackyBaby->ref();

   SoXtExaminerViewer *viewer =
     new SoXtExaminerViewer(myWindow);
   viewer->setSceneGraph(jackyBaby);
   viewer->setTitle("JumpingJackKit");
   viewer->show();
   viewer->viewAll();

   SoXt::show(myWindow);
   SoXt::mainLoop();
}
```

Part II

Extending
Interaction Classes

Chapter 8

Creating Draggers and Manipulators

This chapter shows how to create new draggers and manipulators. The first half of the chapter deals with creating new draggers, which are a special type of node kit with a user interface. The second half of the chapter describes creating new manipulators, which are nodes that employ draggers.

Before reading this chapter, you should first read and thoroughly understand Chapter 15 in *The Inventor Mentor*. Also, because draggers are node kits, you should be familiar with Chapter 14 in *The Inventor Mentor* and Chapter 7 in this book. If you want to create a new manipulator that uses existing draggers, you can skip directly to "Creating a Manipulator" on page 197.

The chapter examples show how to create four new classes:

- A simple dragger, **TranslateRadialDragger**, which allows translation along a line

- A compound dragger, **RotTransDragger**, which allows independent rotation in the *x*, *y*, and *z* directions as well as translation along a line

- A transform manipulator, **RotTransManip**, which uses a **RotTransDragger** for editing its transform fields

- A manipulator, **Coord3Manip**, which is derived from **SoCoordinate3** and which uses an **SoDragPointDragger** for editing its **point** field

The first two classes created in this chapter are derived from the **SoDragger** class. The first class, **TranslateRadialDragger**, shows how to create a *simple* dragger, which typically performs only one operation such as scaling or translating. The second class, **RotTransDragger**, shows how to combine simple draggers into a *compound* dragger that can perform more than one operation. The third class, **RotTransManip**, shows how to create a new manipulator that is a subclass of **SoTransformManip**. The last class, **Coord3Manip**, shows how to create a manipulator that is subclassed from **SoCoordinate3** and uses an existing dragger, the **SoDragPointDragger**.

Creating a Simple Dragger

This section describes the design and implementation of a simple dragger. Simple draggers perform one operation, such as rotating, translating, or scaling, and have a fixed user interface. Although simple draggers can be useful by themselves, they are often combined to make a compound dragger or a manipulator, as described in later sections.

The **TranslateRadialDragger** allows the user to translate the dragger along a line. The direction of the line is determined by the center of the dragger and the point on the dragger that the user first hits. By default, the dragger geometry is a sphere. When the user begins manipulating, an arrow appears in the direction of motion. (Changing the default geometry for a dragger without writing a new dragger is discussed in Chapter 15 of *The Inventor Mentor*. With this technique, any user can replace the arrow with a line or a bolt of lightning, for example.)

Overview

The **SoDragger** class, a node kit, constructs the nodes shown in Figure 8-1. The motion matrix for a simple dragger is typically a translation or a rotation matrix. This matrix is updated by the dragger as it responds to mouse motion. Changes in the motion matrix cause the dragger geometry to move on the screen. In the case of the **TranslateRadialDragger**, the motion matrix is a translation matrix. When this matrix is updated, it moves the dragger along its line in response to the user's dragging the mouse.

Each dragger has a field that reflects its state. The **TranslateRadialDragger** performs translations, so it has a **translation** field. The value of this field must be in sync with the value of the motion matrix. When you construct the dragger, you set it up so that whenever the motion matrix is updated, the dragger's **translation** field is updated, and vice versa. To update the

translation field when the dragger moves, you use a value-changed callback. (This is the typical case.) To update the motion matrix when the **translation** field changes, you attach a field sensor to the **translation** field. (This case is less typical.)

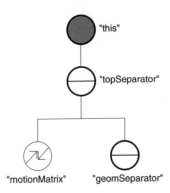

Figure 8-1   Structure of SoDragger

This discussion of draggers and manipulators uses the terms *world space* and *local space*. World space is the transformation space at the top of the scene graph. Local space (for the dragger) is the space after the motion matrix. This is typically where you perform calculations for positioning and moving the dragger. When draggers perform projections, they typically need to know the matrix to convert from local space to world space. The **getLocalToWorldMatrix()** method on **SoDragger** is a convenience method for transforming between these two spaces. Other convenience methods are

- getWorldToLocalMatrix()
- transformMatrixLocalToWorld()
- transformMatrixWorldToLocal()

The **geomSeparator** node also plays an important part in the functioning of the dragger. To facilitate caching, its children should not change during manipulation. (They can, however, change at the start or finish of user manipulation.)

Before you begin writing code for the new class, answer the following questions:

- What should the dragger look like?
- How should the dragger move?
- How do you want to interpret the dragger's motion?

The file SoSubkit.h contains the macros for defining new node-kit classes. Since **SoDragger** is a node kit, you'll be using macros from this file. (Also, because you are deriving a class from a node kit class, you do not need to include this file.) The SO_KIT_HEADER() macro declares type identifier and naming variables and methods that all node kit classes must support. The SO_KIT_SOURCE() macro defines the static variables and methods declared in the SO_KIT_HEADER() macro. Creating a new dragger follows the same general pattern as creating any new node kit, but with some additional steps, as follows:

1. Select a name for the new dragger class and decide what class it is derived from. (It will usually be derived from **SoDragger**.)

2. Determine what kind of motion the dragger will perform and add the appropriate field (for a simple dragger) or fields (for a complex dragger). Examples of fields added to the dragger are **translation**, **rotation**, and **scaleFactor** (see "Creating the Field" on page 160).

3. Design each part in the catalog. Use the SO_KIT_CATALOG_- ENTRY_HEADER() macro in the header file and SO_KIT_ADD_CATALOG_ENTRY() macro in the source file (see "Designing the Parts" on page 155).

4. For the parts in the catalog that determine the user interface:

   a. Define a unique resource name.

   b. Create a default geometry file (see "Creating the Default Geometry File" on page 155).

   c. Create the compiled-in geometry using the special utility program provided (see "Creating the Compiled-in Default Geometry" on page 158).

5. Define an **initClass()** method to initialize the type information (see "Initializing the Dragger Class" on page 159).

6. Determine what kind of projector models your interpretation of the mouse motion. For example, if your dragger moves along a line, use a line projector. It if moves in a plane, use a plane projector. If it rotates about an axis, use a cylinder projector. If it moves along the surface of a sphere, use a sphere projector. (The projector is declared in the .h file, created in the constructor, and used in the drag methods.) See "Creating the Projector" on page 161.

7. Define a constructor (see "Constructor" on page 159).

8. Implement **dragStart()**, **drag()**, and **dragFinish()** methods. These routines perform the dragging (see "Dragging Callback Functions" on page 163).

9. Implement the value-changed callback function. This function updates the dragger's field to reflect the dragger's current position.

10. Implement the field sensor callback function. This function causes the dragger to reposition itself whenever changes are made to its field.

11. Implement the **setUpConnections()** method, which attaches and detaches field sensors.

12. Define a destructor (see "Destructor" on page 162).

Designing the Parts

Our **TranslateRadialDragger** has four public parts and three internal parts. The first two parts, the **translator** part and the **translatorActive** part, are the geometry the user actually interacts with. The second two parts, the **feedback** part and the **feedbackActive** part, are passive parts that indicate the direction of translation. In general, users cannot interact with feedback parts; often, these parts do not appear until after manipulation has begun. The internal parts are the switch nodes that switch between the active and inactive pairs of parts and the **feedbackRotate** part, which orients the feedback geometry.

The subclass **TranslateRadialDragger** adds additional nodes to the base class, as shown in Figure 8-2.

Creating the Default Geometry File

Once we've identified our parts, we need to design the geometry for them. The golden rule here is to *start simple*. For now, use easy primitive shapes for your part geometry; there will be plenty of time to tweak them later. Example 8-1 shows the default geometry file for the **TranslateRadialDragger** (see Chapter 11 in *The Inventor Mentor* for more information on the Inventor file format).

Example 8-1   translateRadialDragger.iv

```
#Inventor V2.0 ascii

# Geometry resource file for the TranslateRadialDragger

DEF translateRadialTranslator Separator {
   Material { diffuseColor .6 .6 .6 }
   DrawStyle { style LINES }
   Sphere { radius 1.732 }
}
DEF translateRadialTranslatorActive Separator {
   Material { diffuseColor .6 .6 0 }
   DrawStyle { style LINES }
   Sphere { radius 1.732 }
}

# Don't show anything for feedback during inactive state
DEF translateRadialFeedback Separator { }

DEF translateRadialFeedbackActive Separator {
   Material { diffuseColor .5  .9 .9 }
   # An arrow aligned with the x axis.

   RotationXYZ {
      axis Z
      angle 1.57079
   }
   Separator {

      #stick
      Cylinder { height 4.0 radius 0.05 }

      #left arrowhead
      Translation { translation 0 2.2 0 }
      Cone { height 0.4 bottomRadius 0.2 }

      #right arrowhead
      Translation { translation 0 -4.4 0 }
      RotationXYZ { axis Z angle 3.14159 }
      Cone { height 0.4 bottomRadius 0.2 }
   }
}
```

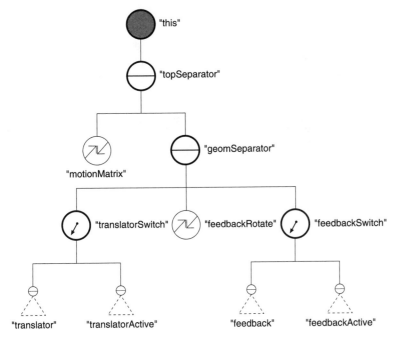

Figure 8-2   Structure of TranslateRadialDragger

In general, follow these conventions when designing the parts of your dragger:

- Give the default geometry file the same name as the dragger. In this case, it is translateRadialDragger.iv.

- In the node-kit catalog, give parts active names like "translator" and "rotator." Don't name them "cube" and "arrow"; the user may change the cube geometry to be a sphere, or the arrow geometry to a be poodle.

- Prefix the resource name (that is, the name used in the default geometry file and the global dictionary) with the base name of the dragger. (Lots of draggers could have a part named "rotator.") Also, if the geometry is for the active portion of a part, suffix it with **Active**. For example, we have **translateRadialTranslatorActive**.

Creating the Compiled-in Default Geometry

It's a harsh, cruel world. The reality of end-user environments is that sometimes resource files, such as a dragger's default geometry file, are accidentally lost or deleted. If the dragger is to continue to operate in this situation, we need to compile in a copy of the default geometry with the dragger.

To compile the default geometry along with the dragger, follow these steps:

1. Use the special utility program provided with Inventor, **ivToIncludeFile**, which translates an .iv file (such as the one shown in Example 8-1) into binary and then writes the binary version as an array of hexadecimal numbers. Once created, you can read this memory buffer directly into Inventor.

    For example, to create the geometry buffer for the translate radial dragger, the command is

    ```
    ivToIncludeFile TranslateRadialDragger::geomBuffer
            < translateRadialDragger.iv
            > TranslateRadialDraggerGeom.h
    ```

    This utility, provided with Inventor, creates a file called TranslateRadialDraggerGeom.h that looks like this:

    ```
    char TranslateRadialDragger::geomBuffer[]= { ... }
    ```

    The braces contain the hexadecimal version of the binary format for the .iv scene graph file. By convention, the name of the file containing the geometry is the name of the manipulator, followed by Geom.h.

2. In the include file, within the class definition of the dragger, declare the static variable *geomBuffer*:

    ```
    static const char geomBuffer[];
    ```

3. In the source file, include the compiled-in version:

    ```
    #include  "geom/TranslateRadialDraggerGeom.h"
    ```

After you've created the dragger, you can modify the resource file (TranslateRadialDragger.iv). See Chapter 15 in *The Inventor Mentor* for information on how to change the resource file without recompiling. When you are finished modifying the resource file, run the translation program and recompile the dragger; the geometry becomes a permanent part of your dragger.

Initializing the Dragger Class

Define the **initClass()** method using the SO_KIT_INIT_CLASS() macro. Note that for existing Inventor draggers, **initClass()** is called by

```
SoInteraction::init()
```

For any draggers or manipulators that you add to the system, you will need to call **yourDragger::initClass()** from the application after the call to **SoInteraction::init()**, or after anything that calls **SoInteraction::init()**, such as **SoXt::init()**.

Constructor

Every simple dragger should declare a constructor that causes the default geometry for this dragger to be used. Let's briefly examine each step in the constructor:

- a. Use SO_KIT_CONSTRUCTOR() to set up the internal variables for the class.
- b. Define the catalog entries for the new dragger (a node kit).
- c. Put the default parts into the global dictionary.
- d. Create the parts list and the parts that are created by default in this dragger using SO_KIT_INIT_INSTANCE().
- e. Create the appropriate field for the dragger—in this case, **translation**.
- f. Create the parts for the dragger.
- g. Set the switches to inactive (if your dragger uses active/inactive pairs of parts).
- h. Create the projector.
- i. Add the dragger callback functions.
- j. Add the value-changed callback function.
- k. Put a sensor on the field.
- l. Call the **setUpConnections()** method to attach the field sensors.

Steps a through d and step f are standard procedure for new node kits. Step g is the recommended convention if your dragger uses active/inactive pairs of parts, but it is not required. The others are required steps for draggers. Here are a few more details about some of these steps.

Defining New Dragger Catalog Entries

As for any node kit, use the SO_KIT_ADD_CATALOG_ENTRY() macro to create the catalog entries for the dragger. This example places the switch nodes and the **feedbackRotate** node below the **geomSeparator** part for improved caching behavior.

Putting Default Parts into the Global Dictionary

When the first instance of the dragger is created, the default scene graph for each part needs to be read and installed in the global dictionary. Use the **readDefaultParts()** method to read the geometry. It takes as arguments the name of the user-changeable resource .iv file, the compiled-in **geomBuffer**, and the size of the **geomBuffer**.

```
if (SO_KIT_IS_FIRST_INSTANCE())
   readDefaultParts
         ("translateRadialDragger.iv", // default geom file
          geomBuffer,                   // compiled-in defaults
          sizeof(geomBuffer));          // size of buffer
```

Creating the Field

Every dragger has a field (or fields) reflecting its state. This dragger performs translations, so you create a **translation** field.

Creating the Parts

Creating the parts is again standard node-kit procedure. Use **setPartAsDefault()** to look up the part in the global dictionary and install the default geometry from the resource file:

```
setPartAsDefault("translator", "translateRadialTranslator");
```

The method **setPartAsDefault()** differs from **setPart()**. If **setPartAsDefault()** is used, then the given subgraph will not be written to file unless it is changed later. If **setPart()** were used, then every subgraph of every part would appear in the file, resulting in lengthy files. Also, when reading the dragger back into Inventor, the geometry written to file would always replace the default. Hence, writing a dragger to file would fix its look forever, even if the default were redesigned.

Setting the Switches

Although the draggers provided with the standard Inventor library use pairs of active and inactive parts, this is not a requirement for your new dragger. However, if you do use similar pairs of parts, the constructor should set the switches to the inactive part to start with:

```
SoSwitch *sw;
sw = SO_GET_ANY_PART(this, "translatorSwitch", SoSwitch);
setSwitchValue(sw, 0);
sw = SO_GET_ANY_PART(this, "feedbackSwitch", SoSwitch);
setSwitchValue(sw, 0);
```

The **setSwitchValue()** method is a convenience routine that checks that the given value is a change before setting it. It also checks whether the switch is NULL.

Creating the Projector

The most common way of turning 2D mouse input into direct 3D interaction is to project the 2D cursor position into a 3D line directed from the eye into the scene and intersect that line with some shape. The classes derived from **SbProjector** are designed to do just that, as well as to simplify the task of interpreting the result of the projection as a translation, rotation, and so on. For more information on **SbProjectors**, see the *Open Inventor C++ Reference Manual*.

In the case of the **TranslateRadialDragger**, we wish the user to be able to translate the dragger along a line. To turn the 2D mouse position into a translation in three dimensions along a line, we make use of an **SbLineProjector**. For now, we just construct an instance of the projector and save a pointer to it. Later, we need to update the projector with the current transform space, the current view volume, and so on. Then, every time the mouse moves, we find out what the mouse position projects to in three dimensions, and how far it moved from the previous position.

To create the projector, the constructor includes the following line:

```
lineProj = new SbLineProjector();
```

Defining the Callback Functions

During construction, the dragger class must also register a set of callback functions that are invoked by the base class when some event or change in state occurs. For the **TranslateRadialDragger** (and most other simple draggers), we need to know these things:

- *When the user initiates dragging*—this happens when the primary mouse button is pressed and a hit occurs on the dragger geometry.

- *When the user drags the mouse*—this happens when the mouse moves, provided dragging has already been initiated and the primary mouse button is still down.

- *When the user completes dragging*—this happens when the primary mouse button is released, provided dragging was already in progress.

Adding a Value-Changed Callback

Whenever the **motionMatrix** changes (for example, as a result of interaction or copying), we must update the **translation** field to correctly reflect this new state (see Figure 8-3). Use a value-changed callback function to update the **translation** field.

Adding a Field Sensor

If the **translation** field changes, the **motionMatrix** must be changed so that the dragger moves to that new position (again, see Figure 8-3). (The dragger's field could change if it is set by the user, by a field-to-field connection, by an engine, or by a value from file.) Put a sensor on the **translation** field to detect and communicate these changes.

Destructor

As with all classes, it is necessary to free any memory that was allocated during construction. Since draggers are a type of node, they are not explicitly deleted; instead, they are automatically deleted when their reference count falls to 0. When this happens, the child nodes of the dragger also have their reference counts decremented and are deleted automatically.

The only things that were created with **new** in the constructor were the projector and the sensor. We explicitly delete the projector and the sensor.

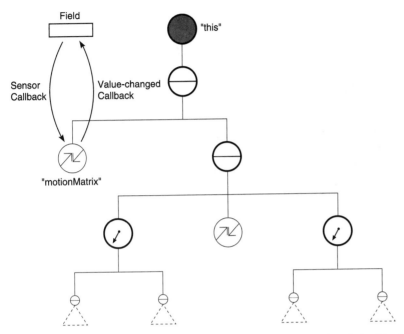

Figure 8-3   Maintaining Consistency Between the Field and the Motion Matrix

Dragging Callback Functions

The source file needs to implement the routines that are called as a result of user interaction: **dragStart()**, **drag()**, and **dragFinish()**. The functions are actually called by small static callback functions (usually called *callback stubs*). Those callback stubs are the functions that we registered in the constructor with the **addCallback** methods on **SoDragger**. (Recall that we need to use callback stubs because there is no notion of the implicit **this** pointer when the callback is invoked.)

Now, we'll look at the functions that do the real work.

Begin Dragging

When the user presses the primary mouse button and causes a hit on the dragger, dragging begins. When this happens, several things must be done by the dragger to prepare for the ensuing dragging by the user:

a. Find out where on the dragger the hit occurred using the **getLocalStartingPoint()** method on **SoDragger**. This is often used to determine a direction of manipulation, or to save an initial point that is used as a marker for successive movements.

b. Set up the projector being used. Projectors need to be initialized, typically with some parameters to set their size and position, a transformation space to work in, and the view volume to use for projecting the mouse position into three dimensions. The projector geometry is usually determined by the dragger based on the initial hit position. The transformation space and the view volume are obtained from methods on **SoDragger** (using **getLocalToWorldMatrix()** and **getViewVolume()**).

c. Set up any feedback geometry that may exist.

d. Set any appropriate switches to display parts as active.

The **TranslateRadialDragger::dragStart()** method accomplishes each of these things. The references to *local* space imply the transformation space that the parts of the manipulator exist in. Example 8-3 includes the code for **dragStart()**.

In the case of the **TranslateRadialDragger**, a special method, **orientFeedbackGeometry()**, is called by **dragStart()** to align the feedback geometry (an arrow) with the direction of translation. This special method is specific to the sample class and is not a requirement for draggers in general.

Continue Dragging

Once dragging has begun, and for as long as the primary mouse button is held down, successive movements of the mouse cause the motion callbacks to be invoked. When motion is detected, the dragger typically does these things:

a. Update the view volume used by any projectors. This is necessary because it is possible for the camera's view volume to change between renderings, either because of viewport cropping or if some external force, such as a viewer, is editing the camera.

b. Update the projector's workspace matrix.

c. Using the current mouse position, project to a new position on the projector. Then using the new position, and perhaps some previously saved positions, determine what kind of motion (scale, rotate, translate) the dragger will perform, in local space.

d. Turn this motion into a matrix and append that matrix to the motion matrix. This results in movement of the dragger.

Here is the code for **TranslateRadialDragger::drag()**. Recall that it is called by **TranslateRadialDragger::motionCB()**, which in turn is invoked by **SoDragger** whenever the mouse moves during dragging.

```
void
TranslateRadialDragger::drag()
{
    // Things can change between renderings. To be safe, update
    // the projector with the current values.
    lineProj->setViewVolume(getViewVolume());
    lineProj->setWorkingSpace(getLocalToWorldMatrix());

    // Find the new intersection on the projector.
    SbVec3f newHitPt
      = lineProj->project(getNormalizedLocaterPosition());

    // Get initial point expressed in our current local space.
    SbVec3f startHitPt = getLocalStartingPoint();

    // Motion in local space is difference between old and
    // new positions.
    SbVec3f motion = newHitPt - startHitPt;

    // Append this to the startMotionMatrix, which was saved
    // automatically at the beginning of the drag, to find
    // the current motion matrix.
    setMotionMatrix(
      appendTranslation(getStartMotionMatrix(), motion));
}
```

Finish Dragging

The last thing a dragger needs to do is reset the state of its geometry when dragging is completed. Example 8-3 includes the code for **dragFinish()**.

Value-Changed Callback

The value-changed callback function updates the dragger's **translation** field when the motion matrix changes. Here is the code for the **TranslateRadialDragger**'s value-changed callback function.

```
void
TranslateRadialDragger::valueChangedCB(void *,
   SoDragger *inDragger)
{
   TranslateRadialDragger *myself
     = (TranslateRadialDragger *) inDragger;

   // Get translation by decomposing motionMatrix.
   SbMatrix motMat = myself->getMotionMatrix();
   SbVec3f trans, scale;
   SbRotation rot, scaleOrient;
   motMat.getTransform(trans, rot, scale, scaleOrient);

   // Set "translation", disconnecting sensor while doing so.
   myself->fieldSensor->detach();
   if (myself->translation.getValue() != trans)
     myself->translation = trans;
   myself->fieldSensor->attach(&(myself->translation));
}
```

Field Sensor

If the dragger's **translation** field changes, the motion matrix must be updated to reflect that change. The callback function for the field sensor performs this task, as follows:

```
// If the "translation" field is set from outside, update
// motionMatrix accordingly.
void
TranslateRadialDragger::fieldSensorCB(void *inDragger,
                                     SoSensor *)
{
   TranslateRadialDragger *myself
     = (TranslateRadialDragger *) inDragger;
```

```
    SbMatrix motMat = myself->getMotionMatrix();
    myself->workFieldsIntoTransform(motMat);

    myself->setMotionMatrix(motMat);
}
```

Note that **workFieldsIntoTransform()** is a special method that changes only the parts of the matrix for which the dragger has fields. In this case, the translation in the matrix changes, but any rotation or scale in the matrix remains undisturbed.

The setUpConnections() Method

When a dragger is read from file or when a copy of a dragger is made, you do not want any of the dragger's sensors to fire. Implement a **setUpConnections()** method to detach and attach the sensors so that draggers can be copied and read correctly. The **SoDragger::copy()** and **SoDragger::readInstance()** methods call **setUpConnections(FALSE)** at the beginning and **setUpConnections(TRUE)** at the end. The constructor also calls **setUpConnections()**. Example 8-3 shows **setUpConnections()** for the **TranslateRadialDragger** class.

Example 8-2 shows the include file for the **TranslateRadialDragger** class.

Example 8-2   TranslateRadialDragger.h

```
//  Resource names and part names for this dragger are:
//       Resource Name:                       Part Name:
//       translateRadialTranslator            translator
//       translateRadialTranslatorActive      translatorActive
//       translateRadialFeedback              feedback
//       translateRadialFeedbackActive        feedbackActive

#include <Inventor/draggers/SoDragger.h>
#include <Inventor/fields/SoSFVec3f.h>
#include <Inventor/sensors/SoFieldSensor.h>

class SbLineProjector;

class TranslateRadialDragger : public SoDragger {
    SO_KIT_HEADER(TranslateRadialDragger);
```

```
// Catalog entries for new parts added by this class.
SO_KIT_CATALOG_ENTRY_HEADER(translatorSwitch);
SO_KIT_CATALOG_ENTRY_HEADER(translator);
SO_KIT_CATALOG_ENTRY_HEADER(translatorActive);
SO_KIT_CATALOG_ENTRY_HEADER(feedbackRotate);
SO_KIT_CATALOG_ENTRY_HEADER(feedbackSwitch);
SO_KIT_CATALOG_ENTRY_HEADER(feedback);
SO_KIT_CATALOG_ENTRY_HEADER(feedbackActive);

public:

  // Constructor
  TranslateRadialDragger();

  // Field that will always contain the dragger's position.
  SoSFVec3f translation;

  // Initialize the class. This should be called once
  // after SoInteraction::init().
  static void initClass();

protected:

  void orientFeedbackGeometry(const SbVec3f &localDir);

  // Projector used for calculating motion along a line.
  SbLineProjector *lineProj;

  // Static callback functions invoked by SoDragger when the
  // mouse button goes down over this dragger, when the
  // mouse drags, and when the button is released.
  static void startCB(void *, SoDragger *);
  static void motionCB(void *, SoDragger *);
  static void finishCB(void *, SoDragger *);

  // These functions, invoked by the static callback
  // functions, do all the work of moving the dragger.
  void dragStart();
  void drag();
  void dragFinish();

  // This sensor watches for changes to the translation field.
  SoFieldSensor *fieldSensor;
  static void fieldSensorCB(void *, SoSensor *);
```

```
// This callback updates the translation field when
// the dragger is moved.
static void valueChangedCB(void *, SoDragger *);

// This will detach/attach the fieldSensor.
// It is called at the end of the constructor (to attach).
// and at the start/end of SoBaseKit::readInstance()
// and on the new copy at the start/end of SoBaseKit::copy().
// Returns the state of the node when this was called.
virtual SbBool setUpConnections(SbBool onOff,
                                SbBool doItAlways = FALSE);


private:

static const char geomBuffer[];

// Destructor.
~TranslateRadialDragger();
};
```

Example 8-3 shows the source code for the **TranslateRadialDragger** class.

Example 8-3   TranslateRadialDragger.c++

```
#include <Inventor/nodes/SoRotation.h>
#include <Inventor/nodes/SoSeparator.h>
#include <Inventor/nodes/SoSwitch.h>
#include <Inventor/projectors/SbLineProjector.h>
#include <Inventor/sensors/SoFieldSensor.h>
#include <Inventor/SoPath.h>

// Include file for our new class.
#include "TranslateRadialDragger.h"

// This file contains the variable
// TranslateRadialDragger::geomBuffer, which describes
// the default geometry resources for this dragger.
#include "TranslateRadialDraggerGeom.h"

SO_KIT_SOURCE(TranslateRadialDragger);
```

```
// Initializes the type ID for this dragger node. This
// should be called once after SoInteraction::init().
void
TranslateRadialDragger::initClass()
{
   SO_KIT_INIT_CLASS(TranslateRadialDragger, SoDragger,
                     "Dragger");
}


TranslateRadialDragger::TranslateRadialDragger()
{
   SO_KIT_CONSTRUCTOR(TranslateRadialDragger);

   // Put this under geomSeparator so it draws efficiently.
   SO_KIT_ADD_CATALOG_ENTRY(translatorSwitch, SoSwitch, TRUE,
                            geomSeparator, , FALSE);
   SO_KIT_ADD_CATALOG_ENTRY(translator, SoSeparator, TRUE,
                            translatorSwitch, , TRUE);
   SO_KIT_ADD_CATALOG_ENTRY(translatorActive,SoSeparator, TRUE,
                            translatorSwitch, , TRUE);
   SO_KIT_ADD_CATALOG_ENTRY(feedbackRotate, SoRotation, TRUE,
                            geomSeparator, , TRUE);
   SO_KIT_ADD_CATALOG_ENTRY(feedbackSwitch, SoSwitch, TRUE,
                            geomSeparator, , FALSE);
   SO_KIT_ADD_CATALOG_ENTRY(feedback, SoSeparator, TRUE,
                            feedbackSwitch, , TRUE);
   SO_KIT_ADD_CATALOG_ENTRY(feedbackActive, SoSeparator, TRUE,
                            feedbackSwitch, , TRUE);

   // Read geometry resources. Only do this the first time we
   // construct one.  'geomBuffer' contains our compiled in
   // defaults. The user can override these by specifying new
   // scene graphs in the file:
   // $(SO_DRAGGER_DIR)/translateRadialDragger.iv
   if (SO_KIT_IS_FIRST_INSTANCE())
     readDefaultParts("translateRadialDragger.iv", geomBuffer,
                      sizeof(geomBuffer));

   // Field that always shows current position of the dragger.
   SO_KIT_ADD_FIELD(translation, (0.0, 0.0, 0.0));

   // Creates the parts list for this node kit.
   SO_KIT_INIT_INSTANCE();
```

```
// Create the parts of the dragger. This dragger has five
// parts that we need to create: "translator",
// "translatorActive", "feedback," and "feedbackActive" will
// be created using the resource mechanism. They are looked
// up in the global dictionary.
// "rotator," used to position the feedback so it points in
// the direction selected by the user, will just be a plain
// old SoRotation node.
// We call 'setPartAsDefault' because we are installing
// default geometries from the resource files. By calling
// 'setPartAsDefault' instead of 'setPart', we ensure that
// these parts will not write to file unless they are
// changed later.
setPartAsDefault("translator",
                 "translateRadialTranslator");
setPartAsDefault("translatorActive",
                 "translateRadialTranslatorActive");
setPartAsDefault("feedback",
                 "translateRadialFeedback");
setPartAsDefault("feedbackActive",
                 "translateRadialFeedbackActive");

// Set the switch parts to 0 to display the inactive parts.
// The parts "translatorSwitch" and "feedbackSwitch"
// are not public parts (i.e., when making the catalog, the
// isPublic flag was set FALSE, so users cannot access them).
// To retrieve the parts we must use the SO_GET_ANY_PART
// macro which calls the protected method getAnyPart().
SoSwitch *sw;
sw = SO_GET_ANY_PART(this, "translatorSwitch", SoSwitch);
setSwitchValue(sw, 0);
sw = SO_GET_ANY_PART(this, "feedbackSwitch", SoSwitch);
setSwitchValue(sw, 0);

// This dragger does motion along a line,
// so we create a line projector.
lineProj = new SbLineProjector();

// Add the callback functions that will be called when
// the user clicks, drags, and releases.
addStartCallback(&TranslateRadialDragger::startCB);
addMotionCallback(&TranslateRadialDragger::motionCB);
addFinishCallback(&TranslateRadialDragger::finishCB);

// Updates the translation field when the dragger moves.
addValueChangedCallback(
                 &TranslateRadialDragger::valueChangedCB);
```

```
        // Updates the motionMatrix (and thus moves the dragger
        // through space) to a new location whenever the translation
        // field is changed from the outside.
        fieldSensor = new SoFieldSensor(
                    &TranslateRadialDragger::fieldSensorCB, this);
        fieldSensor->setPriority(0);

        setUpConnections(TRUE, TRUE);
}


TranslateRadialDragger::~TranslateRadialDragger()
{
        // Delete what we created in the constructor.
        delete lineProj;
        if (fieldSensor!=NULL)
            delete fieldSensor;
}

SbBool
TranslateRadialDragger::setUpConnections(SbBool onOff,
                                            SbBool doItAlways)
{
        if (!doItAlways && connectionsSetUp == onOff)
            return onOff;

        if (onOff) {
            // We connect AFTER base class.
            SoDragger::setUpConnections(onOff, doItAlways);

            // Call the sensor CB to make things up-to-date.
            fieldSensorCB(this, NULL);

            // Connect the field sensor.
            if (fieldSensor->getAttachedField() != &translation)
                fieldSensor->attach(&translation);
        }
        else {
            // We disconnect BEFORE base class.

            // Disconnect the field sensor.
            if (fieldSensor->getAttachedField()!=NULL)
                fieldSensor->detach();

            SoDragger::setUpConnections(onOff, doItAlways);
        }
        return !(connectionsSetUp = onOff);
}
```

```
//  Static callback functions called by SoDragger when the
//  mouse goes down (over this dragger), drags, and releases.
void
TranslateRadialDragger::startCB(void *, SoDragger *dragger)
{
    TranslateRadialDragger *myself =
            (TranslateRadialDragger *) dragger;
    myself->dragStart();
}
void
TranslateRadialDragger::motionCB(void *, SoDragger *dragger)
{
    TranslateRadialDragger *myself =
            (TranslateRadialDragger *) dragger;
    myself->drag();
}
void
TranslateRadialDragger::finishCB(void *, SoDragger *dragger)
{
    TranslateRadialDragger *myself =
            (TranslateRadialDragger *) dragger;
    myself->dragFinish();
}

//  Called when user clicks down on this dragger. Sets up the
//  projector and switches parts to their "active" versions.
void
TranslateRadialDragger::dragStart()
{
    // Display the 'active' parts...
    SoSwitch *sw;
    sw = SO_GET_ANY_PART(this, "translatorSwitch", SoSwitch);
    setSwitchValue(sw, 1);
    sw = SO_GET_ANY_PART(this, "feedbackSwitch", SoSwitch);
    setSwitchValue(sw, 1);

    // Establish the projector line.
    // The direction of translation goes from the center of the
    // dragger toward the point that was hit, in local space.
    // For the center, use (0,0,0).
    SbVec3f startLocalHitPt = getLocalStartingPoint();
    lineProj->setLine(SbLine(SbVec3f(0,0,0), startLocalHitPt));

    // Orient the feedback geometry.
    orientFeedbackGeometry(startLocalHitPt);
}
```

```
// Sets the feedbackRotation node so that the feedback
// geometry will be aligned with the direction of motion in
// local space.
void
TranslateRadialDragger::orientFeedbackGeometry(
                               const SbVec3f &localDir)
{
   // By default, feedback geometry aligns with the x axis.
   // Rotate so that it points in the given direction.
   SbRotation rotXToDir = SbRotation(SbVec3f(1,0,0), localDir);

   // Give this rotation to the "feedbackRotate" part.
   SoRotation *myPart = SO_GET_ANY_PART(this, "feedbackRotate",
                                    SoRotation);
   myPart->rotation.setValue(rotXToDir);
}


// Called when the mouse translates during dragging. Moves
// the dragger based on the mouse motion.
void
TranslateRadialDragger::drag()
{
   // Things can change between renderings. To be safe, update
   // the projector with the current values.
   lineProj->setViewVolume(getViewVolume());
   lineProj->setWorkingSpace(getLocalToWorldMatrix());

   // Find the new intersection on the projector.
   SbVec3f newHitPt =
           lineProj->project(getNormalizedLocaterPosition());

   // Get initial point expressed in our current local space.
   SbVec3f startHitPt = getLocalStartingPoint();

   // Motion in local space is difference between old and
   // new positions.
   SbVec3f motion = newHitPt - startHitPt;

   // Append this to the startMotionMatrix, which was saved
   // automatically at the beginning of the drag, to find
   // the current motion matrix.
   setMotionMatrix(
     appendTranslation(getStartMotionMatrix(), motion));
}
```

```
// Called when mouse button is released and drag is completed.
void
TranslateRadialDragger::dragFinish()
{
   // Display inactive versions of parts...
   SoSwitch *sw;
   sw = SO_GET_ANY_PART(this, "translatorSwitch", SoSwitch);
   setSwitchValue(sw, 0);
   sw = SO_GET_ANY_PART(this, "feedbackSwitch", SoSwitch);
   setSwitchValue(sw, 0);

   // Get rid of the "feedbackRotate" part.  We don't need
   // it since we aren't showing the feedback any more.
   setAnyPart("feedbackRotate", NULL);
}

// Called when the motionMatrix changes. Sets the 'translation'
// field based on the new motionMatrix.
void
TranslateRadialDragger::valueChangedCB(void *,
                                       SoDragger *inDragger)
{
   TranslateRadialDragger *myself =
           (TranslateRadialDragger *) inDragger;

   // Get translation by decomposing motionMatrix.
   SbMatrix motMat = myself->getMotionMatrix();
   SbVec3f trans, scale;
   SbRotation rot, scaleOrient;
   motMat.getTransform(trans, rot, scale, scaleOrient);

   // Set "translation", disconnecting sensor while doing so.
   myself->fieldSensor->detach();
   if (myself->translation.getValue() != trans)
     myself->translation = trans;
   myself->fieldSensor->attach(&myself->translation);
}

// If the "translation" field is set from outside, update
// motionMatrix accordingly.
void
TranslateRadialDragger::fieldSensorCB(void *inDragger,
                                      SoSensor *)
{
   TranslateRadialDragger *myself =
           (TranslateRadialDragger *) inDragger;
```

```
    SbMatrix motMat = myself->getMotionMatrix();
    myself->workFieldsIntoTransform(motMat);

    myself->setMotionMatrix(motMat);
}
```

Creating a Compound Dragger

In this section, you will learn how simple draggers can be combined to make a more complex *compound* dragger. Compound draggers can typically perform several different operations, such as scaling and translating. The **SoCenterBallDragger** and **SoTransformBoxDragger** are examples of compound draggers.

Unlike simple draggers, which can perform only one operation, compound draggers can typically do many things. The operation the user performs is determined by the part of the compound dragger that is first clicked upon.

The steps involved in creating a compound dragger are best illustrated through example. This section shows how to create a **RotTransDragger**, which—as its name implies—allows both rotations and translations. The rotation parts of this compound dragger are made from a set of three **SoRotateCylindricalDraggers**, one for each axis we wish to allow the user to rotate about. The translation part of the dragger is an instance of the **TranslateRadialDragger** that we created in the previous section.

Two nodes are introduced in this section: the **SoAntiSquish** node and the **SoSurroundScale** node. These nodes are often useful in compound draggers and in manipulators. The compound dragger created in this section uses an **SoAntiSquish** node. Its catalog also contains an **SoSurroundScale** node, which is not used by default. The **RotTransManip** manipulator created at the end of this chapter uses a **RotTransDragger** and turns on the **SoSurroundScale** part. This enables the manipulator to have its dragger geometry surround the other objects that will move along with it.

SoAntiSquish Node

The **SoAntiSquish** node makes scaling uniform so that draggers and manipulators retain their shape even if the current transformation contains a nonuniform scale. When an action is applied to this node, it decomposes the current transformation matrix into a rotation, a translation, and a scale.

If the scale is nonuniform, it replaces the current transformation matrix with a new one that uses the same rotation and translation, but a *uniform* scale.

This node has one field, **sizing**, which controls how to make the scale uniform. Possible values for this field are as follows:

AVERAGE_DIMENSION
>
> averages the *x*, *y*, and *z* scale value (default).

BIGGEST_DIMENSION
>
> replaces all three scale values with the largest scale value.

SMALLEST_DIMENSION
>
> replaces all three scale values with the smallest scale value.

LONGEST_DIAGONAL
>
> constructs a unit cube at the origin and transforms it by the current transformation matrix. To do this, it finds the longest diagonal of that transformed cube. Then, it sets the uniform scale to be half the length of this diagonal. (If the cube is being sheared, the LONGEST_DIAGONAL gives you the greatest distance from any point in the cube to the origin. With shearing, this distance could be greater than BIGGEST_DIMENSION.)

SoSurroundScale Node

The **SoSurroundScale** node is used to cause a dragger or manipulator to surround certain objects in the scene. This node is typically used when you create an **SoTransformManip** from a dragger. Although this part is included in the catalog for the **RotTransDragger**, it is not actually constructed by the dragger and is left as NULL.

This node examines what you want it to surround in the scene graph and determines how large the objects are. It then adds a scale and a translation to the current transformation matrix so that it surrounds those objects. For a manipulator, these are usually the objects affected by the movement of the manipulator.

Figure 8-4 shows a scene graph containing a transform manipulator and a cube. The dragger within the manipulator includes a surround-scale node.

The top separator node is the *container* node. In addition to the manipulator, it contains a cube, which the manipulator surrounds. The transform manipulator is the *reset* node. The manipulator surrounds everything below the container node and to the right of the reset node.

The **SoSurroundScale** node has two fields:

numNodesUpToContainer

> number of nodes up the current path to the node that contains the objects to surround

numNodesUpToReset

> number of nodes up the chain to the reset node (that is, the node where the bounding box is emptied)

In Figure 8-4, **numNodesUpToContainer** equals 4 and **numNodesUpToReset** equals 3. (Note that **numNodesUpToReset** must be smaller than **numNodesUpToContainer**, or there will be no reset node.) The result is that the geometry of the dragger now surrounds the cube.

Defining the Parts

Several operations must be completed when you are designing the parts of a compound dragger:

- *Define the desired operations of the dragger*—for this example, the operations are a rotation about each of the three axes, as well as arbitrary translation.

- *Choose the simple dragger to suit each operation*—for rotations about a fixed axis, you can use the **SoRotateCylindricalDragger**. (You could also use the **SoRotateDiscDragger**, which rotates about a fixed axis; however, its behavior is not well suited for this application, since it does not allow rotation when looking edge-on. It is better for dial-type draggers.) For the arbitrary translation part, you can use the **TranslateRadialDragger** created in the previous section.

- *Get the resource names and correlate them to part names*—for example, the **SoRotateCylindricalDragger** is the **XRotator** part in the **RotTransDragger**. The compound dragger needs to create its own resource name for each part of each simple dragger. By convention, Inventor concatenates the part name as follows: compound dragger name/simple dragger part name/name of the part within the simple dragger. In the **RotTransDragger**, the three rotators share the same resources.

- *Determine the geometry of the parts*—by default, the simple draggers use their default part geometry. Typically, what gives compound draggers their flair is the way they redefine this default geometry in an interesting way. This redefinition is done in the Inventor file for the dragger. In the **RotTransDragger**, the default cylinder of each **SoRotateCylindricalDragger** is replaced by a thin ring (actually a thin cylinder with its top and bottom removed). The **RotTransDragger** does not display any feedback for the **SoRotateCylindricalDraggers** because the richer geometry of the compound dragger provides sufficient visual information for the user. (The feedback parts are set to be an empty separator.)

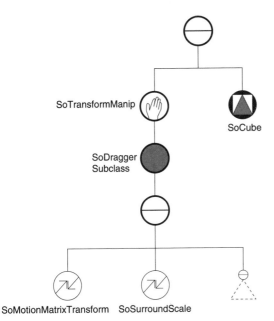

Figure 8-4   Using an SoSurroundScale Node in a Transform Manipulator

Once all of these things have been determined, you can create a default geometry file for the compound dragger. The following geometry file defines the geometry for all parts in the translator and rotators that make up the **RotTransDragger**. It uses the same naming conventions used in the previous section describing the simple dragger. At this point, you also need to create a default include file for the compiled-in geometry. As described in the previous section, run the **ivToIncludeFile** utility to translate the .iv file into an array of hexadecimal numbers.

Example 8-4 shows the default geometry file for **RotTransDragger**.

Example 8-4   rotTransDragger.iv

```
#Inventor V2.0 ascii

# Geometry resource file for the RotTransDragger

# Geometry for the rotating parts.
DEF rotTransRotatorRotator Separator {
    Material {
        diffuseColor  .05 .18 .125
        emissiveColor .05 .18 .125
    }
    DrawStyle { lineWidth 2 }
    Cylinder {
        radius 1.85
        height .15
        parts SIDES
    }
}

DEF rotTransRotatorRotatorActive Separator {
    Material {
        diffuseColor  .05 .2025 .18
        emissiveColor .05 .2025 .18
    }
    DrawStyle { lineWidth 2 }
    Cylinder {
        radius 1.85
        height .15
        parts SIDES
    }
}

# Do not display the axis feedback used
# by the cylinder manips.
DEF rotTransRotatorFeedback Separator { }
DEF rotTransRotatorFeedbackActive Separator { }

DEF rotTransTranslatorTranslator Separator {
    Material { diffuseColor .6 .6 .6 }
    DrawStyle { style LINES }
    Sphere { radius 1.732 }
}
```

```
DEF rotTransTranslatorTranslatorActive Separator {
    Material { diffuseColor .6 .6 0 }
    DrawStyle { style LINES }
    Sphere { radius 1.732 }
}

# Don't show anything for feedback during inactive state.
DEF rotTransTranslatorFeedback Separator { }

DEF rotTransTranslatorFeedbackActive Separator {
    Material { diffuseColor .5 .9 .9 }
    # An arrow aligned with the x-axis.
    RotationXYZ {
        axis Z
        angle 1.57079
    }
    Separator {

        #stick
        Cylinder { height 4.0 radius 0.05 }

        #left arrowhead
        Translation { translation 0 2.2 0 }
        Cone { height 0.4 bottomRadius 0.2 }

        #right arrowhead
        Translation { translation 0 -4.4 0 }
        RotationXYZ { axis Z angle 3.14159 }
        Cone { height 0.4 bottomRadius 0.2 }
    }
}
```

Figure 8-5 shows the scene graph for the **RotTransDragger** class.
Example 8-5 shows the header file for this class.

Example 8-5 RotTransDragger.h

```
//  Geometry resources and part names for this dragger:

//  Resource Names:                    Part Names:
//  rotTransTranslatorTranslator       translator.translator
//  rotTransTranslatorTranslatorActive
//                                     translator.translatorActive
//  rotTransTranslatorFeedback         translator.feedback
//  rotTransTranslatorFeedbackActive   translator.feedbackActive
```

```
// rotTransRotatorRotator            XRotator.rotator
// rotTransRotatorRotatorActive      XRotator.rotatorActive
// rotTransRotatorFeedback           XRotator.feedback
// rotTransRotatorFeedbackActive     XRotator.feedbackActive
// (and similarly for parts of the YRotator and ZRotator)

#include <Inventor/sensors/SoFieldSensor.h>
#include <Inventor/draggers/SoDragger.h>
#include <Inventor/fields/SoSFVec3f.h>
#include <Inventor/fields/SoSFRotation.h>

class TranslateRadialDragger;
class SoRotateCylindricalDragger;

class RotTransDragger : public SoDragger
{
    SO_KIT_HEADER(RotTransDragger);

    // Makes the dragger surround other objects
    SO_KIT_CATALOG_ENTRY_HEADER(surroundScale);
```

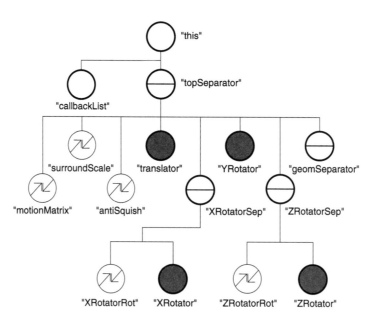

Figure 8-5   Structure of the RotTransDragger

```cpp
// Keeps the dragger evenly sized in all 3 dimensions
   SO_KIT_CATALOG_ENTRY_HEADER(antiSquish);

   // The translating dragger...
   SO_KIT_CATALOG_ENTRY_HEADER(translator);

   // The X and Z rotators need to be turned so as to orient
   // correctly. So create a separator part and put an
   // SoRotation node and the dragger underneath.
   SO_KIT_CATALOG_ENTRY_HEADER(XRotatorSep);
   SO_KIT_CATALOG_ENTRY_HEADER(XRotatorRot);
   SO_KIT_CATALOG_ENTRY_HEADER(XRotator);

   SO_KIT_CATALOG_ENTRY_HEADER(YRotator);

   SO_KIT_CATALOG_ENTRY_HEADER(ZRotatorSep);
   SO_KIT_CATALOG_ENTRY_HEADER(ZRotatorRot);
   SO_KIT_CATALOG_ENTRY_HEADER(ZRotator);

public:

   // Constructor
   RotTransDragger();

   // These fields reflect state of the dragger at all times.
   SoSFRotation rotation;
   SoSFVec3f    translation;

   // This should be called once after SoInteraction::init().
   static void initClass();

protected:

   // These sensors ensure that the motionMatrix is updated
   // when the fields are changed from outside.
   SoFieldSensor *rotFieldSensor;
   SoFieldSensor *translFieldSensor;
   static void fieldSensorCB(void *, SoSensor *);

   // This function is invoked by the child draggers when they
   // change their value.
   static void valueChangedCB(void *, SoDragger *);

   // Called at the beginning and end of each dragging motion.
   // Tells the "surroundScale" part to recalculate.
   static void invalidateSurroundScaleCB(void *, SoDragger *);
```

```
// This will detach/attach the fieldSensor.
// It is called at the end of the constructor (to attach).
// and at the start/end of SoBaseKit::readInstance()
// and on the new copy at the start/end of SoBaseKit::copy()
// Returns the state of the node when this was called.
virtual SbBool setUpConnections( SbBool onOff,
                                 SbBool doItAlways = FALSE);

// This allows us to specify that certain parts do not
// write out. We'll use this on the antiSquish and
// surroundScale parts.
virtual void setDefaultOnNonWritingFields();

private:

static const char geomBuffer[];

// Destructor.
~RotTransDragger();
};
```

Initializing the Compound Dragger

The complete source file for the **RotTransDragger** is shown in
Example 8-6. The process of initializing the compound dragger is identical
to that of the simple dragger (see "Initializing the Dragger Class" on
page 159).

Constructor

Many of the steps for constructing the compound dragger are the same as
those for a simple dragger. This section describes the similarities and
differences. The basic steps for constructing a dragger, described first in
"Constructor" on page 159, are as follows:

    a. Use SO_KIT_CONSTRUCTOR() to set up the internal variables for
       the class.

    b. Define the catalog entries for the new dragger.

    c. Put the default parts into the global dictionary.

    d. Create the parts list and the parts that are created by default in this
       dragger using SO_KIT_INIT_INSTANCE().

e. Create the special-interest field or fields for the dragger.

f. Create the parts for the dragger.

g. Set the switches to inactive (if your dragger uses active/inactive pairs of parts).

h. Create the projector.

i. Add the dragger callback functions.

j. Add the value-changed callback function.

k. Put a sensor on the special-interest field (or fields).

l. Call the **setUpConnections()** method to attach the field sensors.

Steps a through e

Steps a through e are similar for simple and compound draggers.

Step a, using SO_KIT_CONSTRUCTOR(), is the same for simple and compound draggers.

Step b is to define the catalog entries for the dragger, which is actually a node kit. Use the SO_KIT_ADD_CATALOG_ENTRY() macro to define the catalog entries. Arrange the simple draggers relative to each other, as shown earlier in Figure 8-5. Each simple dragger has its own separator, used for caching. The simple draggers can use the cache at the **topSeparator** node if none of the draggers is changing. In compound draggers such as this one, the **geomSeparator**, provided by the base **SoDragger** class, is not used.

Step c is to put the default parts into the global dictionary:

```
if (SO_KIT_IS_FIRST_INSTANCE())
   readDefaultParts("rotTransDragger.iv", geomBuffer,
                   sizeof(geomBuffer));
```

Step d is to create the parts list and the default parts using the macro SO_KIT_INIT_INSTANCE().

Step e is to create the special-interest fields for this compound dragger: a **rotation** field and a **translation** field:

```
SO_KIT_ADD_FIELD(rotation, (0.0, 0.0, 0.0, 1.0));
SO_KIT_ADD_FIELD(translation, (0.0, 0.0. 0.0));
```

Step f: Creating the Parts

Step f is to create the parts for the node kit. This step is more involved for a compound dragger than for a simple dragger. At this point, you need to do the following things:

1. Construct the antisquish node. For the **RotTransDragger**, the sizing field of the **SoAntiSquish** node is set to BIGGEST_DIMENSION. As a result, the largest of the three scale values is used as the uniform scale value.

2. Create the simple draggers.

3. Create the rotation nodes in the **XRotatorRot** and **ZRotatorRot** parts. The rotation node in the **XRotatorRot** part aligns the cylindrical rotate dragger with the *x*-axis (in the default position, it rotates about the *y*-axis). The rotation node in the **ZRotatorRot** part aligns the cylindrical rotate dragger with the *z*-axis.

Steps g through i

Steps g through i are all performed by the child draggers. The parent dragger class does not define these functions.

Step j: Value-Changed Callback Function

Step j is to update the **rotation** and **translation** fields in the dragger when the motion matrix changes (see "Value-Changed Callback" on page 166, where this step was performed for the simple dragger).

The code for the **RotTransDragger** is

```
addValueChangedCallback(&RotTransDragger::valueChangedCB);
```

Step k: Field Sensors

Conversely, you need to update the motion matrix when the **translation** or **rotation** field changes. This dragger places a sensor on the **translation** field and another sensor on the **rotation** field. Both sensors use the same callback function, **fieldSensorCB**, defined later in the source file.

```
// Updates motionMatrix when either field changes.
rotFieldSensor = new SoFieldSensor(
                    &RotTransDragger::fieldSensorCB, this);
rotFieldSensor->setPriority(0);
```

```
translFieldSensor = new SoFieldSensor(
                        &RotTransDragger::fieldSensorCB,this);
translFieldSensor->setPriority(0);

setUpConnections(TRUE, TRUE);
```

Step I: Setting Up Connections

The **setUpConnections()** method is used to connect and disconnect the dragger's field connections, callback functions, and sensors. This method performs the following operations:

1. Calls the base class **setUpConnections()** method.

2. Sets up the geometry of its child draggers.

   For each child dragger in the compound dragger, the **setUpConnections()** method calls **getAnyPart()** to build and return the dragger.

   Then it calls **setPartAsDefault()** after looking up the replacement parts in the global dictionary.

3. Adds the start and finish callback functions.

   The **SoSurroundScale** node does its bounding-box calculations when it is built and when its **invalidate()** method is called. For efficiency, the recalculation is performed only at the beginning and end of a drag. In beween, the dragger continues to draw at the same size. Register the **invalidateSurroundScaleCB()** callback function for each simple dragger.

4. Registers the child draggers.

   It is worth describing in more detail what happens when you call the **registerChildDragger()** method for each simple dragger in the compound dragger. This method binds the child and parent draggers together to function as a unit in two main ways. First, it causes the parent dragger's callback functions to be called after any of the child dragger's callback functions are called. Second, it causes all child draggers to move as a unit: whenever the user clicks and drags on one child dragger, the other draggers move in unison with the first dragger.

   When you call **registerChildDragger()**, the following things happen automatically. A value-changed callback function is added to monitor the motion in the child dragger. When the child dragger moves, the callback transforms that motion into the compound dragger's space, applying it to the compound dragger as a whole. It then zeros out the child dragger's motion so that the child is not moved relative to the whole.

If you create a new dragger and for some reason you don't want the pieces of the compound dragger to move as a whole, you can use the **registerChildDraggerCallbacksOnly()** method, which doesn't transfer the child dragger's motion to the parent dragger. (The spotlight dragger is an example of a dragger that uses this method. When the cone widens, the rest of the dragger remains unchanged.)

5. Attaches the field sensors (as for simple draggers).

Destructor

Since the child draggers are nodes, they are destroyed automatically when the parent node is destroyed. There are no projectors to destroy as with the simple dragger, since no projectors were created here. The destructor merely needs to delete the sensor.

Callback Functions

The **RotTransDragger** uses three callback functions, described above:

invalidateSurroundScaleCB()
called when dragging starts and finishes

valueChangedCB()
called when the motion matrix changes

fieldSensorCB()   called when the special-interest field or fields change

The source file for the compound dragger must define each of these callback functions.

Example 8-6 shows the source code for **RotTransDragger.c++**:

Example 8-6   RotTransDragger.c++

```
#include <Inventor/nodes/SoAntiSquish.h>
#include <Inventor/nodes/SoRotation.h>
#include <Inventor/nodes/SoSeparator.h>
#include <Inventor/nodes/SoSurroundScale.h>
#include <Inventor/nodes/SoTransform.h>
#include <Inventor/sensors/SoFieldSensor.h>
```

```
// Include files for child dragger classes.
#include <Inventor/draggers/SoRotateCylindricalDragger.h>
#include "TranslateRadialDragger.h"

// Include file for our new class.
#include "RotTransDragger.h"

// This file contains RotTransDragger::geomBuffer, which
// describes the default geometry resources for this class.
#include "RotTransDraggerGeom.h"

SO_KIT_SOURCE(RotTransDragger);


//  Initializes the type ID for this dragger node. This
//  should be called once after SoInteraction::init().
void
RotTransDragger::initClass()
{
   SO_KIT_INIT_CLASS(RotTransDragger, SoDragger, "Dragger");
}

RotTransDragger::RotTransDragger()
{
   SO_KIT_CONSTRUCTOR(RotTransDragger);

   // Don't create "surroundScale" by default. It's only put
   // to use if this dragger is used within a manipulator.
   SO_KIT_ADD_CATALOG_ENTRY(surroundScale, SoSurroundScale, TRUE,
                            topSeparator, geomSeparator, TRUE);
   // Create an anti-squish node by default.
   SO_KIT_ADD_CATALOG_ENTRY(antiSquish, SoAntiSquish, FALSE,
                            topSeparator, geomSeparator, TRUE);
   SO_KIT_ADD_CATALOG_ENTRY(translator, TranslateRadialDragger,
                            TRUE, topSeparator, geomSeparator,
                            TRUE);
   SO_KIT_ADD_CATALOG_ENTRY(XRotatorSep, SoSeparator, FALSE,
                            topSeparator, geomSeparator, FALSE);
   SO_KIT_ADD_CATALOG_ENTRY(XRotatorRot, SoRotation, TRUE,
                            XRotatorSep, , FALSE);
   SO_KIT_ADD_CATALOG_ENTRY(XRotator,SoRotateCylindricalDragger,
                            TRUE, XRotatorSep, ,TRUE);

   SO_KIT_ADD_CATALOG_ENTRY(YRotator, SoRotateCylindricalDragger,
                            TRUE, topSeparator, geomSeparator, TRUE);
```

```
SO_KIT_ADD_CATALOG_ENTRY(ZRotatorSep, SoSeparator, FALSE,
                         topSeparator, geomSeparator, FALSE);
SO_KIT_ADD_CATALOG_ENTRY(ZRotatorRot, SoRotation, TRUE,
                         ZRotatorSep, ,FALSE);
SO_KIT_ADD_CATALOG_ENTRY(ZRotator, SoRotateCylindricalDragger,
                         TRUE, ZRotatorSep, ,TRUE);

// Read geometry resources. Only do this the first time we
// construct one. 'geomBuffer' contains our compiled in
// defaults. The user can override these by specifying new
// scene graphs in the file:
// $(SO_DRAGGER_DIR)/rotTransDragger.iv"
if (SO_KIT_IS_FIRST_INSTANCE())
  readDefaultParts("rotTransDragger.iv", geomBuffer,
                   sizeof(geomBuffer));

// Fields that always show current state of the dragger.
SO_KIT_ADD_FIELD(rotation, (0.0, 0.0, 0.0, 1.0));
SO_KIT_ADD_FIELD(translation, (0.0, 0.0, 0.0));

// Creates parts list and default parts for this nodekit.
SO_KIT_INIT_INSTANCE();

// Make the anti-squish node surround the biggest dimension
SoAntiSquish *myAntiSquish =
        SO_GET_ANY_PART(this, "antiSquish", SoAntiSquish);
myAntiSquish->sizing = SoAntiSquish::BIGGEST_DIMENSION;

// Create the simple draggers that comprise this dragger.
// This dragger has four simple pieces:
//     1 TranslateRadialDragger
//     3 RotateCylindricalDraggers
// In the constructor, we just call SO_GET_ANY_PART to
// build each dragger.
// Within the setUpConnections() method, we will
// take care of giving these draggers new geometry and
// establishing their callbacks.

// Create the translator dragger.
SoDragger *tDragger = SO_GET_ANY_PART(this, "translator",
                      TranslateRadialDragger);

// Create the XRotator dragger.
SoDragger *XDragger = SO_GET_ANY_PART(this, "XRotator",
                      SoRotateCylindricalDragger);
```

```
   // Create the YRotator dragger.
   SoDragger *YDragger = SO_GET_ANY_PART(this, "YRotator",
                         SoRotateCylindricalDragger);

   // Create the ZRotator dragger.
   SoDragger *ZDragger = SO_GET_ANY_PART(this, "ZRotator",
                         SoRotateCylindricalDragger);

   // Set rotations in "XRotatorRot" and "ZRotatorRot" parts.
   // These parts will orient the draggers from their default
   // (rotating about Y) to the desired configurations.
   // By calling 'setAnyPartAsDefault' instead of 'setAnyPart'
   // we ensure that they will not be written out, unless
   // they are changed later on.
   SoRotation *XRot = new SoRotation;
   XRot->rotation.setValue(
     SbRotation(SbVec3f(0,1,0), SbVec3f(1,0,0)));
   setAnyPartAsDefault("XRotatorRot", XRot);

   SoRotation *ZRot = new SoRotation;
   ZRot->rotation.setValue(
     SbRotation(SbVec3f(0,1,0), SbVec3f(0,0,1)));
   setAnyPartAsDefault("ZRotatorRot", ZRot);

   // Updates the fields when motionMatrix changes
   addValueChangedCallback(&RotTransDragger::valueChangedCB);

   // Updates motionMatrix when either field changes.
   rotFieldSensor = new SoFieldSensor(
                       &RotTransDragger::fieldSensorCB, this);
   rotFieldSensor->setPriority(0);
   translFieldSensor = new SoFieldSensor(
                         &RotTransDragger::fieldSensorCB,this);
   translFieldSensor->setPriority(0);

   setUpConnections(TRUE, TRUE);
}

RotTransDragger::~RotTransDragger()
{
   if (rotFieldSensor!=NULL)
     delete rotFieldSensor;
   if (translFieldSensor!=NULL)
     delete translFieldSensor;
}
```

```
SbBool
RotTransDragger::setUpConnections(SbBool onOff, SbBool doItAlways)
{
    if (!doItAlways && connectionsSetUp == onOff)
        return onOff;

    if (onOff) {
        // We connect AFTER base class.
        SoDragger::setUpConnections(onOff, doItAlways);

        // For each of the simple draggers that compries this:
        // [a]Call setPart after looking up our replacement parts
        //     in the global dictionary.
        // [b]Add the invalidateSurroundScaleCB as a start and end
        //     callback. When using a surroundScale node, these
        //     trigger it to recalculate a bounding box at the
        //     beginning and end of dragging.
        // [c]Register the dragger as a 'childDragger' of this
        //     one. This has the following effects:
        //     [1] This dragger's callbacks will be invoked
        //         following the child manip's callbacks.
        //     [2] When the child is dragged, the child's motion
        //         will be transferred into motion of the entire
        //         dragger.
        SoDragger *tD =
                (SoDragger *) getAnyPart("translator", FALSE);
        // [a] Set up the parts in the child dragger...
        tD->setPartAsDefault("translator",
                             "rotTransTranslatorTranslator");
        tD->setPartAsDefault("translatorActive",
                             "rotTransTranslatorTranslatorActive");
        tD->setPartAsDefault("feedback",
                             "rotTransTranslatorFeedback");
        tD->setPartAsDefault("feedbackActive",
                             "rotTransTranslatorFeedbackActive");
        // [b] and [c] Add the callbacks and register the child
        tD->addStartCallback(
                &RotTransDragger::invalidateSurroundScaleCB, this);
        tD->addFinishCallback(
                &RotTransDragger::invalidateSurroundScaleCB, this);
        registerChildDragger(tD);
```

```
SoDragger *XD =
        (SoDragger *) getAnyPart("XRotator", FALSE);
// [a] Set up the parts in the child dragger...
XD->setPartAsDefault("rotator",
                     "rotTransRotatorRotator");
XD->setPartAsDefault("rotatorActive",
                     "rotTransRotatorRotatorActive");
XD->setPartAsDefault("feedback",
                     "rotTransRotatorFeedback");
XD->setPartAsDefault("feedbackActive",
                     "rotTransRotatorFeedbackActive");
// [b] and [c] Add the callbacks and register the child
XD->addStartCallback(
        &RotTransDragger::invalidateSurroundScaleCB, this);
XD->addFinishCallback(
        &RotTransDragger::invalidateSurroundScaleCB, this);
registerChildDragger(XD);

SoDragger *YD =
        (SoDragger *) getAnyPart("YRotator", FALSE);
// [a] Set up the parts in the child dragger...
YD->setPartAsDefault("rotator",
                     "rotTransRotatorRotator");
YD->setPartAsDefault("rotatorActive",
                     "rotTransRotatorRotatorActive");
YD->setPartAsDefault("feedback",
                     "rotTransRotatorFeedback");
YD->setPartAsDefault("feedbackActive",
                     "rotTransRotatorFeedbackActive");
// [b] and [c] Add the callbacks and register the child
YD->addStartCallback(
        &RotTransDragger::invalidateSurroundScaleCB, this);
YD->addFinishCallback(
        &RotTransDragger::invalidateSurroundScaleCB, this);
registerChildDragger(YD);

SoDragger *ZD =
        (SoDragger *) getAnyPart("ZRotator", FALSE);
// [a] Set up the parts in the child dragger...
ZD->setPartAsDefault("rotator",
                     "rotTransRotatorRotator");
ZD->setPartAsDefault("rotatorActive",
                     "rotTransRotatorRotatorActive");
ZD->setPartAsDefault("feedback",
                     "rotTransRotatorFeedback");
ZD->setPartAsDefault("feedbackActive",
                     "rotTransRotatorFeedbackActive");
```

```
    // [b] and [c] Add the callbacks and register the child
    ZD->addStartCallback(
          &RotTransDragger::invalidateSurroundScaleCB, this);
    ZD->addFinishCallback(
          &RotTransDragger::invalidateSurroundScaleCB, this);
    registerChildDragger(ZD);


    // Call the sensor CB to make things up-to-date.
    fieldSensorCB(this, NULL);

    // Connect the field sensors
    if (translFieldSensor->getAttachedField() != &translation)
       translFieldSensor->attach(&translation);
    if (rotFieldSensor->getAttachedField() != &rotation)
       rotFieldSensor->attach(&rotation);
}
else {
    // We disconnect BEFORE base class.

    // Remove the callbacks from the child draggers,
    // and unregister them as children.
    SoDragger *tD =
          (SoDragger *) getAnyPart("translator", FALSE);
    tD->removeStartCallback(
          &RotTransDragger::invalidateSurroundScaleCB, this);
    tD->removeFinishCallback(
          &RotTransDragger::invalidateSurroundScaleCB, this);
    unregisterChildDragger(tD);

    SoDragger *XD =
          (SoDragger *) getAnyPart("XRotator", FALSE);
    XD->removeStartCallback(
          &RotTransDragger::invalidateSurroundScaleCB, this);
    XD->removeFinishCallback(
          &RotTransDragger::invalidateSurroundScaleCB, this);
    unregisterChildDragger(XD);

    SoDragger *YD =
          (SoDragger *) getAnyPart("YRotator", FALSE);
    YD->removeStartCallback(
          &RotTransDragger::invalidateSurroundScaleCB, this);
    YD->removeFinishCallback(
          &RotTransDragger::invalidateSurroundScaleCB, this);
    unregisterChildDragger(YD);
```

```
        SoDragger *ZD =
                (SoDragger *) getAnyPart("ZRotator", FALSE);
        ZD->removeStartCallback(
                &RotTransDragger::invalidateSurroundScaleCB, this);
        ZD->removeFinishCallback(
                &RotTransDragger::invalidateSurroundScaleCB, this);
        unregisterChildDragger(ZD);

        // Disconnect the field sensors.
        if (translFieldSensor->getAttachedField()!=NULL)
            translFieldSensor->detach();
        if (rotFieldSensor->getAttachedField()!=NULL)
            rotFieldSensor->detach();

        SoDragger::setUpConnections(onOff, doItAlways);
    }

    return !(connectionsSetUp = onOff);
}

// Called when the motionMatrix changes. Sets the "translation"
// and "rotation" fields based on the new motionMatrix
void
RotTransDragger::valueChangedCB(void *, SoDragger *inDragger)
{
    RotTransDragger *myself = (RotTransDragger *) inDragger;

    // Factor the motionMatrix into its parts
    SbMatrix motMat = myself->getMotionMatrix();
    SbVec3f    trans, scale;
    SbRotation rot, scaleOrient;
    motMat.getTransform(trans, rot, scale, scaleOrient);

    // Set the fields. Disconnect the sensors while doing so.
    myself->rotFieldSensor->detach();
    myself->translFieldSensor->detach();
    if (myself->rotation.getValue() != rot)
      myself->rotation = rot;
    if (myself->translation.getValue() != trans)
      myself->translation = trans;
    myself->rotFieldSensor->attach(&myself->rotation);
    myself->translFieldSensor->attach(&myself->translation);
}
```

```
// If the "translation" or "rotation" field changes, changes
// the motionMatrix accordingly.
void
RotTransDragger::fieldSensorCB(void *inDragger, SoSensor *)
{
   RotTransDragger *myself = (RotTransDragger *) inDragger;

   SbMatrix motMat = myself->getMotionMatrix();
   myself->workFieldsIntoTransform(motMat);

   myself->setMotionMatrix(motMat);
}


// When any child dragger starts or ends a drag, tell the
// "surroundScale" part (if it exists) to invalidate its
// current bounding box value.
void
RotTransDragger::invalidateSurroundScaleCB(void *parent,SoDragger*)
{
   RotTransDragger *myParentDragger = (RotTransDragger *) parent;

   // Invalidate the surroundScale, if it exists.
   SoSurroundScale *mySS = SO_CHECK_PART(
           myParentDragger, "surroundScale", SoSurroundScale);
   if (mySS != NULL)
      mySS->invalidate();
}

void
RotTransDragger::setDefaultOnNonWritingFields()
{
   // The nodes pointed to by these part-fields may
   // change after construction, but we
   // don't want to write them out.
   surroundScale.setDefault(TRUE);
   antiSquish.setDefault(TRUE);

   SoDragger::setDefaultOnNonWritingFields();
}
```

Creating a Manipulator

A manipulator is derived from another class of node, such as an
SoTransform, **SoLight**, or **SoCamera**. It employs a dragger to edit the fields
of that node and adds the dragger to the node as a hidden child. For
example, the **SoPointLightManip** is a subclass of **SoPointLight**. It adds an
SoPointLightDragger as a hidden child of the point light. When this
manipulator is rendered, it draws a point-light dragger and, because it is a
subclass of **SoPointLight**, it also executes the light commands. When an
SoPointLightManip is used, moving the dragger causes the light in the
scene to move because the manipulator is responsible for maintaining the
consistency between its own fields and the fields of its dragger.

Creating a new manipulator involves two kinds of work:

1. First, you need to create a base class for the new kind of manipulator, if
   it does not already exist. The Inventor library provides four base classes
   for manipulators: **SoTransformManip**, **SoPointLightManip**,
   SoSpotLightManip, and **SoDirectionalLightManip**. This step requires
   more work than the following step.

2. Next, you need to derive a new manipulator from this base class to
   employ the new dragger. This step is easy.

Examples 8-7 and 8-8 show the code to create **RotTransManip**, a subclass
of **SoTransformManip**, so you do not need to create the base manipulator
class (that is, you can skip step 1). You may be asking why anyone would
want to derive a new manipulator from one of the existing base classes. The
reason is that your new manipulator can use a different dragger, which
creates a different look and feel for the user interface. For example, the
handle box and trackball manipulators, which you're already familiar with,
both edit the fields of an **SoTransform**. But their user interfaces look and
operate differently from each other.

All you need to do in such cases is to create a new class of node and set the
dragger in the constructor (step 2). If you are creating a manipulator derived
from **SoTransformManip**, you also need to create the surround-scale part,
since transform manipulators typically surround the things they affect (see
"Creating a Compound Dragger" on page 176).

Deriving a Class from SoTransformManip

Examples 8-7 and 8-8 show the **RotTransManip** class, which employs a **RotTransDragger** to edit an **SoTransform** node.

Example 8-7   RotTransManip.h

```
#include <Inventor/manips/SoTransformManip.h>

class RotTransManip : public SoTransformManip
{
   SO_NODE_HEADER(RotTransManip);

 public:
   // Constructor
   RotTransManip();

   // Initialize the class. This should be called once
   // after SoInteraction::init(),
   // TranslateRadialDragger::init().
   // and RotTransDragger::init().
   static void initClass();

 private:
   // Destructor
   ~RotTransManip();
};
```

Example 8-8   RotTransManip.c++

```
#include <Inventor/nodes/SoSurroundScale.h>

SO_NODE_SOURCE(RotTransManip);

//  Initialize the type ID for this manipulator node. This
//  should be called once after SoInteraction::init(),
//  TranslateRadialDragger::initClass()
//  and RotTransDragger::initClass()
void
RotTransManip::initClass()
{
   SO_NODE_INIT_CLASS(RotTransManip, SoTransformManip,
                      "TransformManip");
}
```

```
RotTransManip::RotTransManip()
{
    SO_NODE_CONSTRUCTOR(RotTransManip);

    // Create a new dragger and call setDragger(),
    // a method inherited from SoTransformManip.
    RotTransDragger *myDrag = new RotTransDragger;
    setDragger(myDrag);

    // We want this manipulator to surround the objects it
    // affects when we put it in a scene. So create the
    // surroundScale node.
    SoSurroundScale *mySS = (SoSurroundScale *)
        myDrag->getPart("surroundScale",TRUE);
    mySS->numNodesUpToContainer = 4;
    mySS->numNodesUpToReset = 3;
}

RotTransManip::~RotTransManip()
{
}
```

Overview

Examples 8-9 and 8-10 create the **Coord3Manip** class, which requires more work than the **RotTransManip**. Use the SO_NODE_HEADER() and SO_NODE_SOURCE() macros found in SoSubNode.h. Follow the same basic steps required for any node class, plus some additional ones, as follows:

1. Select a name for the new manipulator class and determine what class it is derived from. The new manipulator will be a subclass of the kind of node you want to provide a user interface for. For example, **Coord3Manip** is a subclass of **SoCoordinate3** because it provides a user interface for editing the **SoCoordinate3** node.

2. Define an **initClass()** method to initialize type information for the manipulator. Use the SO_NODE_INIT_CLASS() macro.

3. Define a constructor for the manipulator. The constructor defines and names any new fields required by the manipulator using the SO_NODE_ADD_FIELD() macro. It also creates the field sensor (see step 7) and uses the **setDragger()** method to add the correct dragger as a child of this manipulator.

4. Define a destructor for the manipulator. If the manipulator created a field sensor in the constructor, it will need to delete it in the destructor.

5. Write the routines for replacing the "regular" node in the scene graph with the editable manipulator node and for putting it back (**replaceNode()** and **replaceManip()**).

6. Write the value-changed callback on the dragger to update the manipulator's field if the dragger's location changes.

7. Write the field sensor callback on the manipulator to update the dragger if the field in the manipulator changes.

8. Implement a **setDragger()** method to allow the dragger to be replaced by another dragger.

9. Implement a **copy()** method. The **copy()** method first copies the manipulator node and its field data. Then it copies the manipulator's children.

10. Implement the actions supported by the manipulator. See "Implementing Actions for the Manipulator" on page 200.

Implementing Actions for the Manipulator

Example 8-10 provides a typical model for how most manipulators implement actions. The **doAction()** method for this new manipulator is similar to that for a group: it simply traverses the manipulator's children.

For most other actions, the manipulator first traverses its children (including the dragger) using **doAction()** and then calls the method on the base class. See the **callback()**, **GLRender()**, **handleEvent()**, and **pick()** methods in Example 8-10.

Exceptions are the **getMatrix()** and **getBoundingBox()** methods. The **getMatrix()** method does not use **doAction()** because it doesn't need to traverse all the children. It performs the same tests as **SoGroup::getMatrix()** (see Chapter 2).

The **getBoundingBox()** method first traverses the children, but it does some extra work to determine the center of the group. Then it traverses the base class (in the example, "this" is **SoCoordinate3**).

Deriving a Class from SoCoordinate3

Example 8-9 shows the header file for the **Coord3Manip** class.
Example 8-10 shows the source code for this new class. Although these
methods are quite lengthy, they are almost identical for all manipulator
base classes. The only difference is the class name used. Also, in the
replaceNode() and **replaceManip()** methods, the appropriate fields must
be transferred from the old node to the new one. In this case, the field,
point, is the only one copied.

The **replaceNode()** method must take care of the case where the child is
owned by a node kit as well as the case where the child is simply a member
of the group. To replace a node that is a part within a node kit, you must set
the part by name:

```
pointFieldSensor->detach();
point = oldPart->point;
Coordinate3Manip::fieldSensorCB(this, NULL);
pointFieldSensor->attach(&point);

lastKit->setPart(partName, this);
```

To replace a node that is not contained in a node kit, you simply call
replaceChild():

```
pointFieldSensor->detach();
point = ((SoCoordinate3 *)myFullPTail)->point;
Coordinate3Manip::fieldSensorCB(this, NULL);
pointFieldSensor->attach(&point);

((SoGroup *)parent)->replaceChild(myFullPTail, this);
```

Similarly, **replaceManip()** must deal separately with nodes that are owned
by node kits and nodes that are not.

Example 8-9   Coord3Manip.h

```
#include <Inventor/draggers/SoDragger.h>
#include <Inventor/fields/SoSFLong.h>
#include <Inventor/nodes/SoCoordinate3.h>
#include <Inventor/sensors/SoFieldSensor.h>

class Coordinate3Manip : public SoCoordinate3
{
    SO_NODE_HEADER(Coordinate3Manip);
```

```
public:
  // Constructor
  Coordinate3Manip();

  // The index of the 'point' field that will be edited
  // by our child-dragger.
  SoSFLong editIndex;

  // Returns the dragger node being employed by this manip.
  SoDragger *getDragger();

  virtual SoNode *copy(SbBool copyConnections = FALSE) const;

  // For replacing a regular SoCoordinate3 node with this
  // manipulator.
  SbBool replaceNode(SoPath *p);

  // For replacing this manipulator with a regular
  // SoCoordinate3 node.
  SbBool replaceManip(SoPath *p, SoCoordinate3 *newOne) const;

  // These functions implement all actions for this manip.
  // They first traverse the children, then use the
  // SoCoordinate3 version of the actions. They traverse first
  // so that the SoCoordinate3 will affect objects which
  // follow it in the tree, but not the dragger-child.
  virtual void doAction(SoAction *action);
  virtual void callback(SoCallbackAction *action);
  virtual void GLRender(SoGLRenderAction *action);
  virtual void getBoundingBox(SoGetBoundingBoxAction *action);
  virtual void getMatrix(SoGetMatrixAction *action);
  virtual void handleEvent(SoHandleEventAction *action);
  virtual void pick(SoPickAction *action);
  virtual void search(SoSearchAction *action);

  // call this after SoInteraction::init();
  static void initClass();

  virtual SoChildList *getChildren() const;

protected:

  // When the dragger moves, this interprets the translation
  // field of the dragger and sets the point field of this
  // node accordingly.
  static void valueChangedCB(void *,SoDragger *);
```

```
// When the point field of this node changes, moves the
// child-dragger to a new location, if necessary.
SoFieldSensor *pointFieldSensor;
static void fieldSensorCB(void *, SoSensor *);

// Establishes the given dragger as the new child-dragger
void setDragger(SoDragger *newDragger);

// The hidden children.
SoChildList *children;

private:

// Destructor
~Coordinate3Manip();

int getNumChildren() const
{ return (children->getLength()); }
};
```

Example 8-10   Coord3Manip.c++

```
#include <Inventor/actions/SoCallbackAction.h>
#include <Inventor/actions/SoGLRenderAction.h>
#include <Inventor/actions/SoGetBoundingBoxAction.h>
#include <Inventor/actions/SoGetMatrixAction.h>
#include <Inventor/actions/SoHandleEventAction.h>
#include <Inventor/actions/SoPickAction.h>
#include <Inventor/actions/SoSearchAction.h>
#include <Inventor/draggers/SoDragPointDragger.h>
#include <Inventor/errors/SoDebugError.h>
#include <Inventor/fields/SoSFLong.h>
#include <Inventor/nodes/SoGroup.h>

// Include file for our new class
#include "Coordinate3Manip.h"

SO_NODE_SOURCE(Coordinate3Manip);
```

```
//  Initializes the type ID for this manipulator node. This
//  should be called once after SoInteraction::init().
void
Coordinate3Manip::initClass()
{
   SO_NODE_INIT_CLASS(Coordinate3Manip, SoCoordinate3,
                      "Coordinate3");
}


Coordinate3Manip::Coordinate3Manip()
{
   children = new SoChildList(this);

   SO_NODE_CONSTRUCTOR(Coordinate3Manip);

   // Create the new 'editIndex' field
   SO_NODE_ADD_FIELD(editIndex, (0));

   // Create the field sensor
   pointFieldSensor = new SoFieldSensor(
           &Coordinate3Manip::fieldSensorCB, this);
   pointFieldSensor->setPriority(0);
   pointFieldSensor->attach(&point);

   // Create a new SoDragPointDragger and use
   // it for our child-dragger.
   setDragger(new SoDragPointDragger);
}

Coordinate3Manip::~Coordinate3Manip()
{
   // Important to do this because dragger may have callbacks
   // to this node.
   setDragger(NULL);

   if (pointFieldSensor!=NULL)
     delete pointFieldSensor;
   delete children;
}
```

```
// Sets the dragger to be the given node...
// Adds it as a child and adds a valueChangedCallback
// on the child to tell this node when the dragger moves.
void
Coordinate3Manip::setDragger(SoDragger *newDragger)
{
   SoDragger *oldDragger = getDragger();
   if (oldDragger) {
     oldDragger->removeValueChangedCallback(
              &Coordinate3Manip::valueChangedCB,this);
     children->remove(0);
   }

   if (newDragger!=NULL) {
     if (children->getLength() > 0)
       children->set(0, newDragger);
     else
       children->append(newDragger);
     // Call the fieldSensorCB to transfer our values
     // into the new dragger.
     Coordinate3Manip::fieldSensorCB(this, NULL);
     newDragger->addValueChangedCallback(
              &Coordinate3Manip::valueChangedCB,this);
   }
}

// Returns value of the current dragger.
SoDragger *
Coordinate3Manip::getDragger()
{
   if (children->getLength() > 0) {
     SoNode *n = (*children)[0];
     if (n->isOfType(SoDragger::getClassTypeId()))
       return ((SoDragger *) n);
     else {
#ifdef DEBUG
       SoDebugError::post("Coordinate3Manip::getDragger",
                          "Child is not a dragger!");
#endif
     }
   }
   return NULL;
}
```

```
// Description:
//     Replaces the tail of the path with this manipulator.
//
//     [1] Tail of fullpath must be correct type, or we return.
//     [2] If path has a nodekit, we try to use setPart() to
//         insert manip. otherwise:
//     [3] Path must be long enough, or we return without
//     [4] replacing.Second to last node must be a group, or we
//         return without replacing.
//     [5] Copy values from node we are replacing into this manip
//     [6] Replace this manip as the child.
//     [7] Do not ref or unref anything. Assume that the user
//         knows what he's doing.
//     [8] Do not fiddle with either node's field connections.
//         Assume that the user knows what he's doing.
//
SbBool
Coordinate3Manip::replaceNode(SoPath *inPath)
{
    SoFullPath *myFullPath = (SoFullPath *) inPath;

    SoNode     *myFullPTail = myFullPath->getTail();
 if (!myFullPTail->isOfType(Coordinate3Manip::getClassTypeId())){
#ifdef DEBUG
     SoDebugError::post("Coordinate3Manip::replaceNode",
                        "End of path is not a Coordinate3Manip");
#endif
     return FALSE;
    }

    SoNode *pTail = inPath->getTail();
    if (pTail->isOfType(SoBaseKit::getClassTypeId())) {

        // Okay, we've got a nodekit here! Let's do this right...
        // If myFullPTail is a part in the kit, then we've got to
        // follow protocol and let the kit set the part itself.
        SoBaseKit *lastKit =
                (SoBaseKit*)((SoNodeKitPath*)inPath)->getTail();
        SbString partName = lastKit->getPartString(inPath);
        if (partName != "") {
          SoCoordinate3 *oldPart =
                (SoCoordinate3 *) lastKit->getPart(partName, TRUE);
            if (oldPart != NULL) {
```

```
          // Detach the sensor while copying the values.
          pointFieldSensor->detach();
          point = oldPart->point;
          Coordinate3Manip::fieldSensorCB(this, NULL);
          pointFieldSensor->attach(&point);

          lastKit->setPart(partName, this);
          return TRUE;
       }
       else {
          // Although the part's there, we couldn't get at it.
          // Some kind of problem going on
          return FALSE;
       }
    }
    // If it's not a part, that means it's contained within a
    // subgraph underneath a part. For example, it's within
    // the 'contents' separator of an SoWrapperKit. In that
    // case, the nodekit doesn't care and we just continue on
    // through...
 }

 if (myFullPath->getLength() < 2) {
#ifdef DEBUG
    SoDebugError::post("Coordinate3Manip::replaceNode",
                       "Path is too short!");
#endif
    return FALSE;
 }

 SoNode        *parent = myFullPath->getNodeFromTail(1);
 if (!parent->isOfType( SoGroup::getClassTypeId() )) {
#ifdef DEBUG
    SoDebugError::post("Coordinate3Manip::replaceNode",
                       "Parent node is not a group.!");
#endif
    return FALSE;
 }

 ref();
```

```
    // Detach the sensor while copying the values.
    pointFieldSensor->detach();
    point = ((SoCoordinate3 *) myFullPTail)->point;
    Coordinate3Manip::fieldSensorCB(this, NULL);
    pointFieldSensor->attach(&point);

    ((SoGroup *) parent)->replaceChild(myFullPTail, this);

    unrefNoDelete();
    return TRUE;
}

// Replaces tail of path (which should be this manipulator)
// with the given SoCoordinate3 node.
//
//      [1] Tail of fullpath must be this node, or we return.
//      [2] If path has a nodekit, we try to use setPart() to
//          insert new node. otherwise:
//      [3] Path must be long enough, or we return without
//      [4] replacing. Second to last node must be a group, or we
//          return without replacing.
//      [5] Copy values from node we are replacing into this manip
//      [6] Replace this manip as the child.
//      [7] Do not ref or unref anything. Assume that the user
//          knows what he's doing.
//      [8] Do not fiddle with either node's field connections.
//          Assume that the user knows what he's doing.
//
SbBool
Coordinate3Manip::replaceManip(SoPath *path, SoCoordinate3
                               *newOne) const
{
    SoFullPath *myFullPath = (SoFullPath *) path;

    SoNode     *myFullPTail = myFullPath->getTail();
    if (myFullPTail != this) {
#ifdef DEBUG
        SoDebugError::post("Coordinate3Manip::replaceManip",
                    "Child to replace is not this manip!");
#endif
        return FALSE;
    }

    SoNode *pTail = path->getTail();
    if (pTail->isOfType(SoBaseKit::getClassTypeId())) {
```

```
    // Okay, we've got a nodekit here! Let's do this right...
    // If myFullPTail is a part in the kit, then we've got to
    // follow protocol and let the kit set the part itself.
    SoBaseKit *lastKit = (SoBaseKit *)
                            ((SoNodeKitPath*) path)->getTail();
    SbString partName = lastKit->getPartString(path);
    if (partName != "") {

      if (newOne != NULL)
        newOne->point = point;

        lastKit->setPart(partName, newOne);
        return TRUE;
    }
    // If it's not a part, that means it's contained within a
    // subgraph underneath a part. For example, it's within the
    // 'contents' separator of an SoWrapperKit. In that case,
    // the node kit doesn't care and we just continue on
    // through...
  }

  if (myFullPath->getLength() < 2) {
#ifdef DEBUG
    SoDebugError::post("Coordinate3Manip::replaceManip",
                        "Path is too short!");
#endif
    return FALSE;
  }
  SoNode      *parent = myFullPath->getNodeFromTail(1);
  if (! parent->isOfType(SoGroup::getClassTypeId())) {
#ifdef DEBUG
    SoDebugError::post("Coordinate3Manip::replaceManip",
                        "Parent node is not a group.!");
#endif
    return FALSE;
  }

  if (newOne == NULL)
    newOne = new SoCoordinate3;
  newOne->ref();
  newOne->point = point;
  ((SoGroup *) parent)->replaceChild((Coordinate3Manip *) this,
                                      newOne);
  newOne->unrefNoDelete();

  return TRUE;
}
```

```
//    Creates and returns an exact copy...
SoNode *
Coordinate3Manip::copy(SbBool copyConnections) const
{
   // Create a copy of the node and fieldData
   Coordinate3Manip *newManip = (Coordinate3Manip *)
     SoCoordinate3::copy(copyConnections);

   // Copy the children
   for (int i = 0; i < children->getLength(); i++)
     newManip->children->append(
        (*children)[i]->copy(copyConnections));

   return newManip;
}


//    Returns the child list...
SoChildList *
Coordinate3Manip::getChildren() const
{
   return children;
}

void
Coordinate3Manip::doAction(SoAction *action)
{
   int        numIndices;
   const int  *indices;

   if (action->getPathCode(numIndices, indices)
     == SoAction::IN_PATH)
     children->traverse(action, 0, indices[numIndices - 1]);
   else
     children->traverse(action);
}
```

```
// These functions implement all actions for Coordinate3Manip.
void
Coordinate3Manip::getMatrix(SoGetMatrixAction *action)
{
   int         numIndices;
   const int   *indices;

   switch (action->getPathCode(numIndices, indices)) {
     case SoAction::NO_PATH:
       break;
     case SoAction::IN_PATH:
       children->traverse(action, 0,indices[numIndices - 1]);
       break;
     case SoAction::BELOW_PATH:
       break;
     case SoAction::OFF_PATH:
       children->traverse(action);
       break;
   }
}

void
Coordinate3Manip::callback(SoCallbackAction *action)
{
   Coordinate3Manip::doAction(action);
   SoCoordinate3::callback(action);
}

void
Coordinate3Manip::getBoundingBox(
   SoGetBoundingBoxAction *action)
{
   SbVec3f      totalCenter(0,0,0);
   int          numCenters = 0;
   int          numIndices;
   const int    *indices;
   int          lastChild;

   if (action->getPathCode(numIndices, indices)
     == SoAction::IN_PATH)
     lastChild = indices[numIndices - 1];
   else
     lastChild = getNumChildren() - 1;
```

```
      // Traverse the children
      for (int i = 0; i <= lastChild; i++) {
        children->traverse(action, i, i);
        if (action->isCenterSet()) {
          totalCenter += action->getCenter();
          numCenters++;
          action->resetCenter();
        }
      }

      // Traverse this as an SoCoordinate3
      SoCoordinate3::getBoundingBox(action);
      if (action->isCenterSet()) {
        totalCenter += action->getCenter();
        numCenters++;
        action->resetCenter();
      }

      // Now, set the center to be the average:
      if (numCenters != 0)
        action->setCenter(totalCenter / numCenters, FALSE);
}

void
Coordinate3Manip::GLRender(SoGLRenderAction *action)
{
   Coordinate3Manip::doAction(action);
   SoCoordinate3::GLRender(action);
}

void
Coordinate3Manip::handleEvent(SoHandleEventAction *action)
{
   Coordinate3Manip::doAction(action);
   SoCoordinate3::handleEvent(action);
}

void
Coordinate3Manip::pick(SoPickAction *action)
{
  Coordinate3Manip::doAction(action);
  SoCoordinate3::pick(action);
}
```

```
void
Coordinate3Manip::valueChangedCB(void *inManip,
   SoDragger *inDragger)
{
   Coordinate3Manip *manip = (Coordinate3Manip *) inManip;

   SbMatrix motMat = inDragger->getMotionMatrix();
   SbVec3f location = motMat[3];

   // Disconnect the field sensor
   manip->pointFieldSensor->detach();

   int ind = (int) manip->editIndex.getValue();

   // Set value of the point if it's different.
   if (ind < manip->point.getNum()) {
     if (manip->point[ind] != location)
       manip->point.set1Value(ind,location);
   }

   // Reconnect the field sensors
   manip->pointFieldSensor->attach(&manip->point);
}

void
Coordinate3Manip::fieldSensorCB(void *inManip, SoSensor *)
{
   Coordinate3Manip *manip = (Coordinate3Manip *) inManip;

   int ind = manip->editIndex.getValue();

   // Set value of the point if it's different.
   if (ind < manip->point.getNum()) {

     SoDragger *dragger = manip->getDragger();

     if (dragger!=NULL) {
       SbVec3f location = manip->point[ind];
       SbMatrix newMat = dragger->getMotionMatrix();
       newMat[3][0] = location[0];
       newMat[3][1] = location[1];
       newMat[3][2] = location[2];

       dragger->setMotionMatrix(newMat);
     }
   }
}
```

## Chapter 9

Creating a Selection Highlight Style

This chapter explains how you can provide your own style of selection highlighting by deriving a new highlight class. The first part of the chapter offers an overview of the steps required to create a new highlight class. When necessary, additional sections explain key concepts in further detail. The chapter examples show how to create two new highlight classes:

- A highlight that renders selected objects as 2D rectangles in the overlay planes

- A highlight that renders only the selected objects

Before reading this chapter, be sure to read Chapter 10 in *The Inventor Mentor*.

Built-in Highlighting

Inventor provides built-in selection highlighting with the **SoXtRenderArea** and with two classes derived from **SoGLRenderAction**: **SoBoxHighlight-RenderAction** and **SoLineHighlightRenderAction**. After a scene graph is rendered, the highlight action renders the path for each object in the selection list. The highlight action is provided to the render area by the application, which calls the **setGLRenderAction**() method.

Overview

Although Inventor provides predefined highlight styles, at times you may want to highlight selected objects with a different style. You can provide your own highlight style in two ways: derive a new highlight class from **SoGLRenderAction** (described here), or make changes directly to the scene graph whenever the selection changes (using **SoSelection** callbacks, as described in Chapter 10 of *The Inventor Mentor*). If you're using manipulators, it's probably easiest to allow the manipulator to make changes to the scene graph through use of selection callbacks. In this case, the manipulator shows which objects are selected.

Creating a new highlight style by deriving a class from **SoGLRenderAction** is basically the same as deriving any new action class, as described in Chapter 4. You can use the action-class macros found in SoSubAction.h. The SO_ACTION_HEADER() macro declares type identifier and naming variables and methods that all node classes must support. The SO_ACTION_SOURCE() macro defines the static variables and methods declared in the SO_ACTION_HEADER() macro.

Creating a new highlight action class requires these steps:

1. Select a name for the new highlight class. It will be derived from **SoGLRenderAction** or another highlight class.

2. Define an **initClass()** method to initialize the type information. Use the SO_ACTION_INIT_CLASS() macro.

3. Define a constructor. Use the SO_ACTION_CONSTRUCTOR() macro.

4. Implement the virtual **apply()** method (see "The apply() Method" on page 216).

5. Implement other methods, if desired, to specify the appearance of the highlight. These optional methods include **setColor()**, **setLinePattern()**, and **setLineWidth()**.

The apply() Method

The **apply()** method of the highlight action renders the scene graph in such a way that selected objects stand out. You could use a two-pass approach, in which the scene is rendered first, and the additional highlights are rendered second. Or your highlight action might render only the selected objects, or render selected objects in a totally different manner (for example, as boxes or spheres). As for any action, the **apply()** method is an overloaded virtual function (it can take a node, a path, or a path list). The derived highlight class provides stubs for the path and path list forms of the **apply()** method. Because selection makes the most sense in the context of a scene graph (since the selection list is a list of paths), highlighting paths and path lists is not defined. The function stubs simply call the corresponding **apply()** method of **SoGLRenderAction** for paths and path lists.

It's also worth examining the **apply()** method of the sample classes in more detail, since it uses caching for improved efficiency. As shown in Example 9-2, the **apply()** method uses a search action to find the selection node and then caches this path. Paths from the root of the scene graph to the selected objects are constructed as follows:

1. The **apply()** method first determines whether the cached path to the selection node is still valid. If the root of the new path is the root of the scene graph and the tail is the selection node, it considers the cached path to be valid (since paths are automatically updated when nodes are added or removed).

2. Next, it checks to be sure that something is selected. The selection node keeps track of the paths to the selected objects. The path from the root to the selection node (in Figure 9-1, the path from Node A to Node B) is prepended to each of the paths maintained in the selection list.

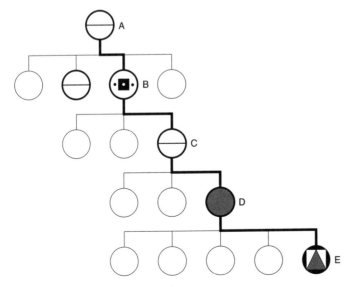

Figure 9-1   Highlight Path

If the selection path ends in a node kit, additional work is performed to extend the path all the way down to the selected object. In Figure 9-1, the selection path is from Node B to Node D (a node kit). First, the last kit in the node kit path is obtained (here, Node D). Then, the node kit path is cast to a full path, and the tail of that path is obtained (Node E). Figure 9-1 shows the complete highlight path, which extends from the root of the scene graph to the selection node (Node A to Node B), and from the selection node to the selected object (Node B to Node E).

Creating a Highlight in the Overlay Planes

The following two examples show a class derived from **SoGLRenderAction** that renders the selected objects as 2D rectangles in the overlay planes. This example illustrates several techniques you will probably use when deriving any new highlight class:

- Using function "stubs" to call the path and pathList forms of the **apply()** method of the parent class

- Caching the path to the selection node

In addition, the **OverlayHighlightRenderAction** class performs some work that is class-specific. For efficiency, its constructor sets up a scene graph that contains a 2D rectangle. Later, the **apply()** method changes the values of the rectangle so that it appears in the correct position for the highlighted object. The **updateBbox()** method is specific to this highlight class. It projects the 3D bounding box for the selected object onto the screen and renders it as a 2D rectangle.

When the constructor creates an **SoGLRenderAction**, it passes in a dummy viewport region. The **SoXtRenderArea** will pass the real viewport region to to **SoGLRenderAction** before the render action's **apply()** method is called.

Example 9-1 shows the class declaration found in the include file OverlayHighlightRenderAction.h.

Example 9-1   OverlayHighlightRenderAction.h

```
#include <Inventor/actions/SoGLRenderAction.h>

class SoCamera;
class SoCoordinate3;
class SoOrthographicCamera;
class SoSeparator;
```

```
class OverlayHighlightRenderAction : public SoGLRenderAction {
    SO_ACTION_HEADER(OverlayHighlightRenderAction);
  public:
   // Constructor and destructor
   OverlayHighlightRenderAction();
   ~OverlayHighlightRenderAction();

   // Applies action to the graph rooted by a node,
   // only drawing selected objects.
   virtual void    apply(SoNode *node);

   // Applies action to the graph defined by a path or path
   // list.
   // These simply invoke the parent class apply() methods.
   // These do NOT highlight the path, whether selected or not.
   // They are implemented to keep the compiler happy.
   virtual void    apply(SoPath *path);
   virtual void    apply(const SoPathList &pathList,
                      SbBool obeysRules = FALSE);

   // This must be called before this class is used.
   static void initClass();

  protected:
   void               updateBbox(SoPath *p, SoCamera *c);

   // Local scene graph
   SoSeparator        *localRoot;
   SoOrthographicCamera *orthoCam;
   SoCoordinate3      *coords;

   // We will cache the path to the first selection node
   SoPath             *selPath;
};
```

Example 9-2 shows the class definition, found in the source file.

Example 9-2   OverlayHL.c++

```
#include <limits.h>
#include <math.h>
#include <Inventor/SbBox.h>
#include <Inventor/SoPath.h>
#include <Inventor/SoNodeKitPath.h>
#include <Inventor/actions/SoGetBoundingBoxAction.h>
#include <Inventor/actions/SoSearchAction.h>
#include <Inventor/nodekits/SoBaseKit.h>
```

```
#include <Inventor/nodes/SoColorIndex.h>
#include <Inventor/nodes/SoCoordinate3.h>
#include <Inventor/nodes/SoDrawStyle.h>
#include <Inventor/nodes/SoFaceSet.h>
#include <Inventor/nodes/SoLightModel.h>
#include <Inventor/nodes/SoOrthographicCamera.h>
#include <Inventor/nodes/SoPickStyle.h>
#include <Inventor/nodes/SoSelection.h>
#include <Inventor/nodes/SoSeparator.h>

#include "OverlayHighlightRenderAction.h"

SO_ACTION_SOURCE(OverlayHighlightRenderAction);

//    Initializes the OverlayHighlightRenderAction class.
void
OverlayHighlightRenderAction::initClass()
{
   SO_ACTION_INIT_CLASS(OverlayHighlightRenderAction,
                        SoGLRenderAction);
}

//   Constructor
OverlayHighlightRenderAction::OverlayHighlightRenderAction()
      : SoGLRenderAction(SbVec2s(1, 1)) // pass a dummy
                                        // viewport region
{
   SO_ACTION_CONSTRUCTOR(OverlayHighlightRenderAction);

   selPath = NULL;

   // Set up the local rendering graph
   localRoot = new SoSeparator;
   localRoot->ref();

   SoPickStyle *pickStyle = new SoPickStyle;
   pickStyle->style = SoPickStyle::UNPICKABLE;
   localRoot->addChild(pickStyle);

   // Set up camera to look at 0 <= x,y <= 1
   orthoCam = new SoOrthographicCamera;
   orthoCam->position.setValue(.5, .5, 1.);
   orthoCam->height = 1.0;
   localRoot->addChild(orthoCam);
```

```
    SoLightModel *lmodel = new SoLightModel;
    lmodel->model = SoLightModel::BASE_COLOR;
    localRoot->addChild(lmodel);

    SoColorIndex *color = new SoColorIndex;
    color->index = 1;
    localRoot->addChild(color);

    SoDrawStyle *drawStyle = new SoDrawStyle;
    drawStyle->style = SoDrawStyle::LINES;
    drawStyle->lineWidth = 3;
    drawStyle->linePattern = 0xffff;
    localRoot->addChild(drawStyle);

    coords = new SoCoordinate3;
    coords->point.setNum(0);
    localRoot->addChild(coords);

    SoFaceSet *fset = new SoFaceSet;
    fset->numVertices = 4;
    localRoot->addChild(fset);
}

// Destructor

OverlayHighlightRenderAction::~OverlayHighlightRenderAction()
{
    localRoot->unref();
    if (selPath != NULL)
        selPath->unref();
}

// Update the bbox to surround the projected bounding box of
// the path.
// Use: protected
void
OverlayHighlightRenderAction::updateBbox(SoPath *p, SoCamera
                                            *camera)
{
    coords->point.deleteValues(0); // clear them all out

    if (camera == NULL) return;
```

```
// Compute the 3d bounding box of the passed path
SoGetBoundingBoxAction bba(getViewportRegion());
bba.apply(p);
SbVec3f min, max;
bba.getBoundingBox().getBounds(min, max);

// Project points to (0 <= x,y,z <= 1) screen coordinates
SbViewVolume vv = camera->getViewVolume();
SbVec3f screenPoint[8];
vv.projectToScreen(SbVec3f(min[0], min[1], min[2]),
                   screenPoint[0]);
vv.projectToScreen(SbVec3f(min[0], min[1], max[2]),
                   screenPoint[1]);
vv.projectToScreen(SbVec3f(min[0], max[1], min[2]),
                   screenPoint[2]);
vv.projectToScreen(SbVec3f(min[0], max[1], max[2]),
                   screenPoint[3]);
vv.projectToScreen(SbVec3f(max[0], min[1], min[2]),
                   screenPoint[4]);
vv.projectToScreen(SbVec3f(max[0], min[1], max[2]),
                   screenPoint[5]);
vv.projectToScreen(SbVec3f(max[0], max[1], min[2]),
                   screenPoint[6]);
vv.projectToScreen(SbVec3f(max[0], max[1], max[2]),
                   screenPoint[7]);

// Find the encompassing 2d box (0 <= x,y <= 1)
SbBox2f bbox2;
for (int i = 0; i < 8; i++)
   bbox2.extendBy(SbVec2f(screenPoint[i][0],
                  screenPoint[i][1]));

if (! bbox2.isEmpty()) {
   float xmin, ymin, xmax, ymax;
   bbox2.getBounds(xmin, ymin, xmax, ymax);

   // Set up the coordinate node
   coords->point.set1Value(0,  xmin, ymin, 0);
   coords->point.set1Value(1,  xmax, ymin, 0);
   coords->point.set1Value(2,  xmax, ymax, 0);
   coords->point.set1Value(3,  xmin, ymax, 0);
}
}
```

```
//  beginTraversal - render highlights for our selection node.
void
OverlayHighlightRenderAction::apply(SoNode *renderRoot)
{
    // Do not render the scene - only render the highlights

    // Is our cached path still valid?
    if ((selPath == NULL) ||
        (selPath->getHead() != renderRoot) ||
        (! selPath->getTail()->isOfType
                            (SoSelection::getClassTypeId()))) {

        // Find the selection node under the render root
        SoSearchAction sa;
        sa.setFind(SoSearchAction::TYPE);
        sa.setInterest(SoSearchAction::FIRST);
        sa.setType(SoSelection::getClassTypeId());
        sa.apply(renderRoot);

        // Cache this path
        if (selPath != NULL)
            selPath->unref();
        selPath = sa.getPath();
        if (selPath != NULL) {
            selPath = selPath->copy();
            selPath->ref();
        }
    }

    if (selPath != NULL) {
        // Make sure something is selected.
        SoSelection *sel = (SoSelection *) selPath->getTail();
        if (sel->getNumSelected() == 0) return;

        // Keep the length from the root to the selection
        // as an optimization so we can reuse this data.
        int reusablePathLength = selPath->getLength();

        // For each selection path, create a new path rooted
        // under our localRoot.
        for (int j = 0; j < sel->getNumSelected(); j++) {
            // Continue the path down to the selected object.
            // No need to deal with p[0] since that is the sel
            // node.
            SoPath *p = sel->getPath(j);
            SoNode *pathTail = p->getTail();
```

```
if ( pathTail->isOfType(SoBaseKit::getClassTypeId())) {
   // Find the last nodekit on the path.
   SoNode *kitTail = ((SoNodeKitPath *)p)->getTail();

   // Extend the selectionPath until it reaches this
   // last kit.
   SoFullPath *fp = (SoFullPath *) p;
   int k = 0;
   do {
      selPath->append(fp->getIndex(++k));
   }
   while'( fp->getNode(k) != kitTail );
}
else {
   for (int k = 1; k < p->getLength(); k++)
      selPath->append(p->getIndex(k));
}

// Find the camera used to render the selected object.
SoNode *camera;
SoSearchAction sa;
sa.setFind(SoSearchAction::TYPE);
sa.setInterest(SoSearchAction::LAST);
sa.setType(SoCamera::getClassTypeId());
sa.apply(selPath);
camera = (sa.getPath() == NULL ? NULL :
                        sa.getPath()->getTail());

// Get the bounding box of the object and update the
// local highlight graph.
updateBbox(selPath, (SoCamera *)camera);

// Make sure the box has some size.
if (coords->point.getNum() == 0) {
  #ifdef DEBUG
  SoDebugError::post
        ("OverlayHighlightRenderAction::apply",
         "selected object has no bounding box - cannot
         render a highlight");
  #endif
}
else {
   // Render the highlight.
   SoGLRenderAction::apply(localRoot);
}
```

```
          // Restore selPath for reuse.
          selPath->truncate(reusablePathLength);
      }
   }
}
// Function stubs: we do not highlight paths and pathLists.

void
OverlayHighlightRenderAction::apply(SoPath *path)
{ SoGLRenderAction::apply(path); }

void
OverlayHighlightRenderAction::apply(const SoPathList &pathList,
                                    SbBool obeysRules)
{ SoGLRenderAction::apply(pathList, obeysRules); }
```

Example 9-3 shows a main program that uses this new highlight class. The highlight is drawn in the overlay planes, and the scene itself is drawn in the normal planes by a different render action.

Example 9-3   Main Program Using OverlayHighlightRenderAction

```
#include <X11/StringDefs.h>
#include <X11/Intrinsic.h>

#include <Inventor/SoDB.h>
#include <Inventor/SoInput.h>
#include <Inventor/Xt/SoXt.h>
#include <Inventor/Xt/viewers/SoXtExaminerViewer.h>
#include <Inventor/nodes/SoSelection.h>

#include "OverlayHighlightRenderAction.h"

void
main(int , char *argv[])
{
   // Initialization
   Widget mainWindow = SoXt::init(argv[0]);
   OverlayHighlightRenderAction::initClass();

   // Open the data file
   SoInput in;
   char *datafile = "monitor.iv";
   if (! in.openFile(datafile)) {
     fprintf(stderr, "Cannot open %s for reading.\n", datafile);
     return;
   }
```

```
// Read the input file
SoNode *n;
SoSeparator *sep = new SoSeparator;
while ((SoDB::read(&in, n) != FALSE) && (n != NULL))
  sep->addChild(n);

// Create a selection root to show off our new highlight.
SoSelection *sel = new SoSelection;
sel->addChild(sep);

// Create a viewer.
SoXtExaminerViewer *viewer = new
                          SoXtExaminerViewer(mainWindow);
viewer->setSceneGraph(sel);

// Set the overlay scene graph same as normal. For viewers,
// we have to cast to render area graph.
viewer->setOverlaySceneGraph(viewer->
                        SoXtRenderArea::getSceneGraph());

viewer->setTitle("Overlay highlight");
viewer->redrawOverlayOnSelectionChange(sel);
viewer->setOverlayGLRenderAction(
                    new OverlayHighlightRenderAction);

// Set up the overlay color map
SbColor red(1, 0, 0);
viewer->setOverlayColorMap(1, 1, &red);

viewer->show();
SoXt::show(mainWindow);
SoXt::mainLoop();
}
```

Rendering Only Selected Objects

Examples 9-3 and 9-4 show a new class that renders only the selected
objects. Rather than drawing a surrogate object as in Examples 9-1 and 9-2,
these examples draw the selected objects themselves.

Example 9-4   ShowSelectionRA.h

```
#include <Inventor/actions/SoGLRenderAction.h>

class SoPath;

class ShowSelectionRenderAction : public SoGLRenderAction {
   SO_ACTION_HEADER(ShowSelectionRenderAction);
  public:
   ShowSelectionRenderAction();
   virtual ~ShowSelectionRenderAction();

   // Applies action to the graph rooted by a node,
   // only drawing selected objects.
   virtual void    apply(SoNode *node);

   // Applies action to the graph defined by a path or path
   // list.
   // These simply invoke the parent class apply() methods.
   // These do NOT highlight the path, whether selected or not.
   // They are implemented to keep the compiler happy.
   virtual void    apply(SoPath *path);
   virtual void    apply(const SoPathList &pathList,
                         SbBool obeysRules = FALSE);
   static void initClass();

  protected:
   // We will cache the path to the first selection node.
   SoPath          *selPath;
};
```

Example 9-5   ShowSelectionRA.c++

```
#include <Inventor/SoPath.h>
#include <Inventor/actions/SoSearchAction.h>
#include <Inventor/nodes/SoBaseColor.h>
#include <Inventor/nodes/SoDrawStyle.h>
#include <Inventor/nodes/SoLightModel.h>
#include <Inventor/nodes/SoNode.h>
#include <Inventor/nodes/SoSelection.h>
#include <Inventor/nodes/SoSeparator.h>
#include <Inventor/nodes/SoTexture2.h>

#include "ShowSelectionRA.h"

SO_ACTION_SOURCE(ShowSelectionRenderAction);
```

```
// Initializes the ShowSelectionRenderAction class.
void
ShowSelectionRenderAction::initClass()
{
   SO_ACTION_INIT_CLASS(ShowSelectionRenderAction,
                        SoGLRenderAction);
}

//   Constructor

ShowSelectionRenderAction::ShowSelectionRenderAction()
     : SoGLRenderAction(SbVec2s(1, 1))
                            // pass a dummy viewport region
{
   selPath = NULL;
}

//   Destructor

ShowSelectionRenderAction::~ShowSelectionRenderAction()
{
   if (selPath != NULL)
     selPath->unref();
}

//   Render the passed scene by searching for the first
//   selection node, then rendering only the selected objects.

void
ShowSelectionRenderAction::apply(SoNode *node)
{
   node->ref();

   // Do we have to search for the selection node?
   // Only if our cached path is NULL,
   // or the action is being applied to a different scene,
   // or the tail of our existing path is no longer a selection
   // node (for instance if that node was removed from the
   // scene).
   if ((selPath == NULL) ||
      (selPath->getHead() != node) ||
      (! selPath->getTail()->isOfType(
          SoSelection::getClassTypeId())))) {
```

```
    // Find the first selection node under the passed root.
    SoSearchAction sa;
    sa.setFind(SoSearchAction::TYPE);
    sa.setInterest(SoSearchAction::FIRST);
    sa.setType(SoSelection::getClassTypeId());
    sa.apply(node);

    // Cache this new path.
    if (selPath != NULL)
      selPath->unref();
    selPath = sa.getPath();
    if (selPath != NULL) {
      selPath = selPath->copy();
      selPath->ref();
    }
  }

  // Render the selected paths!
  if (selPath != NULL) {
    SoSelection *sel = (SoSelection *) selPath->getTail();
    if (sel->getNumSelected() > 0) {
      // Keep the length from the root to the selection
      // as an optimization so we can reuse this data
      int reusablePathLength = selPath->getLength();

      // For each selection path, we need the full path from
      // the passed root to render, else we may not have a
      // camera.
      for (int j = 0; j < sel->getNumSelected(); j++) {
        // Continue the path down to the selected object.
        // No need to deal with p[0] since that is the sel
        // node.
        SoPath *p = sel->getPath(j);
        for (int k = 1; k < p->getLength(); k++)
          selPath->append(p->getIndex(k));

        // Render the selected shape.
        SoGLRenderAction::apply(selPath);

        // Restore selPath for reuse.
        selPath->truncate(reusablePathLength);
      }
    }
  }

  node->unref();
}
```

```
// Function stubs: we do not highlight paths and pathLists.

void
ShowSelectionRenderAction::apply(SoPath *path)
{ SoGLRenderAction::apply(path); }

void
ShowSelectionRenderAction::apply(const SoPathList &pathList,
SbBool obeysRules)
{ SoGLRenderAction::apply(pathList, obeysRules); }
```

Example 9-6 shows a main program that uses this new highlight class. It creates two viewers that share the same selection node. One viewer uses the GLRenderAction, while the other uses the ShowSelectionRenderAction. Selection changes in one viewer are reflected in the other viewer as well.

Example 9-6   Main Program for ShowSelectionRenderAction

```
#include <X11/StringDefs.h>
#include <X11/Intrinsic.h>

#include <Inventor/SoDB.h>
#include <Inventor/SoInput.h>
#include <Inventor/Xt/SoXt.h>
#include <Inventor/Xt/viewers/SoXtExaminerViewer.h>
#include <Inventor/nodes/SoSelection.h>

#include "ShowSelectionRA.h"

void
main(int , char *argv[])
{
   // Initialization
   Widget mainWindow = SoXt::init(argv[0]);
   ShowSelectionRenderAction::initClass();

   // Open the data file
   SoInput in;
   char *datafile = "monitor.iv";
   if (! in.openFile(datafile)) {
     fprintf(stderr, "Cannot open %s for reading.\n", datafile);
     return;
   }
```

```
// Read the input file
SoNode *n;
SoSeparator *sep = new SoSeparator;
while ((SoDB::read(&in, n) != FALSE) && (n != NULL))
   sep->addChild(n);

// Create a selection root to show off our new highlight.
SoSelection *sel = new SoSelection;
sel->addChild(sep);

// Create two viewers, one to show the scene, the other
// to show the selected objects.
SoXtExaminerViewer *viewer1 =
                      new SoXtExaminerViewer(mainWindow);
viewer1->setSceneGraph(sel);
viewer1->setTitle("Scene");

SoXtExaminerViewer *viewer2 = new SoXtExaminerViewer();
viewer2->setSceneGraph(sel);
viewer2->setGLRenderAction(new ShowSelectionRenderAction());
viewer2->redrawOnSelectionChange(sel);
viewer2->setDecoration(FALSE);
viewer2->setTitle("Selection");

viewer1->show();
viewer2->show();

SoXt::show(mainWindow);
SoXt::mainLoop();
}
```

## Chapter 10

Creating a Component

This chapter describes how to create your own Inventor Xt component. Before creating a new Xt component, be sure to read Chapters 10 and 16 in *The Inventor Mentor.*

The first part of this chapter offers an overview of the steps required to create a new component. The second part of the chapter describes the additional steps required to create a new viewer, which is a specific type of component. The chapter examples show creating two new component classes:

- A component derived from **SoXtRenderArea** called **SceneTumble**

- A viewer called **simpleViewer**

Creating a New Component

This section describes the general process of creating a new component. The sample class shown here is derived from **SoXtRenderArea**. The second half of this chapter, beginning with "Creating a New Viewer" on page 245, describes creating a more specialized component, a viewer.

Overview

There are no special macros for creating new component classes. Creating a new component requires these steps:

1. Select a name for the new component class and determine what class it is derived from (see "Overview" on page 246 for a discussion of deriving new viewers).

2. Define a constructor for the new class. If you want other programmers to be able to derive classes from your new class, you need to define two constructors for the class, a public constructor and a protected one (see "Defining the Constructor" on page 234). If no one will be deriving classes from your new class, you can simply define a public constructor.

3. Implement **show**() and **hide**() methods for your component (optional step). The base class, **SoXtComponent**, takes care of showing and hiding your new component. But if your component needs to show *other* components when it is shown, or hide other components when it is hidden, you need to implement these two methods for your new class (see "The show() and hide() Methods" on page 237).

4. Implement the visibility-changed callback function (optional step). This function is called when the component changes state between visible and invisible (see "Visibility-Changed Callback Function" on page 237).

See the SoXtComponent.h file for additional methods you may choose to implement. Possibilities include the following:

windowCloseAction()
>> specifies what happens when the user closes the window using the Window Manager (for example, you could implement this method to exit the program or delete the component)

openHelpCard()   opens a help card for the component

Defining the Constructor

If you are sure that no one will need to derive classes from your new component, you can simply implement one public constructor. This constructor needs to do the following:

- Build the widget (or the widget tree if your component is made up of more than one widget)

- Call **setBaseWidget()** so that the **SoXtComponent** base class methods—such as **show()** and **hide()**—work properly

Defining Public and Protected Constructors

If you want to be sure that programmers can derive new classes from your class, you need to provide a protected constructor in addition to the public constructor. Here's why. The widget tree is built when the component is constructed. If you derive a component subclass, the parent class constructor is called before the constructor of the subclass. This means that the parent class widget is built before the subclass widget. The problem arises if you want the component subclass to provide a container widget for the parent class. The Xt Library requires that a parent widget be supplied when a child widget is created and provides no way to reparent a widget. A little fancy footwork is required for the subclass to provide the parent widget, and that maneuver is provided by the protected constructor.

In Inventor, every **SoXtComponent** class has two constructors: a public constructor and a protected constructor. The protected constructor has one additional parameter, **buildNow**, which is a Boolean value that specifies whether to build the widget tree now or later:

```
protected:
    SoXtComponent(
        Widget parent,
        const char *name,
        SbBool buildInsideParent,
        SbBool buildNow);
```

If you use the protected constructor and specify FALSE for **buildNow**, you can have explicit control over which widgets are built and in what order. For example, your new class may want to build a container widget such as a Motif-style form or bulletin board before it lets the parent class build its widget. In this case, your new class can call its **buildWidget()** method first and then later it can call the **buildWidget()** method of its parent class. In Inventor, the **SoXtFullViewer** class uses this technique. It builds a form widget with user interface trim and then has the parent class, **SoXtRenderArea**, later build its widget inside this form.

In Inventor, and in Examples 10-1 and 10-2, the basic constructor tasks are put into the **constructorCommon()** method, which is called by both constructors. Although this is a useful technique, it is not required. The constructorCommon() method is where the actual building of this widget occurs. This method checks the **buildNow** flag and builds the widget.

Let's analyze the **constructorCommon()** code in Example 10-2 in a bit more detail. After setting up sensors, a camera, and a light for the component, the following calls are made:

```
addVisibilityChangeCallback(visibilityChangeCB, this);
setClassName("SceneTumble");
setTitle("Tumble");

// If we do not build now, the subclass will build when ready
if (buildNow) {
   Widget w = buildWidget(getParentWidget());
   setBaseWidget(w);
}
```

The visibility-changed callback is described in "Visibility-Changed Callback Function" on page 237. The **setClassName()** method sets the name of the class for X resource lookup, which occurs while the widget is being built. The **setTitle()** method sets the title used in the shell window if this is a top-level component. Although not shown here, you can also call **setIconTitle()** to set the title used when the component is iconified.

The constructor then checks the **buildNow** flag. If this flag is TRUE, it builds the widget tree. Also, note that the **buildWidget()** method uses **getParentWidget()** to obtain the parent widget, which is not necessarily the parent widget passed in to the constructor. (The parent passed in to the constructor could be NULL, or the *buildInsideParent* parameter could be FALSE.)

Next, the constructor calls the **setBaseWidget()** method, which lets **SoXtComponent** know what the root of the widget tree is. This widget is used for layout, and by the **show()** and **hide()** methods.

The buildWidget() Method

In Inventor, because we want to allow subclasses to have explicit control over building the widget tree, we implement a separate **buildWidget()** method. If you are providing only the public constructor, you can simply build the widget in the constructor and do not need to create a separate **buildWidget()** method. This method, called by the constructor of your new class (or by subclasses of your new class), builds the widget hierarchy and returns its topmost widget.

If your widget supports X resources, be sure to call **registerWidget()** immediately after you create the topmost container widget and before you build the rest of the widget hierarchy. This method associates the Motif-style widget with the Inventor component to which it belongs. When you create other widgets in the hierarchy, Inventor uses the class name of the component instead of the widget name during resource lookup. For example, the base widget of a render area is a Motif-style bulletin board. Once you have called **registerWidget()**, you can set the background color resource directly on the render area without affecting other bulletin board widgets in your hierarchy.

To define and retrieve your own resources, see the *Open Inventor C++ Reference Manual* on **SoXtResource**. For more information on X resources, see the *Xlib Programming Manual* by Adrian Nye (O'Reilly & Associates, 1990).

The show() and hide() Methods

The base class **SoXtComponent** will show and hide your new component automatically. However, if your component needs to show or hide other components, you must implement your own **show()** and **hide()** methods. In Inventor, if the material editor and color editor are on the screen and the program tells the material editor to hide itself, the material editor needs to tell the color editor to hide itself as well. Similarly, when a viewer hides itself, it also hides the preference sheet if it is visible.

Visibility-Changed Callback Function

Using **addVisibilityChangeCallback()**, your new class can register a callback function with **SoXtComponent** that is called when its visibility changes. A component can be shown, hidden, or iconified; whenever it changes state between visible and invisible (hidden or iconified), the visibility-changed callback function is invoked. This callback is useful, for example, if your component contains a scene with animation. When your component is hidden or iconified, it can stop the animation. Another example of using this callback is the render area, which detaches its redraw sensor when it is hidden or iconified.

See Example 10-2 for an illustration of using **visibilityChangeCB()**.

Creating a Simple Component

The following examples show the header file and source code for a simple component derived from **SoXtRenderArea**. This component animates a camera to rotate the scene. It uses a visibility-changed callback function to stop the tumbling when the component is not visible. A slider at the bottom of the window controls the speed of tumbling.

Example 10-1 shows the include file for the **SceneTumble** class.
Example 10-2 shows the source code for this class.

Example 10-1   SceneTumble.h

```
#include <Inventor/Xt/SoXtRenderArea.h>

class SoPerspectiveCamera;
class SoRotation;
class SoSeparator;
class SoTimerSensor;

class SceneTumble : public SoXtRenderArea {

public:

    // Constructor for public consumption
    SceneTumble(
        Widget parent = NULL,
        const char *name = NULL,
        SbBool buildInsideParent = TRUE);
    ~SceneTumble();

    virtual void setSceneGraph(SoNode *newScene);
    virtual SoNode *getSceneGraph();

    void setTumbling(SbBool onOff);
    SbBool isTumbling() const;
```

```
protected:

    // Constructor subclasses can call if they don't want the
    // widget built right away (i.e. the subclass wants to create
    // a container widget first.)
    SceneTumble(
        Widget parent,
        const char *name,
        SbBool buildInsideParent,
        SbBool buildNow);

    Widget buildWidget(Widget parent);

    void doTumbleAnimation();

    void setSpeed(int s) { speed = s; }
    int getSpeed() const { return speed; }

    Widget speedSlider;

private:

    SoNode * userScene;
        SoPerspectiveCamera *camera;
    SoRotation *rotx;
    SoRotation *roty;
    SoRotation *rotz;
    SoSeparator *root;
    int speed;
    SoTimerSensor *animationSensor;

    void constructorCommon(SbBool buildNow);
    static void visibilityChangeCB(void *userData,
                                   SbBool visible);
    static void animationSensorCB(void *userData, SoSensor *);
    static void speedCB(Widget, XtPointer, XtPointer);
};
```

Example 10-2   SceneTumble.c++

```
#include <Xm/Form.h>
#include <Xm/Scale.h>
#include <Inventor/Xt/SoXtResource.h>
#include <Inventor/nodes/SoDirectionalLight.h>
#include <Inventor/nodes/SoPerspectiveCamera.h>
#include <Inventor/nodes/SoRotation.h>
#include <Inventor/nodes/SoSeparator.h>
```

```
#include <Inventor/sensors/SoTimerSensor.h>
#include "SceneTumble.h"

#define MIN_SPEED 0
#define MAX_SPEED 100

// Speed factor is a small angle
#define SPEED_FACTOR (M_PI/3600.0)

// Public constructor
SceneTumble::SceneTumble(
   Widget parent,
   const char *name,
   SbBool buildInsideParent)
   : SoXtRenderArea(parent, name, buildInsideParent, FALSE,
                    FALSE)
{
   // Passing TRUE means build the component right now
   constructorCommon(TRUE);
}


// Protected constructor for subclasses to call
SceneTumble::SceneTumble(
   Widget parent,
   const char *name,
   SbBool buildInsideParent,
   SbBool buildNow)
   : SoXtRenderArea(parent, name, buildInsideParent, FALSE,
                    FALSE)
{
   // Subclass tells us whether to build now
   constructorCommon(buildNow);
}

// Actual work done at construction time
void
SceneTumble::constructorCommon(SbBool buildNow)
{
   speed = MAX_SPEED/2;

   animationSensor =
        new SoTimerSensor(SceneTumble::animationSensorCB, this);
   animationSensor->setInterval(1/60.0); // 60 frames per second

   userScene = NULL;
   root = new SoSeparator;
   camera = new SoPerspectiveCamera;
```

```
    rotx = new SoRotation;
    roty = new SoRotation;
    rotz = new SoRotation;

    root->addChild(camera);
    root->addChild(new SoDirectionalLight);
    root->addChild(rotx);
    root->addChild(roty);
    root->addChild(rotz);
    root->ref();

    addVisibilityChangeCallback(visibilityChangeCB, this);
    setClassName("SceneTumble");
    setTitle("Tumble");

    // If we do not build now, the subclass will build when ready
    if (buildNow) {
        Widget w = buildWidget(getParentWidget());
        setBaseWidget(w);
    }
}

// Destructor
SceneTumble::~SceneTumble()
{
    root->unref();
    delete animationSensor;
}

// Set the scene graph to tumble. We add this scene graph
// to our local graph so that we can rotate our own camera
// to create the tumbling effect. Our local scene graph
// root is passed to the render area for rendering.
void
SceneTumble::setSceneGraph(SoNode *newScene)
{
    // Replace the existing scene with this one
    if (userScene != NULL)
        root->replaceChild(userScene, newScene);
    else
        root->addChild(newScene);
    userScene = newScene;

    // Make certain the scene is in view
    camera->viewAll(root, getViewportRegion(), 2.0);
```

```
      // Render area will handle redraws for us
      SoXtRenderArea::setSceneGraph(root);
}

// Return the user's scene graph, not our local graph
SoNode *
SceneTumble::getSceneGraph()
{
   return userScene;
}

// Build the widget - create a form widget, and place
// in it a render area and a scale slider to control
// the speed.
Widget
SceneTumble::buildWidget(Widget parent)
{
   Arg args[8];
   int n;

   // Create a form widget as the container.
   Widget form = XtCreateWidget(getWidgetName(),
                                xmFormWidgetClass,
                                parent, NULL, 0);

   // Register the widget, so we can get resources
   registerWidget(form);

   // Get our starting speed from the resource.
   // Resource file should say:
   //     *SceneTumble*speed: <int between 0 and 100>
   short s;
   SoXtResource xr(form);
   if (xr.getResource("speed", "Speed", s)) {
      if (s > MAX_SPEED)
         speed = MAX_SPEED;
      else if (s < MIN_SPEED)
         speed = MIN_SPEED;
      else
         speed = s;
   }
```

```
    // Create render area
    Widget raWidget = SoXtRenderArea::buildWidget(form);

    // Create slider to control speed
    n = 0;
    XtSetArg(args[n], XmNminimum, MIN_SPEED); n++;
    XtSetArg(args[n], XmNmaximum, MAX_SPEED); n++;
    XtSetArg(args[n], XmNvalue, speed); n++;
    XtSetArg(args[n], XmNorientation, XmHORIZONTAL); n++;
    speedSlider =
      XtCreateWidget("Speed", xmScaleWidgetClass, form, args, n);

    // Callbacks on the slider
    XtAddCallback(speedSlider, XmNdragCallback,
                  SceneTumble::speedCB, this);
    XtAddCallback(speedSlider, XmNvalueChangedCallback,
                  SceneTumble::speedCB, this);

    // Layout
    n = 0;
    XtSetArg(args[n], XmNtopAttachment, XmNONE); n++;
    XtSetArg(args[n], XmNleftAttachment, XmATTACH_FORM); n++;
    XtSetArg(args[n], XmNrightAttachment, XmATTACH_FORM); n++;
    XtSetArg(args[n], XmNbottomAttachment, XmATTACH_FORM); n++;
    XtSetValues(speedSlider, args, n);

    n = 0;
    XtSetArg(args[n], XmNtopAttachment, XmATTACH_FORM); n++;
    XtSetArg(args[n], XmNleftAttachment, XmATTACH_FORM); n++;
    XtSetArg(args[n], XmNrightAttachment, XmATTACH_FORM); n++;
    XtSetArg(args[n], XmNbottomAttachment,XmATTACH_WIDGET); n++;
    XtSetArg(args[n], XmNbottomWidget, speedSlider); n++;
    XtSetValues(raWidget, args, n);

    // Make the widgets visible
    XtManageChild(speedSlider);
    XtManageChild(raWidget);

    return form;
}
```

```
// Do the tumble animation. This entails updating our three
// rotation nodes, one each for the x,y,and z axes.
void
SceneTumble::doTumbleAnimation()
{
   SbRotation r;
   float angle;

   // Rotate about three axes in three speeds
   angle = speed * SPEED_FACTOR;
   r = rotx->rotation.getValue() * SbRotation(SbVec3f(1, 0, 0),
                                              angle);
   rotx->rotation.setValue(r);

   angle = speed * SPEED_FACTOR * 1.5;
   r = roty->rotation.getValue() * SbRotation(SbVec3f(0, 1, 0),
                                              angle);
   roty->rotation.setValue(r);

   angle = speed * SPEED_FACTOR * 2.0;
   r = rotz->rotation.getValue() * SbRotation(SbVec3f(0, 0, 1),
                                              angle);
   rotz->rotation.setValue(r);
}

// Turn tumbling on and off. We simply schedule or unschedule
// the animation sensor.
void
SceneTumble::setTumbling(SbBool onOff)
{
   if (onOff)
     animationSensor->schedule();
   else
      animationSensor->unschedule();
}

// Return whether we are tumbling.
SbBool
SceneTumble::isTumbling() const
{
   return animationSensor->isScheduled();
}
```

```
// This is called when the render area visibility changes
// because it is shown, hidden, or iconified. If the
// component is not visible, we turn off the tumble animation.
void
SceneTumble::visibilityChangeCB(void *userData, SbBool visible)
{
    // Set tumbling on when the component is visible,
    // and set it off when the component is not visible.
    SceneTumble *tumbler = (SceneTumble *) userData;
    tumbler->setTumbling(visible);
}

// Animation sensor callback keeps the tumbling going.
void
SceneTumble::animationSensorCB(void *userData, SoSensor *)
{
    ((SceneTumble *) userData)->doTumbleAnimation();
}

// This is invoked when the speed slider changes value.
// We use the value of the slider to change the tumble speed.
void
SceneTumble::speedCB(Widget, XtPointer userData,
                     XtPointer clientData)
{
    SceneTumble *tumbler = (SceneTumble *) userData;
    XmScaleCallbackStruct *data = (XmScaleCallbackStruct *)
                                  clientData;
    tumbler->setSpeed(data->value);
}
```

Creating a New Viewer

Viewers are subclassed from **SoXtRenderArea** and can be thought of as smart rendering windows that respond to events and modify the camera. You can use one of the following classes as a base class for your own viewer:

- **SoXtViewer**

- **SoXtFullViewer**

- **SoXtConstrainedViewer**

SoXtViewer, the lowest base class for viewers, adds the notion of a camera to an SoXtRenderArea. The camera through which the scene is viewed is either found in the scene or created automatically by the viewer. SoXtFullViewer adds a decoration trim around the rendering area, which includes thumbwheels, a zoom slider, and push buttons. This class also creates a pop-up menu and a preference sheet with generic viewer functionality built into them. SoXtConstrainedViewer, the last base class, is used for viewers that have the notion of a world up-direction. These viewers constrain the camera orientation to prevent the user from being upside down relative to the given world up-direction (which defaults to +*y*).

The SoXtViewer class provides basic viewer functionality. This base class provides methods for changing the camera, including setCamera(), getCamera(), viewAll(), saveHomePosition(), and resetToHome-Position(). SoXtViewer also adds a headlight, as well as drawing styles, buffering types, and autoclipping. In addition, SoXtViewer adds support for seek, copy, and paste, enabling subclasses to redefine how a seek or a paste is performed.

Overview

If you create a viewer that is a subclass of SoXtViewer, you perform the following steps. Examples 10-3 and 10-4 illustrate each step.

1. Construct the viewer (required step for all new viewers). See "Defining the Constructor" on page 247.

2. Implement the event-processing routines (required step for all new viewers). These routines include processEvent() and processCommonEvents(), which in turn calls translateCamera() and switchMode(). See "Defining the Event-Processing Routines" on page 247.

3. Implement the seek function (optional step). See "Implementing the Seek Function" on page 248.

4. Modify the cursor to be used for feedback (optional step). See "Using the Cursor for Feedback" on page 250.

If you create a viewer that is subclassed from SoXtFullViewer, you can perform the following steps, in addition to steps 1 through 4. Only step 5 is required; the other steps are optional.

5. Modify how the trim decoration is used (required step). See "Using the SoXtFullViewer Trim Decoration" on page 261.

6. Add push buttons (optional step). See "Adding Push Buttons" on page 262.

7. Change the preference sheet (optional step). See "Changing the Preference Sheet" on page 263.

8. Change the pop-up menu (optional step). See "Changing the Pop-up Menu" on page 265.

9. Change the trim decoration (optional step). See "Changing the Decoration Layout" on page 266.

If you create a viewer that is subclassed from **SoXtConstrainedViewer**, you can perform the following step, in addition to steps 1 through 9. See "Creating a Constrained Viewer" on page 268 for more information on creating a viewer subclassed from **SoXtConstrainedViewer**.

10. Define constraints for the viewer.

Examples 10-3 and 10-4 show how to create a simple viewer derived from **SoXtFullViewer**, similar to the **SoXtPlaneViewer**. The left mouse button is used to translate the camera in the viewer plane and to seek objects. This new viewer redefines the decoration thumbwheels to translate the camera. It also defines mouse cursors to reflect the viewer's current state (viewing, seeking, or picking).

Defining the Constructor

The constructor for the viewer takes an *SoXtViewer::Type* parameter, which specifies whether the viewer is of type BROWSER (the default) or EDITOR. This argument specifies the camera creation policy of the viewer. For more information on component constructors, see "Defining the Constructor" on page 234.

Defining the Event-Processing Routines

Any new viewer must implement the **processEvent()** routine, defined in **SoXtRenderArea**, to send events directly to the scene graph. When viewing is turned on, the new viewer uses those events to manipulate the camera.

The base-class routine **processCommonEvents()**, defined in **SoXtViewer**, is first called when an event is received. This routine is used to handle a set of events that should be common across all viewers. These events are as follows:

- Pressing the Escape key (toggles a viewer between Viewing and Picking mode)

- Pressing the Home key (resets the viewer to Home Position)

- Pressing the S key (toggles Seek mode on and off)

- Pressing any of the four arrow keys (moves the camera left, right, up, or down)

The viewer calls the base class **interactiveCountInc()** and **interactiveCountDec()** methods when the left mouse button is pressed and released. These methods enable the viewer base class to call the user interactive start and finish callbacks and are also used to change the drawing styles and buffering types when interactive styles are chosen (for example, move wireframe).

The code to translate the camera using the new mouse position is called within the **processEvent()** routine (see the **translateCamera()** method in Example 10-4).

The **switchMode()** routine called within **processEvent()** switches between viewer modes. It also sets the correct cursor on the window (see "Using the Cursor for Feedback" on page 250).

In addition to showing how the camera can be translated given the mouse events received, the **processEvent()** routine also shows how seek functionality is supported in the viewer. This topic is explained in detail in the following section.

Implementing the Seek Function

The seek function moves the camera to the picked point (when detail seek is ON) or to the picked object (when detail seek is OFF). The seek functionality for viewers is provided by the base class **SoXtViewer**. The following public methods can be called to set seek parameters:

setDetailSeek()	specifies whether to orient the camera toward the picked point (detail seek is ON), or toward the center of the object's bounding box (detail seek is OFF). The default is ON.
isDetailSeek()	returns whether detail seek is ON.
setSeekTime()	sets the time for a seek to animate the new camera location. The default time is 2 seconds.
getSeekTime()	returns the seek time.

Subclasses can then simply call **seekToPoint()**, passing the mouse location, and the base class **SoXtViewer** performs the seek animation. By default, detail seek is ON, and the base class changes the camera to be the focal distance away from the picked point and aligned to the point normal. When detail seek is OFF, the camera centers itself on the object's bounding box and keeps its orientation the same (the picked point has no real importance; only the picked object is used in this case).

Our simple viewer example uses the seek functionality defined in the base class. If a viewer needs to redefine how seek is performed (**SoXtFlyViewer** and **SoXtWalkViewer** redefine it), the viewer can redefine the **interpolateSeekAnimation()** routine, which changes the camera.

The following protected variables are defined in **SoXtViewer** to help you redefine **interpolateSeekAnimation()** for a new viewer:

seekPoint, seekNormal
point and normal to seek

oldCamOrientation, newCamOrientation
old and new camera orientation

oldCamPosition, newCamPosition
old and new camera position

seekDistance	seek distance (either a percentage or an absolute value)

seekDistAsPercentage
whether the seek distance is a percentage or an absolute value

computeSeekVariables
whether the final camera seek values have been computed. This flag is set to FALSE when **interpolateSeekAnimation()** is first called on a new seek animation.

Using the Cursor for Feedback

It is often desirable to have a viewer change the cursor to reflect the viewer's state. The file SoXtCursors.h defines a set of X bitmaps that can be used for defining cursors. Some of these bitmaps were created for specific viewers, whereas others are generic enough to be reused across viewers. Most viewers have a different cursor during viewing and nonviewing modes. A generic viewer cursor is supplied in the file SoXtCursors.h.

To have a different cursor when viewing is on, the viewer needs to redefine the **setViewing()** method to set the correct cursor on the window. Similarly, if the viewer supports the seek functionality, it also needs to redefine the **setSeekMode()** method to change the cursor. Example 10-4 shows how to change the cursor.

The **defineCursors()** routine, also shown in Example 10-4, needs to be called only once to create the X cursor.

X cursors can be defined only when the widget is actually mapped onto the screen. It is thus a good idea to define the cursors whenever the first event is received in the **processEvent()** routine, since an event guarantees that the window is mapped onto the screen.

Cursors should be defined on the render-area window, not on the window found in the X event structure. This is because the actual window events are received from changes when the viewer switches between single- and double-buffering. The render-area window, however, stays constant, so the cursor is correctly specified.

The following sections deal with more advanced features of viewers, such as the trim decoration around the render area and the viewer pop-up menu.

Example 10-3 shows the header file for the new simple viewer class.

Example 10-3   SimpleViewer.h

```
#include <Inventor/SbLinear.h>
#include <Inventor/Xt/viewers/SoXtFullViewer.h>

class simpleViewer : public SoXtFullViewer {
 public:
   // Constructor/destructor
   simpleViewer(
      Widget parent = NULL,
      const char *name = NULL,
      SbBool buildInsideParent = TRUE,
      SoXtFullViewer::BuildFlag flag = BUILD_ALL,
      SoXtViewer::Type type = BROWSER);
   ~simpleViewer();

   // Redefine this to also change the cursor (viewerCursor)
   virtual void       setViewing(SbBool onOrOff);

 protected:
   // Redefine this to process the events
   virtual void       processEvent(XAnyEvent *anyevent);

   // Redefine this to also change the cursor (seekCursor)
   virtual void       setSeekMode(SbBool onOrOff);

   // Define these thumbwheels to translate in the viewer plane
   virtual void       bottomWheelMotion(float newVal);
   virtual void       leftWheelMotion(float newVal);
   virtual void       rightWheelMotion(float newVal);
   virtual void       bottomWheelStart();
   virtual void       leftWheelStart();

   // Redefine this to customize the preference sheet
   virtual void       createPrefSheet();

   // Define this to bring up the viewer help card
   virtual void       openViewerHelpCard();

 private:
   // Viewer state variables
   int            mode;
   SbBool         createdCursors;
   Cursor         vwrCursor, seekCursor;
   SbVec2s        locator; // mouse position
```

```
                 // Camera translation variables
      SbVec3f          locator3D;
      SbPlane          focalplane;
      float            transXspeed, transYspeed;

      void             switchMode(int newMode);
      void             defineCursors();
      void             translateCamera();
      void             computeTranslateValues();
};
```

Example 10-4   SimpleViewer.c++

```
#include <math.h>

#include <X11/Intrinsic.h>
#include <X11/Xlib.h>
#include <X11/keysym.h>

#include <Inventor/nodes/SoOrthographicCamera.h>
#include <Inventor/nodes/SoPerspectiveCamera.h>
#include <Inventor/Xt/SoXtCursors.h>
#include "simpleViewer.h"

enum ViewerModes {
   IDLE_MODE,
   TRANS_MODE,
   SEEK_MODE,
};

// Constructor for the viewer
simpleViewer::simpleViewer(
   Widget parent,
   const char *name,
   SbBool buildInsideParent,
   SoXtFullViewer::BuildFlag b,
   SoXtViewer::Type t)
      : SoXtFullViewer(
         parent,
         name,
         buildInsideParent,
         b,
         t,
         TRUE) // Tell base class to build (since we don't add
               // anything)
```

```
{
   // Init local vars
   mode = IDLE_MODE;
   createdCursors = FALSE;
   setSize(SbVec2s(520, 360)); //def size

   // assign decoration titles
   setPopupMenuString("Simple Viewer");
   setBottomWheelString("transX");
   setLeftWheelString("transY");
   setRightWheelString("Dolly");
   setPrefSheetString("Simple Viewer Preference Sheet");
   setTitle("Simple Viewer");
}

simpleViewer::~simpleViewer()
{
}

// Call the base class and set the correct cursor
// on the window
void
simpleViewer::setViewing(SbBool flag)
{
   if (flag == viewingFlag || camera == NULL) {
      viewingFlag = flag;
      return;
   }

   // Call the base class
   SoXtFullViewer::setViewing(flag);

   // Set the right cursor
   Widget w = getRenderAreaWidget();
   if (w != NULL && XtWindow(w) != NULL) {
      if (isViewing()) {
         if (! createdCursors)
            defineCursors();
         XDefineCursor(XtDisplay(w), XtWindow(w), vwrCursor);
      }
      else
         XUndefineCursor(XtDisplay(w), XtWindow(w));
   }
}
```

```
// Process the given event to change the camera
void
simpleViewer::processEvent(XAnyEvent *xe)
{
   // Let the base class handle the common set of events
   if (processCommonEvents(xe))
      return;

   // Check if cursors need to be defined (they can only
   // be defined after the window has been mapped.
   // Receiving events guarantees that the window has
   // been mapped.
   if (! createdCursors) {
      defineCursors();
      Widget w = getRenderAreaWidget();
      XDefineCursor(XtDisplay(w), XtWindow(w), vwrCursor);
   }

   XButtonEvent    *be;
   XMotionEvent    *me;
   SbVec2s windowSize = getGlxSize();

   switch (xe->type) {
      case ButtonPress:
         be = (XButtonEvent *) xe;
         locator[0] = be->x;
         locator[1] = windowSize[1] - be->y;
         if (be->button == Button1) {
            switch (mode) {
               case IDLE_MODE:
                  interactiveCountInc();
                  switchMode(TRANS_MODE);
                  break;
               case SEEK_MODE:
                  seekToPoint(locator);
                  break;
            }
         }
         break;

      case ButtonRelease:
         be = (XButtonEvent *) xe;
         if (be->button == Button1 && mode == TRANS_MODE) {
            switchMode(IDLE_MODE);
            interactiveCountDec();
         }
         break;
```

```
        case MotionNotify:
            me = (XMotionEvent *) xe;
            locator[0] = me->x;
            locator[1] = windowSize[1] - me->y;
            if (mode == TRANS_MODE)
                translateCamera();
            break;
    }
}

// Switches to the specified viewer mode. The correct
// cursor is also set on the window.
void
simpleViewer::switchMode(int newMode)
{
    // needed to define new cursors
    Widget w = getRenderAreaWidget();
    Display *display = XtDisplay(w);
    Window window = XtWindow(w);
    if (! createdCursors)
        defineCursors();

    // Switch to new viewer mode
    mode = newMode;
    switch (mode) {
        case IDLE_MODE:
            if (window != 0)
                XDefineCursor(display, window, vwrCursor);
            break;

        case TRANS_MODE:
            {
                // Figure out the focal plane
                SbMatrix mx;
                mx = camera->orientation.getValue();
                SbVec3f forward(-mx[2][0], -mx[2][1], -mx[2][2]);
                SbVec3f fp = camera->position.getValue() +
                    forward * camera->focalDistance.getValue();
                focalplane = SbPlane(forward, fp);
```

```
                // Map mouse position onto the viewing plane
                SbVec2s windowSize = getGlxSize();
                SbLine line;
                SbViewVolume cameraVolume = camera->getViewVolume();
                cameraVolume.projectPointToLine(
                        SbVec2f( locator[0] / float(windowSize[0]),
                        locator[1] / float(windowSize[1])), line);
                focalplane.intersect(line, locator3D);
            }
            if (window != 0)
                XDefineCursor(display, window, vwrCursor);
            break;

        case SEEK_MODE:
            if (window != 0)
                XDefineCursor(display, window, seekCursor);
            break;
    }
}

// Call the base class and set the correct cursor
// on the window.
void
simpleViewer::setSeekMode(SbBool flag)
{
    if (! isViewing())
        return;

    // Call the base class
    SoXtFullViewer::setSeekMode(flag);

    // Switch to the right mode
    switchMode(isSeekMode() ? SEEK_MODE : IDLE_MODE);
}

// Redefine this routine to customize the preference sheet
void
simpleViewer::createPrefSheet()
{
    // Create the preference sheet shell and form widget
    Widget shell, form;
    createPrefSheetShellAndForm(shell, form);
```

```
   // Create most of the default parts
   Widget widgetList[10];
   int num = 0;
   widgetList[num++] = createSeekPrefSheetGuts(form);
   widgetList[num++] = createZoomPrefSheetGuts(form);
   widgetList[num++] = createClippingPrefSheetGuts(form);

   layoutPartsAndMapPrefSheet(widgetList, num, form, shell);
}

// Bring up the viewer help card (called by "?" push button)
void
simpleViewer::openViewerHelpCard()
{
   // Tell the component to open the file for us
   openHelpCard("simpleViewer.help");
}

// Translate the camera right/left (called by thumbwheel).
void
simpleViewer::bottomWheelMotion(float newVal)
{
   if (camera == NULL)
      return;

   // Get camera right vector and translate by wheel
   // delta rotation
   SbMatrix mx;
   mx = camera->orientation.getValue();
   SbVec3f rightVector(mx[0][0], mx[0][1], mx[0][2]);
   float dist = transXspeed * (bottomWheelVal - newVal);
   camera->position = camera->position.getValue() +
      dist * rightVector;

   bottomWheelVal = newVal;
}

// Translate the camera up/down (called by thumbwheel).
void
simpleViewer::leftWheelMotion(float newVal)
{
   if (camera == NULL)
      return;
```

```
    // Get camera up vector and translate by wheel
    // delta rotation
    SbMatrix mx;
    mx = camera->orientation.getValue();
    SbVec3f upVector(mx[1][0], mx[1][1], mx[1][2]);
    float dist = transYspeed * (leftWheelVal - newVal);
    camera->position = camera->position.getValue() +
        dist * upVector;

    leftWheelVal = newVal;
}

// Moves the camera closer/further away from the plane
// of interest, which is defined by the viewing normal
// and the camera focalDistance field value.
void
simpleViewer::rightWheelMotion(float newVal)
{
    if (camera == NULL)
        return;

    // Shorten/grow the focal distance given the wheel rotation
    float focalDistance = camera->focalDistance.getValue();
    float newFocalDist = focalDistance /
                    pow(2.0, newVal - rightWheelVal);

    // Finally, reposition the camera
    SbMatrix mx;
    mx = camera->orientation.getValue();
    SbVec3f forward(-mx[2][0], -mx[2][1], -mx[2][2]);
    camera->position = camera->position.getValue() +
                (focalDistance - newFocalDist) * forward;
    camera->focalDistance = newFocalDist;

    rightWheelVal = newVal;
}

// This routine is used to define cursors, which can
// only be called after the window has been realized.
void
simpleViewer::defineCursors()
{
    XColor foreground;
    Pixmap source;
    Display *display = getDisplay();
    Drawable d = DefaultRootWindow(display);
```

```
   // Set a red color
   foreground.red = 65535;
   foreground.green = foreground.blue = 0;

   // View plane translate cursor
   source = XCreateBitmapFromData(display, d,
          so_xt_flat_hand_bits, so_xt_flat_hand_width,
          so_xt_flat_hand_height);
   vwrCursor = XCreatePixmapCursor(display, source, source,
             &foreground, &foreground, so_xt_flat_hand_x_hot,
             so_xt_flat_hand_y_hot);
   XFreePixmap(display, source);

   // Seek cursor
   source = XCreateBitmapFromData(display, d,
          so_xt_target_bits, so_xt_target_width,
          so_xt_target_height);
   seekCursor = XCreatePixmapCursor(display, source, source,
             &foreground, &foreground, so_xt_target_x_hot,
             so_xt_target_y_hot);
   XFreePixmap(display, source);

   createdCursors = TRUE;
}

// Moves the camera into the plane defined by the camera
// forward vector and the focal point (using the camera
// focalDistance field) to follow the new mouse location.
void
simpleViewer::translateCamera()
{
   if (camera == NULL)
      return;

   SbVec2s windowSize = getGlxSize();
   SbVec2f newLocator(locator[0] / float(windowSize[0]),
      locator[1] / float(windowSize[1]));

   // Map new mouse location into the camera focal plane
   SbLine          line;
   SbVec3f         newLocator3D;
   SbViewVolume cameraVolume = camera->getViewVolume();
   cameraVolume.projectPointToLine(newLocator, line);
   focalplane.intersect(line, newLocator3D);
```

```
        // Move the camera by the delta 3D position amount
        camera->position = camera->position.getValue() +
            (locator3D - newLocator3D);

        // You would think we would have to set locator3D to
        // newLocator3D here.  But we don't, because moving
        // the camera essentially makes locator3D equal to
        // newLocator3D in the transformed space, and we will
        // project the next newLocator3D in this transformed space.
    }

    // Called by the bottom and left thumbwheels to compute
    // the translation factors (how fast should we translate
    // given a wheel rotation).
    void
    simpleViewer::computeTranslateValues()
    {
        if (camera == NULL)
            return;

        float height;

        if (camera->isOfType(
            SoPerspectiveCamera::getClassTypeId())) {
            float angle = ((SoPerspectiveCamera *)
                        camera)->heightAngle.getValue() / 2;
            float dist = camera->focalDistance.getValue();
            height = dist * ftan(angle);
        }
        else if (camera->isOfType(
            SoOrthographicCamera::getClassTypeId()))
            height = ((SoOrthographicCamera *)
                    camera)->height.getValue() / 2;

        // Given the size of the viewing plane, figure out
        // the up/down and right/left speeds for the thumb wheels.
        transYspeed = height / 2;
        transXspeed = transYspeed * camera->aspectRatio.getValue();
    }
```

```
// Thumbwheels start callbacks
void
simpleViewer::bottomWheelStart()
{
    computeTranslateValues();

    // call parent class
    SoXtFullViewer::bottomWheelStart();
}

void
simpleViewer::leftWheelStart()
{
    computeTranslateValues();

    // call parent class
    SoXtFullViewer::leftWheelStart();
}
```

Using the SoXtFullViewer Trim Decoration

SoXtFullViewer is used as the base class for most viewers. This abstract class adds a decoration around the render area, a pop-up menu with viewer functions, and a preference sheet that can be used to customize a specific viewer. The decoration around the render area includes thumbwheels that duplicate direct viewing manipulation, a slider to change the camera zooming factor, and viewer/application push buttons. By default, the base class creates push buttons for viewing, home, set home, view all, and seek. Subclasses can easily add viewer-specific push buttons, as well as change the look of the decoration and the preference sheet. The creation of the decoration and preference sheet is accomplished by many small routines, so subclasses can redefine as much or as little as necessary.

SoXtFullViewer provides three thumbwheels around the render area. By default, these thumbwheels do nothing in the **SoXtFullViewer** base class and should therefore be implemented by each subclass. The subclass should implement functions so that the bottom and left thumbwheels duplicate the right-left and up-down functionality of the mouse during direct viewing. The right thumbwheel is used to dolly the camera (move forward and backward).

The simple viewer example defines the thumbwheel functionality by redefining methods from the base class as shown in Example 10-4.

For convenience, when you are defining thumbwheel functionality and redefining the decoration layout, the base class **SoXtFullViewer** provides the following thumbwheel variables. These variables include thumbwheel widgets, previous values (helpful for obtaining incremental rotation), and labels:

rightWheel, bottomWheel, leftWheel
> thumbwheel widget variables

rightWheelStr, bottomWheelStr, leftWheelStr
> string label for each thumbwheel

rightWheelVal, bottomWheelVal, leftWheelVal
> previous value of each thumbwheel

rightWheelLabel, bottomWheelLabel, leftWheelLabel
> widget label for each thumbwheel

When a viewer is derived from **SoXtFullViewer**, it should set the correct labels on the thumbwheels, the pop-up menu, the preference sheet, and the window title. This needs to be done only once and therefore should be done in the constructor. Example 10-4 shows the code to fully support the **SoXtFullViewer** base class.

Adding Push Buttons

By default, the base class **SoXtFullViewer** creates a list of push buttons (**XmPushButton** widgets with pixmaps). The method **buildViewer-Buttons()**, which subclasses do not need to redefine, uses a list of push buttons to construct all the buttons within a form widget. The button's form widget is then laid out within the right-trim form widget. Subclasses can easily add or remove any number of buttons from the existing list of buttons by redefining the **createViewerButtons()** method and appending, inserting, and removing from the **SbPList** of buttons.

Our simple viewer example does not add any new viewer buttons, but here is some sample code that adds a push button to the existing list.

```
void
SoXtExaminerViewer::createViewerButtons(Widget parent)
{
    // Get the default buttons
    SoXtFullViewer::createViewerButtons(parent);
```

```
// Allocate our buttons - this simple case doesn't
// set the XmNlabelType to be a pixmap, just a simple letter.
Arg args[2];
int n = 0;
XtSetArg(args[n], XmNshadowThickness, 2); n++;
XtSetArg(args[n], XmNhighlightThickness, 0); n++;
Widget button = XmCreatePushButtonGadget(parent, "P", args,
                                           n);

XtAddCallback(button, XmNactivateCallback,
              (XtCallbackProc)
              SoXtExaminerViewer::pushButtonCB,
              (XtPointer) this);

// Add this button to the list to have it laid out by the
// parent class (removing a widget from the list will
// prevent the corresponding push button from being laid
// out and managed; therefore it will not show up in the
// decoration).
viewerButtonWidgets->append(button);
}
```

Look at the file SbPList.h for a description of methods available on the **SoXtFullViewer::viewerButtonWidgets** protected variable.

Note: The viewer default push buttons all have a 24-by-24-pixel size, and the decoration trim is designed with that in mind. It is therefore recommended that you create pixmaps of this size for viewer or application push buttons.

Changing the Preference Sheet

Preference sheets allow the user to customize the behavior of a viewer. A default preference sheet is created by the **SoXtFullViewer** class. Subclasses typically make changes to the default preference sheet to give the user control over viewer-specific parameters. Like the decoration in **SoXtFullViewer**, the preference sheet is made up of many small building blocks to make it easier for subclasses to redefine it. The following protected methods are used to build the different parts of the preference sheet:

void **setPrefSheetString**(const char *name);

virtual void **createPrefSheet**();

void **createPrefSheetShellAndForm**(Widget &shell, Widget &form);

void **createDefaultPrefSheetParts**(Widget *widgetList*[ ], int &*num*,
                                      Widget *form*);

void **layoutPartsAndMapPrefSheet**(Widget *widgetList*[ ], int *num*,
                                      Widget *form*, Widget *shell*);

Widget **createSeekPrefSheetGuts**(Widget *parent*);

Widget **createSeekDistPrefSheetGuts**(Widget *parent*);

Widget **createZoomPrefSheetGuts**(Widget *parent*);

Widget **createClippingPrefSheetGuts**(Widget *parent*);

Widget **createStereoPrefSheetGuts**(Widget *parent*);

To change only the preference-sheet title, use the **setPrefSheetString()**
method. Use the **createPrefSheet()** method to redefine the preference sheet
for a subclass, as follows:

```
// This creates the preference sheet in a separate window. It
// calls other routines to create the actual content of the
// sheet.
void
SoXtFullViewer::createPrefSheet()
{
    // Create the preference sheet shell and form widget
    Widget shell, form;
    createPrefSheetShellAndForm(shell, form);

    // Create all of the default parts
    Widget widgetList[10];
    int num = 0;
    createDefaultPrefSheetParts(widgetList, num, form);

    layoutPartsAndMapPrefSheet(widgetList, num, form, shell);
}

// This simply creates the default parts of the pref sheet.
void
SoXtFullViewer::createDefaultPrefSheetParts(
                    Widget widgetList[], int &num, Widget form)
{
    widgetList[num++] = createSeekPrefSheetGuts(form);
    widgetList[num++] = createSeekDistPrefSheetGuts(form);
    widgetList[num++] = createZoomPrefSheetGuts(form);
    widgetList[num++] = createClippingPrefSheetGuts(form);
    widgetList[num++] = createStereoPrefSheetGuts(form);
}
```

When a subclass creates its own preference sheet, it only needs to redefine the **createPrefSheet()** routine and write it like the base class routine. The simple viewer example redefines the preference sheet to omit some of the default parts. Example 10-4 shows the **createPrefSheet()** method for **simpleViewer**.

Subclasses can easily add new items to the preference sheet by adding them to the widget list that is passed to the **layoutPartsAndMapPrefSheet()** method, just like the default parts. The custom items should all be built within a form widget that is automatically laid out and managed within the **layoutPartsAndMapPrefSheet()** method. The layout is from top to bottom in the shell widget.

The preference-sheet widget and all of its child widgets are destroyed when the preference-sheet window is closed by the user. This behavior is intended, since the preference sheet is only a temporary window, and we don't want to carry the unwanted widget around when it is no longer needed.

Changing the Pop-up Menu

The **SoXtFullViewer** pop-up menu, which includes a rich set of viewer functions, can be changed in subclasses by redefining any of the following pop-up menu build routines:

void **setPopupMenuString**(const char *name);

virtual void **buildPopupMenu**();

Widget **buildFunctionsSubmenu**(Widget popup);

Widget **buildDrawStyleSubmenu**(Widget popup);

To change the pop-up menu title, use the **setPopupMenuString()** method. To change the pop-up menu, subclasses can redefine the **buildPopupMenu()** method. Subclasses can also append new entries to the pop-up menu by directly adding a Motif-compliant **xmToggleButton** or **xmPushButton** to the pop-up menu widget.

Changing the Decoration Layout

On rare occasions, you may want to change the decoration surrounding the rendering area. The **SoXtWalkViewer** class, for example, adds an extra thumbwheel and label in the left-hand trim. To simplify the redefining of the decoration, the base class **SoXtFullViewer** constructs the decoration in many small and manageable steps. The following functions are used to create the decoration and can be redefined by subclasses at any level:

Widget **buildWidget**(Widget *parent*);

virtual void **buildDecoration**(Widget *parent*);

virtual Widget **buildLeftTrim**(Widget *parent*);

virtual Widget **buildBottomTrim**(Widget *parent*);

virtual Widget **buildRightTrim**(Widget *parent*);

virtual Widget **buildZoomSlider**(Widget *parent*);

virtual Widget **buildViewerButtons**(Widget *parent*);

virtual Widget **buildAppButtons**(Widget *parent*);

void **setBottomWheelString**(const char **name*);

void **setLeftWheelString**(const char **name*);

void **setRightWheelString**(const char **name*);

Example 10-5 contains pseudocode that shows how the decoration is built in the base class **SoXtFullViewer**. Only important parts of the code are given to illustrate how the decoration is built.

Example 10-5   Building the Viewer Decoration in SoXtFullViewer

```
// Build the render area and the decoration trim within the
// given parent widget.
Widget
SoXtFullViewer::buildWidget(Widget parent)
{
   // Create a form to hold everything together
   mgrWidget = XtCreateWidget(getWidgetName(),
                              xmFormWidgetClass, parent,
                              args, n);
```

```
    // Build the render area and the decoration
    raWidget = SoXtRenderArea::buildWidget(mgrWidget);
    if (decorationFlag)
        buildDecoration(mgrWidget);

    // Lay out and manage the render area and decoration
    ...

    return mgrWidget;
}

// Build the viewer decoration (left, right and bottom trim)
void
SoXtFullViewer::buildDecoration(Widget parent)
{
    // Build the trim sides
    leftTrimForm = buildLeftTrim(parent);
    bottomTrimForm = buildBottomTrim(parent);
    rightTrimForm = buildRightTrim(parent);

    // Lay out the trims but let the buildWidget() manage them
    ...
}

// Build the left trim decoration
Widget
SoXtFullViewer::buildLeftTrim(Widget parent)
{
    // Create a form to hold all the parts
    Widget form = XtCreateWidget("LeftTrimForm",
                                 xmFormWidgetClass, parent,
                                 NULL, 0);

    // Create all the parts
    buildLeftWheel(form);
    Widget butForm = buildAppButtons(form);

    // Lay out and manage the parts
    ...

    return form;
}
```

SoXtWalkViewer redefines only the **buildLeftTrim()** routine in order to build the default parts as well as the extra thumbwheel and label. The viewer then simply returns a form containing its new left trim to the **buildDecoration()** routine, and everything works as before. Only the new trim has to be modified.

Creating a Constrained Viewer

The **SoXtConstrainedViewer** base class adds the notion of a world up-direction, with methods like **setUpDirection()** and **getUpDirection()**. New viewers that require the notion of an up-direction should be derived from this base class. With the notion of a world up-direction (which defaults to $+y$), a viewer can constrain the camera to prevent the user from looking upside down. This constraint is currently used in **SoXtFlyViewer** and **SoXtWalkViewer**.

SoXtConstrainedViewer redefines some of the routines, such as **saveHomePosition()** and **resetToHomePosition()**, to save and restore the original camera up-direction. This base class redefines the **paste()** and **setCamera()** methods to guarantee that the original camera up-direction is preserved whenever new camera values are given. **SoXtConstrainedViewer** also provides some convenience routines to allow the user to interactively specify the world up-direction (the **findUpDirection()** method) and constrain the camera to the current up-direction (the **checkForCameraUpConstrain()** method).

The world up-direction can be changed with the **setUpDirection()** method and can also be changed interactively by the user while viewing a model using the **findUpDirection()** method, defined in **SoXtConstrainedViewer**.

The base class **SoXtConstrainedViewer** also provides a convenient way to check that the current camera values are consistent with the up-direction and to tilt the camera up or down while constraining to +/− 90 degrees from the eye-level plane. This prevents the camera from ever looking upside down. Those protected methods are as follows:

void **checkForCameraUpConstrain()**;

> checks the camera orientation and makes sure that the current right vector and ideal right vector (cross between the view vector and world up-direction) are the same and corrects it if they are not the same. This method keeps the up-direction valid.

virtual void **tiltCamera**(float *deltaAngle*);

> tilts the camera, restraining it to within 180 degrees from the up-direction. A positive angle tilts the camera up.

For convenience, **SoXtConstrainedViewer** defines the decoration thumbwheels, which can also be redefined by subclasses. These are defined as follows:

virtual void **bottomWheelMotion**(float *newVal*);

> rotates the camera around the world up-direction

virtual void **leftWheelMotion**(float *newVal*);

> tilts the camera up and down, constraining it to within 180 degrees of the world up-direction

virtual void **rightWheelMotion**(float *newVal*);

> moves the camera forward and backward

Note: A viewer that is constrained to a world up-direction should always rotate the camera around that world up-direction when rotating left and right. It is important to rotate around the world up-direction—as opposed to the current camera up-value, which is not the same if the camera is tilted up or down—to prevent rolling. This rolling disturbs the camera alignment and eventually causes the camera to look upside down.

## Chapter 11

Creating an Event and Device

This chapter describes how to create a new event and a new Xt device. The examples show how to subclass events and Xt devices and how to translate X events into Inventor events.

This chapter focuses on translating X events into Inventor events. This general process can be applied to the translation of any window-specific events into Inventor events, which are independent of the window system. Examples 11-1 and 11-2 show how to create the **DialEvent**, which is used by the dial and button device.

The details of setting up an **SoXt** device to work with a render area are also explained here. Note that new devices can be added only if you are using the Inventor Component Library. Examples 11-4 and 11-5 use the **DialNButton** device to show how to translate events and communicate with the render area.

Note that new events will not automatically be understood by existing manipulators. You can create new manipulators (or other objects that respond to events) to recognize the new events. Or you can register a new static method for an existing manipulator in the method list for the **SoHandleEventAction**. Then your new method for the manipulator can handle the new events appropriately (see Chapter 4).

Before reading this chapter, be sure to read Chapters 10 and 16 in *The Inventor Mentor.*

Creating an Event

This section describes creating a new event and offers background information on translating an event. For information on creating a new device, see "Creating a Device" on page 279. The device's main responsibility is translating events, which is described in more detail in "Dispatching Events" on page 276.

Overview

The file SoSubEvent.h contains the macros for defining new event classes. The SO_EVENT_HEADER() macro declares type identifier and naming variables and methods that all event classes must support. The SO_EVENT_SOURCE() macro defines the static variables and methods declared in the SO_EVENT_HEADER() macro.

Creating a new event requires these steps:

1. Select a name for the new event class and determine what class it is derived from.

2. Define an **initClass()** method to initialize the type information. Use the SO_EVENT_INIT_CLASS() macro. The application needs to call the event's **initClass()** method immediately after **SoXt::init**.

3. Define a constructor.

4. Define a destructor.

5. Implement **set()** and **get()** methods for the additional information your event provides. For example, the dial event needs to include information on which dial was turned, and what its value is.

6. Write convenience routines for the event to perform common queries and tasks (optional step). For the dial box, the convenience routine is **isDialEvent()**.

7. Write convenience macros for the event (optional step). These are static functions that are used in event callback functions. For the dial, the macro is DIAL_EVENT(). Note that it uses the convenience routines defined in step 6.

Translating Events

When an event is dispatched, the event translator creates an Inventor event from an X event and sets its values (see "Dispatching Events" on page 276). It provides all the information about the event, including the following:

- Time the event occurred
- Position of the locator when the event occurred
- State of the modifier keys (Shift, Control, Alt) when the event occurred
- Any additional information required by the event (for example, if a keyboard key is pressed, which key is it?)

Inventor includes three subclasses of **SoEvent**. **SoButtonEvent** includes additional information about the button state (is it up or down?). Subclasses of **SoButtonEvent** provide information about which button was pressed. **SoMotion3Event** includes information on translation and rotation values generated by an input device such as the spaceball. **SoLocation2Event** includes information on the absolute location of the cursor in window coordinates.

A value such as the event's time or position is read-only during event traversal because the event is passed as a **const** pointer. Only the creator of an event can set its values.

Creating a Dial Event

The dial and button input device generates two X events that need to be translated into Inventor events and handled by the database:

XDeviceMotionEvent
  provides value changes of the eight dials

XDeviceButtonEvent
  provides information about the state of the device's 32 buttons

The information provided by **XDeviceMotionEvent** is translated into a **DialEvent**. The **XDeviceButtonEvent** is translated into a **ButtonBoxEvent**, which is subclassed from **SoButtonEvent** and has button information specific to the button box.

This section discusses the code for the **DialEvent**, which describes the state of any of the eight dials. Note, however, that you could instead choose to create a more generic event that could be used for other devices in addition to the dial box. For example, you could create a **ResetToHomePositionEvent** that would be used when the user presses a button box button, clicks on a Home button on the screen, or performs some other designated action.

❖ **Tip:** Be sure to call **initClass()** on the event after initializing Inventor.

Example 11-1 shows the code for the dial event include file.

Example 11-1   DialEvent.h

```
#include <Inventor/SbBasic.h>
#include <Inventor/events/SoEvent.h>
#include <Inventor/events/SoSubEvent.h>

// Convenience macro for determining if an event matches
#define DIAL_EVENT(EVENT, WHICH) \
    (DialEvent::isDialEvent(EVENT, WHICH))

class DialEvent : public SoEvent {

    SO_EVENT_HEADER();

  public:
    // Constructor
    DialEvent();

    // Which dial generated the event, 1-8
    void      setDial(int d)   { dial = d; }
    int       getDial() const  { return dial; }

    // Value of the dial turned
    void      setValue(int v)  { value = v; }
    int       getValue() const { return value; }

    // Convenience routines to see if an SoEvent is a turn of
    // the passed dial. Passing -1 matches any button.
    static SbBool      isDialEvent(const SoEvent *e,
                                       int which = -1);

      static void          initClass();
```

```
private:
  int                   dial;              // Which dial
  int                   value;             // Value of dial
};
```

Example 11-2 shows the complete source code for the dial event.

Example 11-2   DialEvent.c++

```
#include "DialEvent.h"

SO_EVENT_SOURCE(DialEvent);

// Class initialization
void
DialEvent::initClass()

{
    SO_EVENT_INIT_CLASS(DialEvent, SoEvent);
}

// Constructor
DialEvent::DialEvent()
{
    dial = 0;
    value = 0;
}

// Convenience routine - this returns TRUE if the event is a
// dial turn event matching the passed dial.
SbBool
DialEvent::isDialEvent(const SoEvent *e, int whichDial)
{
    SbBool isMatch = FALSE;

    // is it a dial event?
    if (e->isOfType(DialEvent::getClassTypeId())) {
      const DialEvent *de = (const DialEvent *) e;

      // did the caller want any dial turn? or do they match?
      if ((whichDial == -1) ||
          (de->getDial() == whichDial))
        isMatch = TRUE;
    }

    return isMatch;
}
```

Dispatching Events

Using the **DialNButton** device as an example, this section outlines in more detail how the event translator works with the X Server and the **SoXt** main loop to obtain X events and translate them into Inventor events.

Note: The way **SoXt** main loop works with the event translator is slightly complex, for the following reasons. The X Window System provides compile-time event types only for the mouse and keyboard devices. The X input extension provides events for all other devices. The complication arises because the Xt Library ignores the X input extension. For this reason, we must get the complete list of events at runtime. **SoXt** sets up its own event handler to dispatch the extension events, and Xt dispatches the standard events (see "SoXt Main Loop" on page 278). For more information, see the MIT X Consortium Standard, "X11 Input Extension Library Specification," X Version 11, Release 5.

Translating an Event

Figure 11-1 shows the general sequence for translating an event. (Because the device's main responsibility is to translate events, it is referred to here simply as *the translator*.) Before events can be translated, certain information must be conveyed:

1. The application registers its software devices with the render area. (See *The Inventor Mentor*, Chapter 16.) Mouse and keyboard devices are handled automatically. All additional devices must be explicitly registered using the **SoXtRenderArea::registerDevice()** method.

2. The translator tells the X Server which event classes it is interested in.

3. The translator tells the **SoXt** main loop which event types it is interested in.

After these entities have been notified, the translator is ready to receive and translate events. The following steps describe this process. Remember that the dispatching of events is slightly complicated because X input extensions must be dealt with separately in the main loop routine:

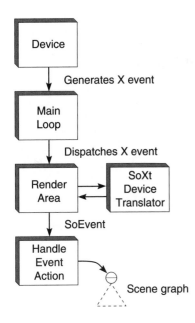

Figure 11-1   Sequence for Translating an Event

4. The physical input device generates events.

5. If these are X events, they are sent to the **SoXt** main loop for dispatching. (If the device doesn't generate X events, your event translator needs to do some extra work.)

6. Within the **SoXt** main loop, Xt dispatches standard X events to the appropriate widget (the corresponding render area will then use the correct translator). **SoXt** dispatches the X input extension events to the render area, which in turn employs the translators to translate the event.

7. The translator translates the event into an Inventor **SoEvent** subclass.

8. The **SoEvent** is sent to the scene manager, which uses a handle event action to traverse the scene database until a node is found to handle the event (typically a manipulator or selection node).

SoXt Main Loop

The code for the **SoXt** main loop is shown in Example 11-3 so that you can see how the main loop dispatches both standard X events and X input extension events. You shouldn't have to modify this code.

Example 11-3   SoXtMainLoop

```
void
SoXt::mainLoop()
{
   XtAppContext context = getAppContext();
   XEvent event;

   for (;;) {
      SoXt::nextEvent(context, &event);
      SoXt::dispatchEvent(&event);
   }
}

void
SoXt::nextEvent(XtAppContext appContext, XEvent *event)
{
   XtAppNextEvent(appContext, event);
}

Boolean
SoXt::dispatchEvent(XEvent *event)
{
   Boolean success = True;

   if (event->type >= LASTEvent) {
      XtEventHandler proc;
      XtPointer clientData;
      Widget w;
      Boolean dummy;

      // Get the event handling function which was
      // registered with Inventor for handling this
      // event type in this widget
      SoXt::getExtensionEventHandler(event, w, proc, clientData);
```

```
    // Call the event handler!
    if (proc == NULL)
        success = False;
    else
        (*proc)(w, clientData, event, &dummy);

}

// else it is not an extension event - let Xt dispatch it
else
    success = XtDispatchEvent(event);

return success;
}
```

Creating a Device

This section provides detailed information on creating a new device, using the dial and button box as a sample.

Overview

Creating a new **SoXt** device class requires these steps:

1. Select a name for the new device class and determine what class it is derived from.

2. Define a constructor (see "Constructor" on page 280).

3. Define a destructor.

4. Define an **enable()** method, which enables the device for a certain widget or render area (see "Enable Method" on page 280).

5. Define a **disable()** method, which disables the device when the widget is destroyed.

6. Define a **translateEvent()** method, which translates X events into Inventor events (see "Translate Event Method" on page 280).

Constructor

First, the constructor for the device obtains a list of the input devices currently attached to the display. In our example, it loops through the list and looks for a device named "dial+buttons." If found, it opens that device (using **XOpenDevice**).

Next, the device queries the X Server for the event types it generates. (Recall that these **const** values are available only at runtime because they are part of the X input extension.) The **DeviceMotionNotify()** function returns the event class and event type for motion events. The **DeviceButtonPress()** and **DeviceButtonRelease()** functions return the event class and event type for the button-press and button-release events.

Enable Method

In its **enable()** method, the **DialNButton** device calls **XSelectExtensionEvent()** to register interest in its event classes with the X Server.

The device also must inform Inventor's main loop about the extension events it is prepared to translate. To do this, it calls **addExtensionEventHandler()** on **SoXt** main loop and passes in the event types (obtained earlier with **DeviceMotionNotify()**, **DeviceButtonPress()**, and **DeviceButtonRelease()**).

Translate Event Method

The **DialNButton translateEvent()** method contains two routines:

translateMotionEvent()
> translates an **XDeviceMotionEvent** into a **DialEvent**

translateButtonEvent()
> translates an **XDeviceButtonEvent** into a **ButtonBoxEvent**

First, the **translateMotionEvent()** sets the position, time, and the state of the Shift, Control, and Alt keys at the time of the event. Then, it sets the dial and value. The variables in the **XDeviceMotionEvent** are stored differently for different devices. Check the documentation for your device driver for information on how data is stored in this event. The

XDeviceMotionEvent for the dial box stores which dial was turned in its **first_axis** field, and the value of that dial in its **axis_data[0]** variable.

As described in "Translating Events" on page 273, the **translateEvent()** method creates the **SoEvent** and then sets the time, state of the modifier keys, and so on.

Example 11-4 shows the code for DialNButton.h.

Example 11-4   DialNButton.h

```
#include <X11/X.h>
#include <X11/extensions/XInput.h>
#include <Inventor/Xt/devices/SoXtDevice.h>
#include <Inventor/events/SoButtonEvent.h>

class ButtonBoxEvent;
class DialEvent;

class DialNButton : public SoXtDevice {
  public:
    // The first constructor uses the display set when
    // SoXt::init is called.
    DialNButton();
    DialNButton(Display *d);
    ~DialNButton();

    // These functions will enable/disable this device for the
    // widget. The callback function f will be invoked when
    // events occur in w. data is the clientData which will be
    // passed.
    virtual void       enable(Widget w, XtEventHandler f,
                            XtPointer data, Window win = NULL);
    virtual void       disable(Widget w, XtEventHandler f,
                            XtPointer data);

    // This converts an X event into an SoEvent,
    // returning NULL if the event is not from this device.
    //
        virtual const SoEvent * translateEvent(XAnyEvent *xevent);

    // Return whether or not the dial+button device exists for use.
    // The first uses the display set when SoXt::init is called.
    static SbBool      exists()
                            { return exists(SoXt::getDisplay()); }
    static SbBool      exists(Display *d);
```

```
protected:
  // Initialize the device.
  static void          init(Display *d);
  static SbBool        firstTime;

  // These event types are retrieved from the X server at run
  // time.
  static int           motionEventType;
  static int           buttonPressEventType;
  static int           buttonReleaseEventType;

  // Event classes passed to XSelectExtensionEvent.
  static XEventClass    eventClasses[3];//max of 3 event classes
  static int            eventTypes[3]; // max of 3 event types

  // Device id is set at runtime.
  static XDevice       *device;

  // Inventor events generated by this device.
  ButtonBoxEvent       *buttonEvent;
  DialEvent            *dialEvent;

  // Event translators!
  DialEvent        *translateMotionEvent(XDeviceMotionEvent *me);
  ButtonBoxEvent   *translateButtonEvent(
                       XDeviceButtonEvent *be,
                       SoButtonEvent::State whichState);
};
```

Example 11-5 shows the source code for DialNButton.c++.

Example 11-5 DialNButton.c++

```
#include <X11/Xlib.h>
#include <X11/extensions/XI.h>

#include <Inventor/SbTime.h>
#include <Inventor/Xt/SoXt.h>
#include <Inventor/events/SoButtonEvent.h>

#include "ButtonBoxEvent.h"
#include "DialEvent.h"
#include "DialNButton.h"
```

```
extern "C" {
XDeviceInfo *XListInputDevices(Display *, int *);
XDevice     *XOpenDevice(Display *, XID);
int         XSelectExtensionEvent(Display *, Window, XEventClass *,
int);
}

#define DEVICE_NAME "dial+buttons"

// There are 3 event classes for this device:
// motion, button down, button up.
static const int numEventClasses = 3;

// Static members
SbBool DialNButton::firstTime = TRUE;
int DialNButton::motionEventType;
int DialNButton::buttonPressEventType;
int DialNButton::buttonReleaseEventType;
XEventClass DialNButton::eventClasses[3];
int DialNButton::eventTypes[3];
XDevice *DialNButton::device;

// Description:
//   Initialize the dial+button device.
//   We only need to do this once.

void
DialNButton::init(Display *display)
{
    // If already initialized, return.
    if (! firstTime)
        return;

    firstTime = FALSE;

    // Get the list of input devices that are attached to the
    // display now.
    XDeviceInfoPtr  list;
    int             numDevices;

  list = (XDeviceInfoPtr) XListInputDevices(display, &numDevices);
```

```
      // Now run through the list looking for the dial+button
      // device.
      device = NULL;
      for (int i = 0; (i < numDevices) && (device == NULL); i++) {
        // Open the device - the device id is set at runtime.
        if (strcmp(list[i].name, DEVICE_NAME) == 0) {
          device = XOpenDevice(display, list[i].id);
        }
      }

      // Make sure we found the device
      if (device == NULL) {
        fprintf(stderr, "DialNButton::init",
        "Sorry there is no dial and button attached to this display");
        return;
      }

      // Query the event types and classes
      unsigned long eventClass;

      DeviceMotionNotify(device, motionEventType, eventClass);
      eventClasses[0] = eventClass;
      eventTypes[0] = motionEventType;

      DeviceButtonPress(device, buttonPressEventType, eventClass);
      eventClasses[1] = eventClass;
      eventTypes[1] = buttonPressEventType;

      DeviceButtonRelease(device, buttonReleaseEventType,
                          eventClass);
      eventClasses[2] = eventClass;
      eventTypes[2] = buttonReleaseEventType;

      // Init all dial values to 0
      static int vals[8] = {0, 0, 0, 0, 0, 0, 0, 0};
      XSetDeviceValuators(display, device, vals, 0, 8);
    }

    // Constructor using default display
    DialNButton::DialNButton()
    {
        init(SoXt::getDisplay());

        buttonEvent = new ButtonBoxEvent;
        dialEvent = new DialEvent;
    }
```

```
// Constructor
DialNButton::DialNButton(Display *d)
{
    init(d);

    buttonEvent = new ButtonBoxEvent;
    dialEvent = new DialEvent;
}

// Destructor
DialNButton::~DialNButton()
{
    delete buttonEvent;
    delete dialEvent;
}

// Returns whether the dial+button device exists for use or
// not.
SbBool
DialNButton::exists(Display *display)
{
    // Get the list of input devices that are attached to the
    // display now.
    XDeviceInfoPtr  list;
    int             numDevices;

  list = (XDeviceInfoPtr) XListInputDevices(display, &numDevices);

    // Now run through the list looking for the dial + button
    // device.
    for (int i = 0; (i < numDevices) &&
                (strcmp(list[i].name, DEVICE_NAME) != 0); i++)
      ; // keep looping

    // If we broke out of the loop before i reached numDevices,
    // then the dial + button does in fact exist.
    return (i < numDevices);
}
```

```
// This selects input for dial + button device events which
// occur in w.
// The callback routine is proc, and the callback data is
// clientData.
void
DialNButton::enable(
   Widget w,
   XtEventHandler proc,
   XtPointer clientData,
   Window window)
{
   if (numEventClasses == 0)
      return;

   Display *display = XtDisplay(w);
   if (display == NULL) {
     fprintf(stderr, "DialNButton::enable",
           "SoXt::init not properly called (Display is NULL).");
     return;
   }

   if (w == NULL) {
     fprintf(stderr, "DialNButton::enable",
           "widget is NULL.");
     return;
   }

   if (window == NULL) {
     fprintf(stderr, "DialNButton::enable",
           "widget must be realized (Window is NULL).");
     return;
   }

   // Select extension events for the dial + button which the
   // user wants.
   XSelectExtensionEvent(display, window,
                         eventClasses, numEventClasses);

   // Tell Inventor about these extension events!
   for (int i = 0; i < numEventClasses; i++)
     SoXt::addExtensionEventHandler(
       w, eventTypes[i], proc, clientData);
}
```

```
// This unselects input for dial + button device events which
// occur in w,
// i.e. dial + button events will no longer be recognized.
void
DialNButton::disable(
    Widget w,
    XtEventHandler proc,
    XtPointer clientData)
{
    // Tell Inventor to forget about these classes.
    for (int i = 0; i < numEventClasses; i++)
        SoXt::removeExtensionEventHandler(
            w, eventTypes[i], proc, clientData);
}

// Translate X events into Inventor events.
const SoEvent *
DialNButton::translateEvent(XAnyEvent *xevent)
{
    SoEvent *event = NULL;

    // See if this is a dial + button event.
    if (xevent->type == motionEventType) {
        XDeviceMotionEvent *me = (XDeviceMotionEvent *) xevent;
        if (me->deviceid == device->device_id)
            event = translateMotionEvent(me);
    }
    else if (xevent->type == buttonPressEventType) {
        XDeviceButtonEvent *be = (XDeviceButtonEvent *) xevent;
        if (be->deviceid == device->device_id)
            event = translateButtonEvent(be, SoButtonEvent::DOWN);
    }
    else if (xevent->type == buttonReleaseEventType) {
        XDeviceButtonEvent *be = (XDeviceButtonEvent *) xevent;
        if (be->deviceid == device->device_id)
            event = translateButtonEvent(be, SoButtonEvent::UP);
    }

    return event;
}
```

```
// This returns a DialEvent for the passed X event.
DialEvent *
DialNButton::translateMotionEvent(XDeviceMotionEvent *me)
{
   setEventPosition(dialEvent, me->x, me->y);
   dialEvent->setTime(SbTime(0, 1000*me->time));
   dialEvent->setShiftDown(me->state & ShiftMask);
   dialEvent->setCtrlDown(me->state & ControlMask);
   dialEvent->setAltDown(me->state & Mod1Mask);

   // the dial that turned is stored as first_axis in the X event.
   // the value is always in axis_data[0].
   dialEvent->setDial(me->first_axis);
   dialEvent->setValue(me->axis_data[0]);

   return dialEvent;
}

// This returns a ButtonBoxEvent for the passed X event.
ButtonBoxEvent *
DialNButton::translateButtonEvent(
   XDeviceButtonEvent *be,
   SoButtonEvent::State whichState)
{
   setEventPosition(buttonEvent, be->x, be->y);
   buttonEvent->setTime(SbTime(0, 1000*be->time));
   buttonEvent->setShiftDown(be->state & ShiftMask);
   buttonEvent->setCtrlDown(be->state & ControlMask);
   buttonEvent->setAltDown(be->state & Mod1Mask);

   // Set which button along with its state.
   buttonEvent->setButton(be->button);
   buttonEvent->setState(whichState);

   return buttonEvent;
}
```

Index

deriving new classes. *See* creating nodes, creating
   elements, etc.

designing draggers, 153

destroying draggers, 162

destructor
   actions, 75
   draggers, 188
   elements, 89
   manipulators, 159

detail seek, 248

details, creating, 34

DeviceButtonPress(), 280

DeviceButtonRelease(), 280

DeviceMotionNotify(), 280

devices
   constructor, 280
   creating, 279 to 288
   example, 281 to 288
   registering, 276

DialEvent, 273, 280

disable(), 279

disabling outputs, 112, 116 to 117

dispatching events, 276

doAction(), 25, 29, 76, 200

drag(), 163

dragFinish(), 163

dragger switches, 161, 164

draggers
   and manipulators, 197
   child and parent, 187
   compound
      children, 187
      constructor, 184 to 188
      creating, 176 to 196
      designing parts, 178 to 181
      example, 181 to 196
   constructor, 159
   creating simple, 152 to 176
   designing, 153
   destructor, 162, 188
   initializing, 159

draggers *(continued)*
   parts
      default geometry, 155, 158, 180
      designing, 155, 157
      feedback, 155
   resources, 178
   simple
      creating, 152 to 176
      example, 167 to 176
   structure, 153
   uniform scaling, 176
   writing to file, 160

dragging, 162, 163 to 165

dragStart(), 163

E

editor viewers, 247

element bundles, 28

element stacks, 7

elements
   accessing, 9, 27
   actions, 12 to 17
   actions and nodes, 8
   class tree, 86 to 88
   creating, 85 to 98
   defaults, 90
   deriving from existing, 94
   destructor, 89
   enabling, 6 to 7, 23, 74, 77
   example, 96 to 98
   GL versions, 11 to 12, 89, 94
   initializing, 86, 89
   listed, 9 to 12
   macros, 85
   pushing and popping, 95
   setting, 7 to 8, 27

enable field, 113

enable(), 279, 280

enabling elements, 6 to 7, 23, 74, 77

enabling outputs, 112

endShape(), 34

engine network, 110, 111

fields *(continued)*
   multiple-value, creating, 69 to 71
   reading, 67
   single-value, creating, 66 to 69
   touching, 110
   writing, 67
fieldSensorCB(), 188
file format, 155
   unknown nodes, 58
finishing manipulation, 165
flags
   buildNow, 235, 236
   isBuiltIn, 59
   Override, 8, 27
form widget, 235, 265
free(), 70
freeing memory, 89

G

gate engines, 113
generateDefaultNormals(), 63
generatePrimitives(), 32, 33, 35
geometry
   dragger parts, 155, 180
   feedback, 164
   for manipulators, 158
geomSeparator, 153
get(), 27, 90
getAnyPart(), 187
getBoundingBox(), 32, 36
getCamera(), 246
getChildren(), 50
getClassTypeId(), 18
getElement(), 93
getInput(), 121
getInstance(), 27
getLocalStartingPoint(), 164
getLocalToWorldMatrix(), 153, 164
getNodekitCatalog(), 126
getNum(), 27, 108

getOutput(), 121
getParentWidget(), 236
getPart(), 130
getPathCode(), 50
getSeekTime(), 249
getTypeId(), 18
getValue(), 110, 112, 113
getViewVolume(), 164
GetVolumeAction, 77
GL versions, of elements, 11 to 12, 89, 94
global dictionary, 160, 185
global variable, 17
Glow property node, 28, 29, 58
glPushMatrix(), 96
GLRender(), 32, 34
groups
   creating, 49 to 58
   example, 53 to 58
   hidden children, 50
   path code, 50 to 52

H

handle box, 197
headlight, 246
help card, for components, 234
hidden children, 50, 127, 197
hide(), 234, 237
hiding components, 237
hierarchy, widget, 236
highlight path, 217
highlight styles, creating, 215 to 231
highlights
   appearance, 216
   overlay planes, 218
     example, 218 to 226
   selected objects
     example, 226 to 231

realloc(), 70
realTime global field, 117
redraw sensor, 111
registerChildDragger(), 187
registerChildDraggerCallbacksOnly(), 188
registerDevice(), 276
registering
    child draggers, 187
    devices, 276
    static methods, 75
    widgets, 237
registerWidget(), 237
render area, 237, 276
rendering, 34
replaceManip(), 200
replaceNode(), 200
replicating field values, engines, 105
reset node, 178
resetToHomePosition(), 246
resources
    draggers, 178
    X, 237
rightSiblingName parameter, node kit parts, 130
root
    scene graph, 217
    widget tree, 236
RotTransDragger, 176
RotTransManip, 197
runtime type checking, 66, 89
runtime types, 18

S

saveHomePosition(), 246
SbLineProjector, 161
SbPList, 262
SbProjector, 161
scaling, draggers and manipulators, 176

scene graph, 6
    changes in, 110
    icons for nodes in, xxiv
    root, 217
    traversing, 76
search action, 217
search(), 5
second-ticker engine, 116
seek function, 248
seekDistance variable, 249
seekDistAsPercentage variable, 249
seeking, and viewers, 246
seekNormal variable, 249
seekPoint variable, 249
seekToPoint(), 249
selection
    and manipulators, 216
    and node kits, 218
selection callback functions, 216
selection highlight styles. *See* highlights
selection list, 217
selection node, 277
selection path, 217
sensor, redraw, 111
sensors
    attaching and detaching, 64, 167
    field, 153, 162, 166, 186
separators, 86
sequence, of notification, 112
set(), 7, 27, 90
setBaseWidget(), 235, 236
setCamera(), 246
setClassName(), 236
setColor(), 216
setDetail(), 34
setDetailSeek(), 249
setDragger(), 199
setElt(), 91, 94